School Personnel Administration

— *A Practitioner's Guide* —

Richard T. Castallo, Editor
State University of New York at Cortland

Matthew R. Fletcher
Cayuga-Onondaga Board of Cooperative Educational Services

Andrew D. Rossetti
Syracuse University

Robert W. Sekowski
Oneida-Madison Board of Cooperative Educational Services

Allyn and Bacon
Boston   London   Toronto   Sydney   Tokyo   Singapore

Dedication

The purpose for writing this book was simple. Our colleague and co-author, the late Andy Rossetti, believed that students of educational administration should have what he called a "hands-on" resource for personnel administration. He envisioned a practical book that they, as well as practicing administrators, could put on a shelf by their desks for easy access.

If we have learned little else from our experiences, we have at least become aware that every successful project must have a driving force behind it. Ideas are plentiful, but good ideas that can actually become realities are too rare. Andy Rossetti was the force behind this project. He showed us what it should be and provided much of the outline of how to go about it. We will always remember him and appreciate his inspiration, energy, and vision.

Copyright © 1992 by Allyn and Bacon
A Division of Simon & Schuster, Inc.
160 Gould Street
Needham Heights, Massachusetts 02194

Library of Congress Cataloging-in-Publication Data

School personnel administration : a practitioner's guide / Richard T.
  Castallo . . . [et al.].
    p. cm.
  Includes index.
  ISBN 0-205-13135-2
  1. School personnel management—United States.   I. Castallo,
Richard T., 1950-
LB2831.58.S36   1991
371.2'01'0973—dc20   91-9914
                                                                          CIP

Printed in the United States of America

10 9 8 7 6 5 4 3 2 1   95 94 93 92 91

Contents

iii

adult stage
adult learner

just cause 148
disc. steps
letter reprimand
158

CHAPTER — 10 —

Conditions of Employment   231

CHAPTER — 11 —

Employee Data   247

CHAPTER — 12 —

Administering Support Staff 257

CHAPTER — 13 —

Empowering Teaching Staff 269

CHAPTER — 14 —

Policy and Procedure 297

CHAPTER — 15 —

Career Paths 313

Preface

A few years ago the authors of this publication were engaged in a discussion about the need for a book that could serve as a text for future school administrators, as well as a ready desk reference for those already practicing. Our collective experiences as practitioners had as a common thread the fact that we had learned most of what we knew about personnel administration by trial and error. Most of the books we had used as students had been so general that they provided little meaningful assistance in dealing with the daily problems with which we were confronted on the job. For the most part we had been fortunate enough to avoid getting into much trouble along the way. However, as we reflected on some of the mistakes we had made, we realized that many of them could have been avoided. This led to further discussion about some of the "fatal" errors made by colleagues over the years. In some cases, these mistakes were serious enough that administrators had to leave their positions; in others, they were serious enough that they had to leave the field altogether.

It also seemed that much of what we had learned about what to do in given situations was consistent with what some of our colleagues had done in similar circumstances. This led quite naturally to the idea that perhaps the laws, regulations, and common sense behind certain actions could and should be shared. If these were put into a book, perhaps students would have the opportunity to learn earlier the steps to take when confronted with personnel-related problems. Further, we reasoned that students and practitioners would find such a book to be a useful daily reference while engaged in the rigors of their positions.

In planning *School Personnel Administration: A Practitioner's Guide*, we were determined to discuss topics that we believed were of real interest to school administrators. As a result, emphasis was placed on contemporary concerns related to daily practices. With today's demand for improvement in the performance of schools, serious attention is given to the need for systematic planning, involving virtually all members of the school community. The role of today's administrators has shifted. They are no longer asked to be responsible only for planning for their districts, but also for coordinating and directing in such a way that those involved are empowered in the decision-making process. This book suggests who should be included in these efforts and discusses processes for their accomplishment.

Traditional responsibilities for personnel administrators have been maintained; recruitment, selection, training, and orientation of staff continue to be primary duties. To conduct these efforts most effectively, administrators must be aware of the legal parameters constraining them, and of practices that can help them identify the most appropriate candidates.

The administration of personnel has become increasingly complex and legalistic. Administrators must be educated in various aspects of law that relate to school operation. These include the ability to negotiate and administer contracts and to develop and implement personnel policies for various groups in school districts—instructional, support, administrative, and board of education.

Besides their responsibilities to their school districts, administrators must also pay attention to their own careers—an often ignored topic. *School Personnel Administration: A Practitioner's Guide* addresses various career paths, including those related to school administration. The text also contains suggestions for locating positions, interviewing, and working up through the career ladder in administration.

We wish to express our genuine thanks to our colleagues from around the country who provided in-depth and constructive feedback on the chapters in the book. We extend our gratitude to the following reviewers: Bob Thompson, Lamar University; Hal Rowe, East Lyme Public Schools, East Lyme, CT; and Beverly Dryden, a practitioner in Lawrenceville, GA.

Appreciation is extended to the New York State School Boards Association for allowing us to excerpt sample provisions from their book, *Negotiations Proposals to Achieve/Avoid—1989.*

We also acknowledge the assistance of the New York State Association of School Personnel Administrators in supporting this project.

Special thanks is given to Ms. Mari Gibbore-Geisenhof for her assistance in doing a little bit of everything: reviewing, editing, and proofreading.

The authors

CHAPTER

– 1 –

The Personnel Function—
Past and Present

It is difficult to represent the personnel function in a school district with a specific job description. This difficulty is based in part on the fact that the majority of school districts in the United States do not have full-time personnel managers. Even within the districts that do have a designated person in this role, his or her exact responsibilities and day-to-day activities vary a great deal. For instance, in smaller districts, which may only employ a superintendent, a business manager, and a principal or two, the personnel function is often decentralized; each member of the administrative staff takes responsibility for those areas that most affect his or her primary job concerns. The greatest concerns of principals tend to involve the employment function—recruitment, selection, orientation, and separation. Business managers are usually most concerned with areas such as compensation, organization of employee data, and collective bargaining. Superintendents, of course, have the responsibility of overseeing all of these, in addition to planning, contract administration and other duties.

Without question, personnel management includes all of these things and more. It involves the recording and cataloging of "nitty gritty" details about all employees in the school district, from their recruitment to their final separation. It means providing opportunities for staff development that will allow employees to grow and expand intellectually and professionally. One of the most critical personnel functions, and one that until recently received less attention than others, is its importance in creating and communicating a healthy organizational climate to staff, students, and the school and community at large.

The personnel function is best characterized as diverse. It includes a number of disparate and unrelated activities. This lack of definition has provided many skilled administrators with the flexibility to be creative and even daring in trying out new ideas. In other situations, the lack of definition has been the Sword of Damocles, finally falling and cutting short a career because an administrator either did not realize his or her responsibility to carry out a function or did not know how to fulfill that function in a satisfactory manner. This, perhaps more than any other reason, makes personnel administration the most critical managerial activity in any school district.

— THE PERSONNEL FUNCTION IN THE PUBLIC SECTOR —

Understanding the evolution of the personnel function means going back to its development in government and business. Many students correlate the emergence of personnel management with the late 1800s and early 1900s and the theory of scientific management. However, personnel management was greatly influenced by government, particularly the civil service system.

Birth of the Federal Civil Service System

The federal civil service in the United States started in 1789 with the first president of the United States, George Washington. With the birth of a new nation, a system was needed for administering the government. Originally the system was strictly controlled by the president without much involvement by the Congress. The system employed only about 350 people, an inconsequential number compared to the almost 4 million federal civil servants employed at the close of World War II.

George Washington's popularity and reputation for fairness allowed the civil service system to develop with little criticism. He made an effort to make appointments based primarily on factors such as ability and reputation. Most appointments were of members of the gentry rather than the general population. Everything considered, the civil service did an admirable job in its early years, and there was little call for changes in its structure or operation. Jefferson made the first notable changes in the system and attempted to achieve balance between the numbers of Republicans and Federalists appointed. Although sensitive to political balance, Jefferson continued to support the practice of his predecessors in requiring civil servants to be capable. Jefferson was also open to recommendations by members of Congress for appointments. This allowed for more influence from party members, but the office of the president continued to maintain primary control.

In the 1800s, under James Madison, Congress began to take more control of civil service appointments. A greater demand for civil servants occurred during the War of 1812. Because of his inability to pacify various factions, some of Madison's appointments were not approved by Congress. In some cases, Madison left appointments to department heads, increasing the possibility for positions being obtained on the basis of patronage. This practice flourished through the mid-1800s, with mass hirings and firings often occurring with the beginning of a new presidential term.

As a result of these practices, the civil service was viewed by many as promoting gross favoritism. The system's flaws were many: lack of stability in critical and sensitive positions, appointment of men and women incompetent to fulfill job duties, politicians acting as bargaining agents, and inaccessibility of positions to individuals who were interested and competent to fill them.

Reforming the Civil Service System

Growing displeasure with the civil service system resulted in a series of Congressional bills in the mid-1860s; recommended changes required competitive examinations, promotions based on seniority and performance, and removal from office based on justifiable cause. According to Kaufmann,[1] a final report was presented by the Joint Committee on Retrenchment in 1868. The report "contained extensive analyses of the civil service systems of China, England, France, and Prussia and summaries of the opinions of almost 450 American supervisory officials." This report was accompanied by yet another bill calling for reform of the system, but the bill was defeated. However, the report became the basis for the reforms that ultimately occurred.

In 1881 the assassination of President James A. Garfield, by a man who believed Garfield had refused him an appointment, gave impetus to changes in the civil service system. Garfield's murder occurred when there was growing public disfavor with the spoils system of political appointments. In 1883 the Civil Service Act, also known as the Pendleton Act, was signed into effect by President Chester A. Arthur, establishing the Civil Service Commission. Those concerned with change believed that the spoils system was corrupt and needed to be abolished; the Civil Service Commission was seen as a means of doing this through the use of standard examinations administered by the commission. Those who produced this legislation based it largely on their interpretation of the British system. The Civil Service Act required that the commission be made up of three persons appointed by the president and approved by Congress. These individuals could not hold any other office. The law also required a number of major reforms, among them:

Open, competitive examinations related to the duties of the position for
   which the individual applies;

Noncompetitive examinations for positions when qualified persons are
   not required to compete;

Appointments given to those with the highest examination scores;

Establishment of a probationary period before an appointment becomes
   final;

A restriction preventing an individual in public service from being required to contribute to any political fund or provide any political
   service;

A restriction preventing any individual from using his or her position
   for political influence.

These efforts were aimed at bringing fairness to a corrupt system, but
little more than 10 percent of civil service positions were affected by the
legislation when it was first enacted. The percentage has increased
dramatically since 1884, and today only a little more than 10 percent of existing federal civil service positions do *not* require examinations. Although
any system as large as the United States Civil Service is likely to contain
frustrating layers of bureaucracy, its operation in the 1990s is unquestionably
more objective than it was during the early 1800s. As a result, the civil service system provided a model for the organization of personnel management in the private sector.

— PERSONNEL ADMINISTRATION IN THE PRIVATE SECTOR —

As the new century approached, many industries began to recognize the
importance of the non-work-related needs of employees. By the 1890s, social
secretaries, also known as welfare secretaries, were hired to help employees'
families with financial, housing, medical, recreational, and other personal
matters.

The Era of Scientific Management

Students of management often refer to the era of scientific management,
a period from the 1880s through the 1930s. This time was also associated
with the industrial revolution and the genesis of industrial psychology,
fostered by an interest in increased production. According to Patten,[2] personnel management was an outgrowth of this new field. Interest in personnel
administration grew, and in 1900 the Goodrich Company had the first

"employment department" in America. National Cash Register established a "labor department" in 1902. According to Wren,[3] Plimpton Press established a "personnel department" in 1910.

In the era of scientific management, specialists were concerned with employee-related matters such as welfare, rate setting, training, and health and safety. The focus was placed on the completion of tasks through division of labor, an identifiable hierarchy of management, specific rules and procedures governing the responsibilities and rights of workers, and a promotion system based on technical ability.

Scientific managers saw the completion of tasks as their ultimate goal. As a result, methods for completing these tasks in the most efficient manner were emphasized. Proponents of this school felt that observation of people in the workplace would provide ideas for improving the way specific jobs were being accomplished. Physical conditions such as lighting, designation of job responsibilities, organization of tasks, and other concerns related to physical aspects of jobs were given prominent consideration.

Given less attention was the human element, in terms of individuals and their personal needs and in how individual employees related to other employees in the workplace.

The Human Relations Era

Probably the greatest contribution of the scientific management period was that it brought attention to the study of management. Its greatest deficit was the lack of attention devoted to individual workers and their relationship with other workers and with the organization itself. During the human relations period, from the early 1930s through approximately 1950, researchers believed that most organizations had failed to develop and maintain effective human relationships with and among their employees. The most recognized contribution from this period was the Hawthorne studies at the Western Electric Company's Hawthorne Plant in Chicago.

The Hawthorne studies. A series of research studies took place over a period of several years, to determine the effects of illumination on quality and quantity of work output. While the amount of illumination varied through several different experimental conditions, the researchers were unable to find any consistent correlation between amount of lighting and output. The one exception occurred when workers were asked to function under .06 foot-candle, about the same amount of light provided by moonlight.[4]

A number of other variables that might affect output (amount of sleep, diet, health) were also studied in detail, but no relationships seemed to correlate. Confused by the inconclusive results, the researchers finally realized that one factor had not been given consideration: during the study, employees had been consulted about their working conditions. Previously, employees were rarely asked about working conditions, but during the study their bosses gave them attention and showed concern. Workers felt their opinions had begun to matter and were considered important. The conclusion of researchers focused on an unexpected factor: that a new social order had been formed in the workplace, and that the way supervisors and workers interacted in that social order affected output.

Informal structure.   The Hawthorne studies pointed out the importance of social behavior in the work setting. The idea that an informal structure exists which is not identifiable on any organizational chart was a significant conclusion. Other important conclusions were:

The informal organization is used as a means of protection against arbitrary management decisions.

Output and morale are not directly correlated to working conditions and wages, but attention by supervisors can affect production and morale.

Specialization is not necessarily the most efficient means of operation.

A narrow focus of control is not required to maintain effective supervision.

Informal leaders may be as important as the formal leaders in an organization.

During this same period, the impact of World War II resulted in attention to a number of other personnel-related functions. Testing in connection with the selection and training of employees became more critical with the shortage of skilled workers. Wage and hour administration became important as a result of concern with retaining workers and with wage and price controls. Factors such as fringe benefits and safety became more important during worker negotiations with management.

Testing.   The wide use of tests in employment situations became more popular during this period, but their first broad application took place starting in 1912, when the U.S. Public Health Service began testing immigrants who wished to enter the United States at Ellis Island. The Binet test, along with other tests, was used to screen immigrants. This resulted in overwhelming "evidence" that many new citizens were feeble-minded, so many were rejected and returned to their homelands. Sadly, this procedure was applauded by a number of members of the scientific community, and the validity of the tests was not questioned until years later. Even today the ability of a test to predict something as complex as the potential of individuals to adapt to a new society is highly questionable. However, tests have continued to play a major role in various areas of American society, and their incorporation into the employment field has been established in both private and government organizations.

The Behavioral Science Era

The late 1950s and early 1960s ushered in the behavioral science era. During this period, the technology boom brought the need for more college-trained engineers and technicians. Industries found themselves competing for the skilled help they required; active recruiting on college campuses became popular. At this same time, a shift of focus took place, from the employee to the manager and his relationship with the employee. Methods for improving the motivation and retention of those in the managerial ranks became a greater concern.

Advocates of this school disagreed with some of the principles of those who supported scientific management. Those supporting behavioral science believed that scientific management was not responsive enough to employees; jobs had become overspecialized; people were underutilized; too much management control took place; and employees felt a lack of self-fulfillment because they did not receive sufficient recognition for their work. To remedy some of these concerns, steps were taken to give greater recognition to employees. Newsletters, morale surveys, employee training, and meaningful involvement in studying quality-of-work factors were extended to workers.

Further attention to employee protection and rights was sometimes the result of external forces. In the late 1960s and early 1970s, civil rights legislation, equal opportunity, and affirmative action employment came to pass. The use of ombudsmen to act as agents between labor and management became fashionable, to encourage more consideration of employee concerns. At this same time, "organizational development" became a popular field of study, both in factories and in universities. Attitude surveys, exit interviews of employees separating from their company, and joint problem-solving and conflict-resolution efforts were tested and adopted by many organizations.

Behavioral science had roots in both scientific and human relations theory. Chester Barnard, President of New Jersey Bell, was closely identified with this stage. Advocates of this approach believed that worker commitment to an organization was critical and that managers should pay close attention to managing the informal organization. Barnard was one of the first to talk about the importance of the chief executive in molding and managing the shared values of an organization.

The Era of Productivity Management

The period from the mid-1980s through the present has not yet been formally titled, but it might be considered a period of productivity management, because of the national cry for improved worker productivity, the country's falling below European countries in quality-of-life indicators, and declining student test scores, among other factors. In addition, concerns with education identified at the federal level have resulted in proposals to disestablish the federal education department; encouragement of institutional competition through tuition tax credits, vouchers, and awards programs; increases in minimum standards for teachers and students; emphasis on acquisition of content; and attempts to reinstitute prayer, character education, and stronger discipline.[5]

The Formal and Informal Organization

Contemporary studies have found that many effective organizations borrow from all of the approaches previously discussed. Perhaps the most significant outcome of the attention given to the study of management, particularly the results of the Hawthorne studies, was recognition of the duality of organizational functioning. Beyond the management charts, illustrations, and other schematics that outline how organizations function, came the realization that the sum total of the formal and informal structures determines the difference between good and bad organizations or good and bad schools.

School Culture

Webster's defines culture as "the totality of socially transmitted behavior patterns characteristic of a people." Academicians refer to values, traditions, beliefs, and behavior when discussing this concept. How a culture becomes established was discussed by Kilmann,[6] who states that a corporate culture is based on the "organization's mission, setting and requirements for success: high quality, efficiency, product reliability, customer service, innovation, hard work, and loyalty."

– PERSONNEL MANAGEMENT IN THE SCHOOLS –

The history of the civil service and the various schools of management reflect the importance of the personnel field. As the United States grapples with important national economic concerns, personnel management is seen as a key in overcoming many of these problems. School administrators have often preceded their counterparts in business and industry in understanding the importance of positive personnel relations. Education has also provided a forum for initiating changes in personnel management. Education benefits from having highly educated staff, and insights and contributions from these employees can be helpful in analyzing needs and formulating possible solutions. Stability in the market being served is another advantage for educators; school boards, administrators, teachers, and support staff can always count on there being children in need of education. In addition, a regular amount of support provided by taxpayers and state and federal agencies can be taken for granted.

Factors Affecting the Personnel Function

At the same time, personnel administrators may view a number of factors as impeding their efforts. Teachers' unions have become very powerful in the last twenty years. Once these organizations were considered professional associations, but their main purpose today relates to improving the conditions under which their members labor. Many administrators feel that unions show little concern for the welfare or education of children and that when they do, it is only for public relations purposes.

The reform efforts of the early and mid-1980s called upon schools to change the way education takes place. Some schools have responded to this call by adopting the idea of school-based or site-based management; others have explored and are trying out ideas related to teacher empowerment. Interestingly enough, these approaches are not exclusively seen in the schools, but are being used in a number of businesses and industries today. Many popular management books, such as *In Search of Excellence,*[7] have described organizations that have adopted the equivalent of teacher-empowerment efforts.

Regardless of the label, education in the late 1990s will be changed more than it has been since the days of one-room schoolhouse. America's decline in the world marketplace, low student SAT scores, and poor performance on international tests will combine with the demands of technology, the changing marketplace, and the call by teachers to take part in decision making. All of these phenomena, taking place at the same time, will require a change in the way schools go about their business, and the personnel management function is at the center of these changes. What changes will be adopted, how they take place, who will be involved in them, and when they will occur are all questions that must be coordinated and orchestrated so that change efforts are effective.

— DEFINING THE PERSONNEL FUNCTION —

As noted, the personnel administration function carries a number of responsibilities. How those responsibilities are assigned varies from school district to school district. This text identifies those areas in which every student of personnel administration should have a good working knowledge. These areas have been determined by experience, a survey of fellow administrators, and a review of literature related to personnel management. To make this more than just an introductory text for students of the field of educational administration, model materials, references, and explanations make this book a useful reference for the practicing administrator.

For a full appreciation of the functioning of personnel offices in today's schools, an understanding of the events which shaped and influenced these operations is necessary. School personnel administration is not an isolated field, but a composite of what has been learned from federal and state civil service and from private sector organizations.

Planning.   As we enter the next decade and the next century, school administrators must be ready to prepare boys and girls for a world that is vastly different from the one in which their teachers grew up. As noted by John Naisbitt,[8] the United States has moved from an agricultural to a manufacturing to an information society. Identifying the needs of the marketplace, providing the correct educational programming, and educating school boards and staff members regarding the changes that are needed will take skill.

Recruitment.   Probably most members of the general population, if asked to define the job of personnel administrator, would respond that the job involves hiring and firing people. Although the job includes many more areas, hiring and firing are critical responsibilities that will continue to be administered by personnel managers. The difference is in the increasing number of external controls in recent years. Personnel administrators must have a complete understanding of laws and regulations that dictate the latitude they are allowed and their responsibilities. Recruitment policy must clearly outline how potential employees will be identified for consideration;

activities related to solicitation must be implemented; questions regarding internal candidates must be addressed; and planning for interviews and communications with all applicants should occur.

Selection. Once recruitment activities have been initiated, the selection process begins. Collecting and checking references, conducting interviews, observing laws and regulations regarding hiring procedures, and making final appointments are all part of personnel management. As a result, the administrator in charge of this area must have a comprehensive knowledge of laws affecting the selection and employment of staff.

Orientation. How new employees are introduced to the school system may have a long-term effect on how those employees feel about their jobs. A structured orientation program to assist new staff members in becoming acclimated to their positions, schools, and the district and community is likely to result in an easier adjustment in the job itself. This effort should be well-coordinated and involve members from various areas of the school and community. Done correctly, it will help in enhancing staff development efforts and retaining personnel.

Staff development. The identification, employment and orientation of new staff members are key procedures in the personnel administration process. However, these are only the start or initiation phase of employment. Staff members should keep up with trends and changes in their business. In recent years greater attention has been given to the need for staff (or personnel) development activities for both professional and support staff members in school districts. Not only do such efforts help to keep staff current, but they also provide opportunities for renewal through intellectual stimulation and colleague interaction.

Personnel procedures. Personnel administrators are responsible for following appropriate procedures after hiring takes place. Paper trails to keep track of probationary and tenure periods must be maintained. Proper actions, in terms of time lines as well as status, related to appointment and separation should take place to avoid potential problems later.

Compensation. One of the calls of reform advocates has been the need for better pay for educators. Personnel administrators must have an understanding of pay standards, scales, arguments for merit pay plans, and merit programs that have been initiated.

Bargaining and administering the negotiated agreement. A matter of importance to all staff members is the negotiated agreement. Preparation for negotiations, making as well as evaluating demands, and bringing a negotiation to closure are all critical activities in which personnel managers are expected to show leadership. Further, once negotiations have been brought to closure, administrators must know how to interpret what has been agreed upon and put it into practice. In any school district, the personnel administrator is the key person in educating staff about their rights and responsibilities in the negotiated agreement.

Conditions of employment. When educators first met to discuss forming teachers into associations, one of the primary reasons for doing so was to improve the conditions under which teachers were asked to work. While other interests have been added, this overall concern has remained constant, and its administration is a primary responsibility of the personnel manager.

Employee data. Because of the rights afforded staff members, personnel offices are required to maintain updated, accurate information on each employee. Data to be collected, means of collection, and methods for cataloging are important for later decisions regarding issues such as reassignment, evaluation, and staff development.

Support staff. The role of support staff in schools is often understated. This employee group is critical to the daily operation of the school district and influential in shaping the perception of the district in the community. Recognition of members of this group and support for their ongoing development are significant responsibilities of the personnel administrator.

Empowering teaching staff. Without question, the 1990s will be the decade of teacher empowerment. The call for radical change in education has been felt in schools by requests or demands for the involvement of teaching staff in decision making. Pressure to respond to this movement may come through various channels, from staff themselves, school boards, and even legislatures and state education departments. Such changes can have critical effects on how schools operate. Personnel administrators will be asked for leadership in understanding and interpreting this concept to members of school districts, and in determining what initiatives are most appropriate for the districts' participation.

Policy and procedure. While the education of staff members most often comes to mind when discussing personnel in schools, education of the board of education is also critical. The role of the board, to establish policy in a school district, is distinct from the administration's role in carrying out policy. An increasing responsibility of the personnel administrator is the ongoing education of school board members to help them in carrying out their roles.

Career paths. One important form of assistance provided by personnel administrators is the support of those who are interested in moving into other positions within the field of education. Opportunities for support staff exist within the support function. Likewise, many teachers are interested in considering opportunities that will allow them to take on increased instructional and support responsibilities without having to leave the classroom entirely. Others may pursue opportunities in administration. The personnel administrator is looked upon as a local expert to provide advice and assistance to those interested in pursuing career changes.

– REFERENCES –

1. Kaufmann, Herbert. "The Growth of the Federal Personnel System." In Wallace S. Sayre (Ed.), *The Federal Government Service*, p. 33. Englewood Cliffs, NJ: Prentice-Hall, 1965.
2. Patten, Thomas H., Jr. (Ed.), *Classics of Personnel Management*, pp. 1–3. Oak Park, IL: Moore, 1979.
3. Wren, Daniel A. "Origins of Industrial Psychology and Sociology." In Thomas H. Patten, Jr. (Ed.), *Classics of Personnel Management*, pp. 4–12. Oak Park, IL: Moore, 1979.
4. Roethlisberger, F.J. "The Hawthorne Experiments." In Thomas H. Patten, Jr. (Ed.), *Classics of Personnel Management*, pp. 16–26. Oak Park, IL: Moore, 1979.
5. Clark, David L., and Astuto, Terry A. "The Significance and Permanence of Changes in Federal Education Policy." *Educational Researcher*, Vol. 15, No. 8 (October 1986), pp. 4–13.
6. Kilmann, Ralph H. "Corporate Culture." *Psychology Today* (April 1985), pp. 63–68.
7. Peters, Thomas J., and Waterman, Robert H., Jr. *In Search of Excellence.* New York: Harper & Row, 1982.
8. Naisbitt, John. *Megatrends: Ten New Directions Transforming Our Lives.* New York: Warner Books, 1982.

CHAPTER

— 2 —

Planning

Probably the most popular metaphor for planning is one that compares the process to taking a trip. A traveler would rarely consider such a venture without knowing where he or she was planning to go. It would also be necessary to consider what highways to use to reach the destination and where to stop for food and lodging. The wise traveler would also make sure to have enough cash and credit for any foreseeable expenses.

Good planning in schools is certainly complex and, because of this complexity, not always well conceived and implemented. In fact, the steps involved in planning are fairly simple. However, the process itself is time-consuming, challenging, and subject to change, depending on the size and complexity of the organization in which it is carried out.

— A CHANGING SOCIETY —

We often hear adults refer to "the way it was when we were growing up." The changes occurring in society as we approach the twenty-first century will call for schools to educate students in a different manner. The students coming into classrooms today have often grown up in family situations much different from those in which their teachers and administrators grew up. Educators may have difficulty identifying with the values of students whose experiences are so different from their own. For example, the U.S. Census Bureau and National Center for Health Statistics tell us that while the marriage rate since 1950 has remained relatively constant, the divorce rate has almost tripled. As a result, one third of the children born in the 1980s may be living in a stepfamily before the age of eighteen. Additionally, approximately 22 percent of the children born in the late 1980s were born to single mothers, with about one third of those mothers being teenagers.[1]

family changes

These numbers point up that the family unit that provided the psychological and emotional base for the children of the postwar baby boom has changed drastically. According to the U.S. Census Bureau, almost 55 percent of today's working women are married. In addition, many of these working mothers are having their first children when they are older than their counterparts of twenty years ago. The National Center for Health Statistics reports that this trend appears to be the result of a desire to complete their education and begin careers; the number of women aged thirty to thirty-four with college degrees went from 40 percent to 48 percent between 1975 and 1986. In addition, the number of first births to women between ages thirty and thirty-four went from 42,404 in 1970 to 181,504 in 1986. The first births for women aged thirty-five to thirty-nine increased from 11,704 to 44,427. Since many of these mothers intend to return to work after having their children, schools must determine how they will adapt to these changes in community makeup. Movement to a philosophy of schools as community centers has been popular since the late 1960s. Many interpreted this to mean opening the doors at night for adult education programs and on weekends for parent organization craft shows and other community functions. Today, many school boards face bigger and more complicated questions: Should the schools offer such services as day-care programs, medical services, child and family services, and job search assistance? Should local taxpayers be asked to support some of these services? Will schools and other agencies find they can provide better and more efficient services to their clients through joint planning?

economic changes

Not only are educators forced to deal with the changes caused by shifting family structures, but certain economic realities must also be considered. At the turn of the century, 6 percent of the total population graduated from high school. By the middle of the century, this number had increased to approximately 75 percent and remained relatively constant. However, the 1980s brought renewed interest in the school dropout problem, as approximately one million students dropped out of American schools annually. The cost of these dropouts in terms of welfare funding and lost revenue is incalculable, but is estimated to be billions of dollars annually. Also the cost of educating a student in the late 1980s would be approximately $5,000 to $6,000 per year, while the average cost of keeping an inmate in prison would exceed $30,000 annually. Since the majority of prison inmates lack at least a high school education, and the business community regularly releases statistics outlining the critical need for labor, a strong message about the demand for an educated work force is evident.

In addition to the profound problem of school dropouts, other factors dictate the need for a more productive work force. Whereas seventeen workers supported each retiree in 1956, it is estimated that between three and four workers will support each retiree by the year 2000, when many postwar baby-boomers will be at or near retirement. This shift will be felt by almost all age groups. According to the U.S. Census Bureau, 36 percent of the population was under eighteen in 1960, approximately 26 percent will fall into this category in 1990, and a further decline to 22 percent is projected for 2030. At the other extreme, 9.3 percent of the population was sixty-five years of age or older in 1960, 12.7 percent fall into this category in 1990, and a significant increase to 20.7 percent is forecast for 2030. The impact of these shifts, on the employment pool for what are presently lower-paying jobs for teenagers and on filling management and executive positions, is significant for how business, industry, and education prepare for the future.

Another major demographic change to be considered involves the shift in the racial and ethnic makeup of the population. The U.S. Census Bureau estimates an increase of 24.8 percent of whites between 1980 and 2030, with an increase of blacks by 68.3 percent; other minorities by 78.7 percent (American Indians, Eskimos, Aleuts, Asians, and Pacific Islanders); and Hispanics by 186.8 percent in the same period.[2]

– STEPS IN THE PLANNING PROCESS –

Some variation may occur, depending on the approach taken, but the process and results involved in planning are relatively similar:

1. Determining the philosophy, vision, and mission of the system;
2. Identifying "where we want to be" (goals and objectives);
3. Identifying "where we are" (baseline information);
4. Determining options for reaching goals and objectives;
5. Determining necessary human and material resources;
6. Identifying barriers to achieving goals and objectives;
7. Determining how to evaluate accurately and repeat the cycle.

While this sequence provides a logical structure, good planning must also allow for flexibility. In other words, effective administrators must be flexible enough to apply new information as it becomes available, not just at the conclusion of the steps outlined. Further discussion will be provided in the evaluation section.

– PHILOSOPHY/VISION/MISSION/GOALS/OBJECTIVES –

Before initiating any type of planning effort, a school administrator must have an accurate idea of the district's beliefs and priorities. Today's school administrator is familiar with such terms as "vision" and "mission." Education is prone to the use of "buzz words," which become embedded, at least for brief periods, in the vocabulary of teachers, administrators, and college personnel, and are used to describe the latest popular programs. At other times, old practices are described through new terminology.

Philosophy

As a course assignment, students in personnel administration classes are routinely asked to bring copies of their school district's philosophy statements to class. Often the statements cannot be located. One student reported that, "The superintendent's secretary has been in the district for over thirty years. She said she knows there use to be one, but . . .". Another student said, "Here's something we found on the front of the teacher handbook [or contract, or board of education policy book], is this what you mean?" These comical responses are quite common. Even when statements of philosophy do exist, and students are asked to note the last time they read them, the typical answer is, "Never."

A school district philosophy usually contains the board of education's beliefs on the purpose of education. Such statements tend to be so general that they could easily be interchangeable from one district to the next. Statements are often ideological, rooted in Western tradition, and permanent. While open to review, they are rarely significantly modified.

Vision

In recent years more has been heard about the concept of vision in both the private and public sectors. The term is generally used to describe a state of being which the leader of an organization is able to articulate to subordinates, clients, and anyone else willing to listen.

In education, vision describes an ideal state of affairs, built upon beliefs that school and community members hold for their schools. Ideally, this vision is developed by school leaders after a lot of listening and discussion with people both inside and outside of the school, including parents, community members, students, school staff, and perhaps even prospective employers and political, business, industrial, and educational leaders. Involved parties at local levels talk together about what is important for their schools and children. While this use of "vision" is relatively new, good administrators have utilized it for years. The best example of a vision was provided by a man who was not a professional educator. The eloquence of

Martin Luther King's "I Have a Dream" speech provides us with a very clear picture of his vision.

Few people can actually define "vision." Some school staff members are indeed able to articulate the vision they have for their school. In one school, the vision was clearly academic excellence for all. Students were grouped heterogeneously throughout elementary and junior high grades. Students were also placed in heterogeneous groups for English and social studies classes throughout their high school years. Every student was expected to pass English and social studies examinations developed for college-bound students. The number of students taking at least three years of course work in college preparatory math and science in this school was more than double the state average. Because middle-class working parents expected their children to attend reputable colleges and universities, parents supported the principal and teachers in the few instances of serious disciplinary concerns. The administrator in this school saw his job as one of supporter/orchestrator. Although much of his time revolved around the daily demands of operating the school, strong community support and the high expectations of the staff made it possible for him to use much of his time and energy to support learning-related activities rather than in walking halls and dealing with disciplinary problems.

In another school, an elementary facility located in an inner city, the students, parents, and teachers had become resigned to the negative climate in their school. A new principal, dedicated to a vision of excellence and equity, convinced his staff that such a vision could be reached. Slogans, programs, and buttons developed by the staff and principal were shared with central office personnel, parents, and children. Although these symbols helped convey the vision of the school, the staff would agree that the major factor that brought them success in attaining the vision was hard work. Staff members put in an extraordinary number of hours to improve school climate and student achievement. When asked how they dealt with staff members unwilling to put in comparable time, one teacher responded, "They felt so uncomfortable being around us that they left on their own."

Although schools are educational institutions, the assumption that the vision will be much the same, centered around educational achievement, is not necessarily true. As in the second example, equity issues warrant attention in many schools. In others, social welfare issues may play an important role. Although concepts such as academics, equity, social welfare, leadership, and self-concept are considered in virtually every school, the emphasis that is finally selected should play an important part in the school's vision.

One of the best explanations of the concept of vision and how it becomes part of a leader's style is provided by Warren Bennis, who studied chief executive officers in private enterprise, and noted:

. . . they view themselves as leaders, not managers. . . . They do not spend their time on the "How to". . . . In short, they are concerned not with "doing things right" [the overriding concern of managers] but with "doing the right thing."[3]

Bennis went on to note some of the common characteristics of effective leaders he studied. They included the ability to develop and communicate a *vision* of a desirable state of affairs for their organizations; ability to *communicate and align* the organization according to the vision; *persistence, consistency,* and *focus* to continue the direction of their organizations even during difficult times; *empowerment* to develop climates that would help bring about the results being sought; and "organizational learnings," which Bennis considered to be the means to monitor, evaluate progress towards objectives, and continuously review past efforts while developing future ones. Included also is the ability to review the structure of the organization and its personnel, to be able to rearrange them when faced with new challenges.

Mission Statements

Mission statements are narrower than statements of vision or philosophy. A mission statement should be brief, conveying its message in one or two sentences. Statements are value-based and summarize the specific beliefs of a school or district. Although correctly developed mission statements may be changed, such changes are usually incremental.

The mission does not belong to the principal, the teachers, the students, or the parents. The mission is an outgrowth of the perceived needs of students in relation to the values of the school community.

Establishing a mission statement should be a developmental process. By identifying and verbalizing the mission of the school district, each person involved in the educational process is put on notice about the district's priorities. Why is a clear understanding of the district's mission so important? Responding to this question in relation to business, Mark B. Roman noted:

> The nature of companies is to self-destruct. This is the second law of thermodynamics applied to business. Companies are in a natural state of entropy. They are collections of individuals, each with a slightly different idea about what the company should do. If left to their own devices, people would cause chaos. The company would pull itself apart. It's the leader's job to keep that from happening and get people thinking along the same lines. Mission statements help channel the energy of every employee in the same direction.[4]

A good way to develop a mission statement is to first develop a number of "belief statements," such as the following:

All students are capable of learning.
Students are the primary purpose of our schools
Discipline is an opportunity for learning, not punishment.

Goals (long-range) and objectives (short-range) focus on specific changes in the operations or behaviors of persons in the school. Changes in statements of goals and objectives are much more common than changes in mission statements. While goals are established for longer periods of time, objectives are usually accomplished in a shorter time—months or perhaps a year and a half at most.

Goals and objectives, when originally determined, are outgrowths of the mission of the school. Likewise, the mission is determined by the ideas expressed in the philosophy of the district. (See Figure 2.1.)

Developing a District Mission Statement

Process. Many managers, in schools and businesses, have jumped onto the "philosophy-mission-belief statements" bandwagon because it seems, based on what is being written and discussed in graduate classes, the right thing to do. In fact, in one district the superintendent and assistant

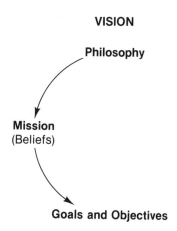

VISION

Philosophy

Mission
(Beliefs)

Goals and Objectives

FIGURE 2.1

superintendent came to a school board meeting (at which some staff members were also in attendance) and presented the board with the new district mission statement they had developed. They proudly handed it over and proclaimed, "This is our new mission statement." The response of one staff member in the audience was "That may be their mission statement, but it sure isn't mine!" The moral of the story is obvious. While the content and substance of philosophy and mission statements are important, the process of developing the statements is equally important.

Members of a school community must be involved in the development of statements. This might be accomplished by a format we have used in consulting with districts on the development of statements.

1. Determine, with the board of education, who will be invited to participate. This might be through direct invitations to individuals or indirectly, by asking the president of teacher, administrator, or support staff associations to identify people who should participate, or a combination. Once participants are identified, invitations should be sent, to explain the purpose of the group and the one-day meeting they are being asked to attend. Approximately thirty people should be involved, including community leaders, business people, board members, students, teachers, and administrators. One district found it useful to include a member of the press.

2. Once the group has formed for its meeting, those attending should be told why the development of a mission and philosophy statement is so important: the statement is a vehicle for informing the community about the purpose of the school district; it is useful for planning; it is an effective communications mechanism, especially for problem solving; it provides a basis for dealing with crises; it makes *all* school people accountable; and it provides direction and cohesion.

3. Conduct an "ice-breaker" exercise to mix the individuals. Allowing all administrators or teachers to remain together in one group should be avoided. Once the ice-breaker is concluded, divide the group into three teams (not competitive teams) or sub-groups. Each should be asked to develop a set of belief statements related to what they *believe* to be the mission of their school district. Once completed, these statements are written on large sheets of newsprint and explained by a spokesperson from each team.

4. Ask the whole group to review all of the statements and to combine those that are similar. Next, ask the group to determine which statements they wish to include or eliminate. Once the elimination

process is completed, each team should look at the list of belief statements that has been agreed upon.

5. Using the agreed-upon statements, ask each team to develop a draft mission statement.

6. Next, a volunteer from each team should be asked to join an ad hoc committee. This committee takes the sample mission statements and list of belief statements and drafts a mission statement to send to all participants.

7. The participants are asked to screen the statement and return it with any comments. The next draft would then be prepared by the ad hoc committee and sent out. After that, representatives from the group of thirty would meet with various constituents to share the draft.

8. Once comments are received from each constituent group, a final version of the statement would be developed and presented to the board of education for adoption.

9. Once adopted, the mission statement should be well publicized in the school and community through any available sources, including newspapers, radio, and television. In addition, and most important, copies of the statement should be printed, framed, and hung in each room in the district's administrative offices and schools.

The belief statements and mission statement that are adopted by the board of education may also provide a basis for the board of education to review the district's philosophy statement. The existing statement may work well in its present form, or some minor revisions may be necessary. The group of thirty might be asked to meet again to assist in the review or development of the philosophy statement, but the philosophy statement is usually within the province of the board of education, who can use the mission statement and accompanying belief statements as a basis of understanding.

The final statement.   While most professional planners agree that a mission statement should be brief and contained in one or two sentences, organizations will tailor their statements to their own needs. Some districts refer to their efforts as mission statements, others call them belief statements, and still others consider them to be working or operating philosophies. Exactly what a statement is called or what it looks like is less important than its ability to convey a message to the organization's audience. See the accompanying statements from the Wellsville Central School District and the Madison-Oneida BOCES (a regional education agency).

WELLSVILLE CENTRAL SCHOOLS
MISSION STATEMENT

The Wellsville Central School District is committed to providing students with a balanced education enabling them to be responsible, contributing members of society. Our goals are to develop self-esteem, respect for others, cooperation, and the ability to think, reason, and communicate. Each individual within the community—students, school personnel, families, citizens, and support organizations—has potential and shares in the responsibility for a successful educational experience.

To fulfill this commitment, the district will . . .

- Provide an educational environment which is nurturing and productive.
- Utilize the resources of the community.
- Foster flexibility and growth by being responsive to concerns, recommendations, and changing needs.
- Be accountable to its students, staff, and the community.

Reprinted by permission of Wellsville Central School District, Superintendent Thomas McGowan.

MADISON-ONEIDA BOCES OPERATIONAL PHILOSOPHY

1. The Madison-Oneida Board of Cooperative Educational Services (BOCES) is responsible for the delivery of requested educational and related services to local school districts and the learners they may entrust to us.
2. Local schools and learners are entitled to high quality services, at a responsible cost, delivered on time as promised.
3. Local schools and learners are to be encouraged to evaluate, comment upon, and commend BOCES services; such feedback will be used to improve and enhance services and will be accepted constructively.
4. Local school personnel and learners are entitled to frequent visits and consultations with BOCES to encourage review, enhancement, and development of BOCES services.
5. BOCES staff members are entitled to equitable pay, pleasant and safe working conditions, and ongoing training.

6. BOCES staff members are entitled to frequent written feedback about their performance based upon a predetermined set of standards.

7. BOCES staff members are expected to evaluate and comment upon operational procedures and practices for the improvement of services. This dialogue can be expected to occur in an environment of acceptance and trust.

8. All BOCES staff members are entitled to recognition for efforts to enhance and develop practices, procedures, and services in addition to payroll remuneration.

9. All BOCES staff members are managers in their own right. As such, they are expected to continually experiment with improved practices and procedures in the delivery of services.

10. Local school representatives, learners, advisory committees, and representatives of other BOCES are to be constantly surveyed about the quality, cost, and development of BOCES services.

Reprinted by permission of the Madison-Oneida Board of Cooperative Educational Services, Superintendent Edward Shafer.

Developing Individual School Mission Statements

In addition to district mission and philosophy statements, a number of individual schools have found it valuable to undergo a similar process at the school level. This process is a valuable means of drawing together the staff in a school to discuss priorities, goals, and even specific activities for meeting agreed-upon goals.

One principal, Cynthia Westbrook, shared her approach to developing a school mission statement, noting eight steps an administrator should take in helping members of the school community identify their mission. The process was titled by using the mnemonic "GIS ASC ME" as a means for designating the steps to be followed. Suggestions in brackets have been added by the authors.

1. *Generate* ideas from the school, culture, and structure. [Talk to people; find out what they believe to be important in the school and community.]

2. Develop an *image* of the desirable future state. [What the school or program should be in relation to how it presently functions.]
3. Formulate a mission *statement* that is clear and concise. [Involve all parties and share each draft for criticism and revision. The steps outlined above for school districts would also be appropriate at the school level.]
4. Develop a plan of *action*. [Get those involved in #3 to "buy in" through commitment and involvement.]
5. Design and use *symbols:* metaphors, insignias, songs. [Capitalize on this step by involving people creatively and by recognizing others for their ideas.]
6. *Communicate* the mission constantly. [Use the symbols to carry forth the mission to the school and community.]
7. *Monitor* the implementation and progress. [Use internal as well as external methods for assessing progress.]
8. *Evaluate* and revise according to changes in environment. [Be honest. Use tools sensitive to the types of changes being attempted.]*

Ramifications. Philosophy and mission statements can have critical ramifications, both practically and legally. On a practical level, such statements will give those involved some idea of what the school is "about." They can also be a valuable reference in planning. For instance, in one district the staff in a middle school agreed on a mission statement that included the point that middle school students should be segregated physically from senior high students as much as practically possible. While room assignments were being scheduled, two special-area teachers came to the principal and argued that they wanted to keep their own rooms (one in the middle school wing, the other in the high school wing), even though they were both involved in teaching at both levels. If their request had been granted, middle school students, at least one period per day, would have had to enter the high school section of the building. The principal referred the teachers to the mission statement that they had helped to draft, to explain that the school would continue to support the physical segregation of middle school and high school students.

Because broad statements may work against boards of education, boards and administrators should be careful about supporting idealized statements that may run counter to the reality in which the schools operate. A potential grievance might be based on the fact that districts have stated certain ideals in philosophy or mission statements that are inconsistent with decisions made by board of education members or administrators.

---

*Reprinted by permission of Cynthia Westbrook.

The process of developing statements is as important as their actual substance. Unless staff are involved and committed to what has been put on paper, they will put the statement on a shelf, never to be seen again. This has happened in many school districts in the past.

Identifying Goals and Objectives

A flow should occur from the *philosophy, mission,* and *vision* (value-based, long-term) statements to the *goals* (long- and intermediate-term) and *objectives* (short-term) of the school. These goals and objectives are the result of a *need* or gap between the present state of being and the desired state of being. According to Lipham and Fruth,[5] goals describe general states or behaviors that a school or district continuously works toward, and objectives are specific behaviors, skills, or outcomes that the school attempts to achieve.

Various units in the school are usually responsible for developing goals and objectives. Some districts require that objectives be developed at all levels, including the board of education, school administrators, and individual staff. How objectives are developed varies from district to district. Board goals and objectives may be constructed by the board of education with the assistance of the school superintendent. Superintendent goals may be developed in conjunction with the board. Administrators of individual schools, as middle managers, may develop their goals in conjunction with the superintendent, or their own staff, or both. Recently, more schools are asking teachers to develop annual goals and objectives as well.

As with the development of philosophy and mission statements, the *process* involved in the development of goals and objectives is as important as their substance. This process should be both "top down" and "bottom up." Involvement from the board, superintendent, and district administrators is necessary to ensure support. Those closest to the ultimate implementation of plans are most familiar with the problems to be solved, and their expertise is critical. The school superintendent and personnel administrator need to work closely with the board in regularly reviewing progress toward meeting goals.

One of the greatest difficulties in the way educational planners operate involves *when* goals and objectives are developed. Educators tend to work on a different calendar than "normal" people, and consider the year to run from July 1st to June 30th. As a result, educators' personal time (determining vacations, setting dates for the year, etc.) is usually based on a year that begins on July 1st. Their professional time (planning on conferences to attend, gearing up to deal with changes in board and staff members, starting a new budget cycle) is also based on a year that begins on July 1st.

Unfortunately, educators also begin activities intended to meet new goals and objectives on July 1, with the understanding that the criteria outlined in their goals and objectives statements must be met by the next June 30th in order to be successful. This is counterproductive for a number of reasons. First, because of the difference between goals and objectives. The time necessary for reaching goals should be longer than the time needed for meeting objectives. A goal is not necessarily going to be reached by meeting one objective, but may require the successful completion of a number of objectives. As a result, goals take longer to meet than objectives. In establishing goals and objectives, administrators should plan on some taking months to complete, and others taking years. In fact, some administrators make a point of having dates for accomplishment set during the school year, rather than at the traditional end of the year on June 30th. This reinforces the message that once the year ends, the goal or objective should not be dismissed as also concluded, and never to be considered again.

Another weakness of educational planners is to think in terms of minimum goals rather than goals that will move their systems toward higher levels of achievement. The vast majority of school district goals make statements concerning minimum competency levels for children, minimum numbers of students who should pass certain tests and/or grade levels, minimum percentages of students expected to go on to college or work, etc. Administrators who are progressive will plan for achievement in terms of the maximum that can be accomplished. For instance, one goal might be to increase the number of students who qualify for the honor roll. Another might be to increase the number of students who meet the requirements to enroll in advanced courses. If schools are to improve as institutions, it is critical that educators begin to think in terms of how students at all levels can be encouraged to achieve, not just how those performing at lower levels can be raised to a basic minimum.

Additionally, goals and objectives should precede budget development. Ironically, educators often operate backwards, developing an annual budget at the midpoint of one year and goals and objectives at the start of the next school year.

Objectives provide short-term benchmarks. A well-written objective should contain at least five specific criteria:

1. *Who* will change.
2. *What* will occur.
3. The *date* by which the change will occur.
4. The *evaluation tool* by which the change will be judged.

5. The *criteria* by which the change will be measured.

Using this model, a sample objective might be: "By June 30, 199__, 95 percent of the sixth graders will pass the State Reading test with a score of at least 75 percent."

The Goal-Setting Process

Many school administrators appreciate the wisdom of having members of the board of education and administration periodically take the time to meet and discuss the status of the district. Sometimes these groups meet individually, sometimes together. The best approach is the one that works for a particular district. Taking the opportunity to discuss and plan in a non-crisis environment is critical to the good health of a school district.

Methods for approaching the process may vary. In some districts the superintendent is asked to act as the coordinator/facilitator for the process. In others, a consultant has been found to be valuable, since an outsider is often able to make observations that an administrator or other "member of the family" would find difficult. Several useful procedures for initiating the goal-setting process are available to school boards. One includes steps calling for discussion, brainstorming and prioritizing.

1. Break participants (administrators and/or community members) into sub-groups of three to five individuals.

2. Ask each sub-group to develop a description of the model school.

3. Ask all sub-groups to share their descriptions with the whole group.

4. Ask members of the full group what gaps exist between the "ideal" description and the present state of the district.

5. Explain to members of the group that they will be asked to generate a list of *potential* topics for district goals and objectives. Using a round-robin approach, ask each member to share one concern which might be a potential goal. If nothing comes to mind, a person may pass until the next time around. Maintain the round robin until all potential topics have been mentioned.

6. Once topics have been listed, go through the list and ask for clarification on any point that might be confusing.

7. Ask members of the group if any of the topics might be combined.

8. Next, ask each member of the group to choose the three topics he or she believes are the most important.

9. Note the number of people who voted for each. Erase topics that draw fewest votes. This method will substantially reduce the list and focus on topics that members see as priorities. Depending on the number of topics generated, it may be necessary to reduce the list even further. This may be done by asking participants to vote again on the *two* topics they believe are most critical. No more than four to six topics should be generated for a single year. However, some topics might be delegated by the board to the administration.

Once priority topics have been identified, they should be interpreted in the goal-objective format outlined in the preceding section on "Identifying Goals and Objectives." Periodic meetings between the superintendent and appropriate administrators should be established to review progress. In turn, those administrators should meet with any other appropriate individuals to monitor their progress and provide assistance.

With the many demands on them, school administrators can easily get caught up in day-to-day activities and fail to remember the long-range goals and objectives that are important to the life and health of the school. Constant consideration of goals is critical, as shown by Bennis and Nanus,[6] who studied executives identified as visionaries. Bennis and Nanus noted that these strong leaders continued to work toward their "vision" regardless of any roadblocks that occurred.

Identifying Baseline Information

Several pieces of information are important to educators concerned with planning changes in their school districts. Depending on the issue under consideration, various types of data are considered; test scores, school completion rates, and percentage of students going on to college are often reviewed in determining the success of local efforts. Success or need for improvement in these areas will vary; for example, in a given year a 60 percent rate for continuing on to college may be excellent in one school district and considered poor in another. Other concerns are constant; decisions related to capital construction, staffing, and program offerings will always

VISION

Philosophy

Mission
(Beliefs)

Goals and Objectives
• Baseline information

FIGURE 2.2

have to be reviewed annually. Planning to meet these needs begins by determining the number of students who will be served.

Forecasting population trends. A popular method of determining population changes in schools, the cohort survival formula, considers the number of students in each grade level in the district over a number of previous years. It also requires consideration of the number of students expected to enter the kindergarten over the next five years, based on census data of children between the ages of 0 and 4 living in the district. Using this information, an average ratio is calculated for each class from year to year, based on available data. Using that average, enrollments for future years are estimated.

While the cohort formula has proven useful, some problems exist and should be acknowledged. First, due to a change in birthrate trends, many communities are seeing an increase in kindergarten enrollments. Some of these increases are attributed to "older mothers," products of the baby boom who waited until they were in their thirties to have their first child. These rises followed what was a general decline in the number of students in American schools over the last decade. As a result, many districts now find themselves in the position of having to locate more space. Unfortunately, many of these same districts closed down and sold off school buildings during the period of decreasing enrollments, thinking they would never need those buildings again. In the meantime, the rise in elementary populations just noted, statutory requirements for improved special education programming, and other external demands such as those resulting from the reform movement have become critical problems for many educational planners.

In estimating locally, administrators should also request information from agencies such as town planning boards, to determine the number of requested building permits, as well as plans by local businesses and industries for expansion or cut-backs. Other factors should also be considered, such as retention rates in the schools. Projecting is an inexact science; the cohort method is as good a tool as any other available, but no method will consistently forecast student enrollments with total success. Most state education departments have bureaus that will help districts make their forecasts. Personnel in these agencies are knowledgeable and willing to assist staff in local districts.

A few additional points are worth noting. Changes presently affecting society, such as first births to baby boom mothers, and changes in economic factors, such as job opportunities, make it more difficult to forecast elementary enrollments than secondary. Secondary forecasts are based on students already attending school; elementary forecasts are based on census information, which tends to be less accurate, making projections of primary grade enrollments more vulnerable to error. Thus, secondary projections are usually more accurate than elementary ones.

To improve accuracy, some districts have determined ways to allow for consistent inaccuracies in elementary projections. For example, some districts have found that census data for three- and four-year-olds are consistently 20 percent below the number of students who actually enroll. They have also found that their data are usually 30 percent below the actual number of zero- to two-year-olds. As a result, these districts find that their most accurate projections come about by adding the appropriate percentage to the census findings. Likewise, some districts have found that using the cohort from a particular grade level (i.e., second grade for zero- to six-year-olds) provides them more accurate projections, because migration in and out of the district is more frequent with younger families.

In summary, there is no method that will consistently provide a school district with accurate enrollment projections. Barring a major change in the conditions in a district, the cohort approach has proved a relatively good method, especially for secondary students. At the primary level, districts should review their projections over the last several years, determine the degree of accuracy, and then determine whether there is consistency in their inaccuracy. Once identified, various means of modifying present procedures can be tested until the best method is determined.

ENROLLMENT PROJECTING

The following directions outline the procedure for projecting enrollments using a cohort survival formula. Following the directions is a partially completed worksheet which includes the necessary background data needed to complete the projections and the projections for the first and second grades. . . .

Using the Cohort Survival Formula

1. Begin by using the 1984–85 data. In figuring, set your calculator to round up (>.5) or down.
2. Note that the kindergarten enrollment for 1984–85 is 53. The 1st grade enrollment for 1985–86 is 66.
3. Divide the 1985–86 1st grade enrollment by the 1984–85 kindergarten enrollment—ratio of 1.25.
4. Figure the ratio for each set of numbers.
5. After figuring all of them, add the four ratios in each column and divide by 4 to get an AVERAGE RATIO. The AVERAGE RATIO for the first column should be 1.08.
6. Multiply 1988–89 Kindergarten enrollment (68) × AVERAGE RATIO (1.08) = 1st grade (73) for the 1st grade in 1988–90.
7. Do for each grade for 1989–90.
8. Do the same thing for 1990–91, multiplying the kindergarten enrollment × AVERAGE RATIO. Do NOT figure ratios for years starting with 1988–89.
9. Add across to get the total student population for each year.

Source: Adapted from New York State Education Department's *Cohort Survival Formula.*

Program mandates. In addition to increased enrollments in many school districts, program mandates have also affected planning by school decision makers. Requirements such as additional foreign language courses, opportunities for accelerating junior high school students, instruction in special areas in the middle school years, and additional instruction in

COHORT PROJECTION WORKSHEET

Year	Kd	1	2	3	4	5	6	7	8	9	10	11	12	Total
1984	53	65	56	66	64	85	79	93	77	96	70	87	78	969
1985	50	66	62	63	62	69	85	86	90	70	94	67	88	952
1986	52	52	65	60	58	64	68	93	85	87	78	89	68	919
1987	68	54	55	67	53	56	64	75	95	90	91	74	90	934
1988	68	68	57	59	76	52	58	67	74	95	92	88	68	924
Average Ratio														
1989	60	73												
1990	62	64												
1991	55	60												
1992	50	59												
1993	50	59												

Handwritten annotations:

66/53

1.25 1.04 1.07 1.00

.95 .98 1.06 1.09

X 1.08

Y2/Y1

BOYS SUMS

various secondary areas such as social studies, math, and science, will require added space and personnel. In addition, other program offerings have become desirable, as parents and students both expect that students should be computer literate.

Enrollments and program mandates are primary concerns to planners, but other local issues must also be considered. For instance, the removal of asbestos has, or will have, a major impact on the use of school funds. This impact will undoubtedly be felt in many other areas of a school. As an example, it is likely to affect the number of dollars available for personnel (number of personnel employed and how those who are employed will be compensated). The ability to finance new programs or to supplement existing ones will also be affected. In reality, virtually every aspect of district operation is apt to feel the impact of a major financial demand.

The addition of classrooms is yet another consideration. The increased number of elementary students, along with greater secondary program requirements, have required many districts to ask voters to approve building projects. In some cases these have been additions, in others, entire new schools.

In the ideal situation, building and program needs drive staffing and resource needs. Based on this, decisions are made and implemented. However, in the not-so-ideal world of reality, cost is a factor many school boards and administrators must confront. The ability to support programs is critical and often difficult. When a fiscal shortfall occurs, administrators who have planned well and are able to present convincing evidence to their school boards and communities are often able to establish and maintain the programming that they believe is important. In other cases, regardless of how critical the educational needs may be, communities may refuse to support budget requests, and funding is much more restricted.

Strategies and Resources for Reaching Goals and Objectives

The numerous goals and objectives that many school administrators adopt annually are unrealistic if the purpose is to make real changes in the school systems. Certain objectives, such as instituting a new math curriculum in the high school, may be viewed as "mechanical." In other words, if the decision to adopt the change has been made, the objective can be achieved after planning the steps to be taken. While important and time-consuming, the process will not significantly affect the organization or operation of the school. On the other hand, improvement of school climate, student discipline, or management-labor relations are goals that take a tremendous amount of planning, day-to-day attention, and sensitive evaluation.

Without question, one of the most demanding tasks for administrators is determining how to reach their goals and objectives. As we approach the end of the century, many veteran budget watchers are forecasting more difficult financial times for education. If this forecast is accurate, meeting goals and objectives will be even more difficult.

The role of the personnel manager, whether a full-time individual or a line administrator with personnel functions assigned to him or her, is at the center of a school district's planning. This individual must provide leadership to help determine how goals and objectives, visions, missions, and philosophies are to be reached by use of available resources.

Factors. One major responsibility of a board of education is to determine whether to fund particular programs. If a board accepts proposed goals and objectives, planners should have some confidence that needed resources will be made available. However, if new board members run on a platform of fiscal conservatism, or if concerned citizens' groups pressure present board members, financial commitments can be, and often are, rescinded. Thus, the bottom line message for administrators is a simple one: never take anything for granted.

Life on this seesaw provides some administrators with their greatest challenges. Many enjoy the opportunity to be tested, to see how well they can move the system toward established goals and objectives, especially in difficult times. Research on visionary leaders shows that those who are true visionaries are able to keep their organizations on track even through the tough periods.[6] So it is with strong educational leaders.

Facility and program resources are of increasing concern in many school districts. The demands made by the reforms of the 1980s, along with special education mandates that many states have adopted, have called upon schools to offer more programs. However, increased student populations or a lack of space result in instances of some unmet mandates. When faced with the threat of losing their ability to offer comprehensive programs, some districts are forced to consider cutting back services such as full-day to half-day kindergartens and use of buildings by the community, or the possibility of scheduling split sessions, merging, or other options not considered attractive by the public. In addition, demands from the marketplace for students with skills such as computer literacy have meant yet another mandate for educators.

The best strategy for ensuring ongoing program development is through good planning. While the board of education approves philosophy and mission statements, program goals and objectives are usually developed by those in the schools—administrators and teachers. The personnel administrator must keep the superintendent and board of education abreast of progress being made in meeting the district's goals and objectives. In doing so, the personnel administrator constantly reminds them of the correlation between daily functioning and district mission. Without question, board support is critical to program functioning. By reminding the board of the priorities it has set, the personnel administrator, and consequently the program, should be able to maintain better support.

In addition to the important role of the board, staff support, particularly that of instructional personnel and school administrators, is also of critical importance. A number of studies have pointed out the need for staff involvement for a project to succeed. Active support by the district superintendent is also important. Without his or her willingness to provide release time, recognition, and needed resources, a program's chance for success is minimal.

Community involvement is also a concept practiced in many school districts, and one which will probably receive even more attention in coming years. The twenty-first annual Gallup Poll (1989) indicated that 20 percent of the population surveyed did *not* favor parent involvement in establishing standards for schools but also that 60 percent of those surveyed favored pupils and parents having the option to choose which public schools in their communities students will attend. Only 8 percent gave public schools an "A" rating and 33 percent a "B." The majority of residents in most school districts do not have children, so there is certainly a need to inform and solicit the support of those subsidizing education but having no children in the school.[7]

Most educators would agree that involvement by community members should be sought by the schools, but the extent of involvement is often a subject for debate. Many school people can recall stories of athletic coaches and music directors who formed "booster clubs," and two or three years later members of the booster clubs called for the dismissal of the same coach or band director who helped organize them in the first place.

Advisory groups can be helpful and should be utilized. To be successful, such groups should have the following:

1. *Specific purpose:* Groups should not be formed for the purpose of sharing information and gathering opinions. Such generality leads to problems. Some people may feel they were not given all the information they desire. In addition, a lack of guidelines regarding what opinions are to be collected can lead to a group of people who are willing to give opinions on any imaginable topic, even those outside of their area of direct involvement.

2. *Membership destined for success:* Any school administrator can attest

to the fact that having the wrong cross section of people on a committee can quickly kill any effort to solve important problems. Certainly, any task force should represent various views. What such a group should not include is a contingent likely to support one view regardless of what ideas might emerge during the life of the group. Do administrators sometimes manipulate membership on committees? Absolutely. A group should not be packed with people likely to support the board's or administrators' viewpoints, but selection should include people who are objective, will bring different points of view, and will not promote a personal agenda, regardless of the facts.

3. *Starting and ending dates:* By keeping groups aware of what is expected and by when, administrators are more likely to keep them on task. This helps prevent wasting time on incidentals or getting caught up in minutiae.

4. *A prescribed number of meetings:* Predetermine the number of meetings necessary, if possible. Throughout the planning process, it often becomes necessary for planning staff to meet for extended periods without interruption. This is particularly important during the initial stage, when the philosophy and mission statements are developed, and near the conclusion after activities have been developed. If absolutely necessary, additional meetings can always be called, but by keeping the group aware of their purpose, unnecessary meetings can more easily be avoided.

5. *Awareness of responsibility:* Probably nothing can damage the reputation and credibility of an administrator or board of education more than giving a community group an erroneous impression of their level of authority. Groups must know exactly how their final recommendations will be considered. This may include:

   a. Recommendation will be adopted.
   b. Recommendation will be given *strong* consideration.
   c. Recommendation will be considered.

In addition, members should know who will be handling their recommendation. Using a school-based group as an example, this too may vary:

   a. Recommendation goes from group to school or program administrator who will recommend to the superintendent.
   b. Recommendation goes from group to superintendent who will recommend to the board.
   c. Recommendation will be made directly to the board.

Depending on what is to be accomplished, as well as who endorsed the formation of the committee, these determinations should be made before the first meeting of the committee, so all individuals and groups are fully aware of their limits and responsibilities.

In addition, some internal decisions must be made in the group itself, such as how leadership of the group will be determined. Administrative representation on any committee is strongly recommended.

— CHARTING PROGRESS —

A team approach to program development and planning is recommended. Without question, the collective expertise and insights of teachers and administrators will enrich any effort at program implementation. By outlining what a program should look like once in place, the planning team can determine what needs to be done, by whom, and when. A Program Review Chart outlines these responsibilities. (See the box on p. 40.) It can be used to illustrate progress and help the personnel administrator and those on the planning team to map their efforts.

Identifying Barriers

No set formula can identify blockages that must be eliminated to implement change in a school district. A number of standard reactions to change efforts are well known. "We've tried that before," and "That will never work here" are heard in many schools when someone suggests an effort that might call for change from the status quo. Involvement of respected, veteran staff members in any important project is always advisable. Having these staff members discuss challenges is a useful method of identifying potential difficulties and possible responses.

A systematic approach to problem identification is advised. Categories should first be identified: What human resources will be needed? Offices for support? Individuals? Are there contract or policy limitations to be considered? What personnel (groups or individuals) are likely to resist this effort and why? What information exists to support a recommendation for change? What information must still be gathered and who will go about getting it? Undoubtedly, other categories and questions will also exist and should be identified as part of the team effort by those involved. Once potential problems are determined, staff members should work together to prepare for resistance by developing planning strategies.

PROGRAM REVIEW CHART

The following is an example of objectives a district office staff might adopt in a given year and a calendar administrators could use to monitor and plan.

The key used (PD, P, I, etc.) can be altered based on the individual. For instance, some administrators might use "R" to designate the month during which a *report* of progress must be filled.

Objectives Calendar

Objectives

1.0 Develop a process and program for inservice for new school board members—Supt.
2.0 Complete a review of the district testing program—Dir., Pupil Services.
3.0 Develop a district public relations program—Asst. Supt., Personnel Services.
4.0 Initiate a joint labor management committee for problem solving—Asst. Supt. Mgmt.

Objective	Jul	Aug	Sep	Oct	Nov	Dec	Jan	Feb	Mar	Apr	May	Jun	Jul
1.0	PD	P	—	P	—	—	—	—	—	—	PO	E	
2.0		P	P	P	P	—	—	—	—	—	E		
3.0	P	P	—	—	—	—	—	—	—	PO	E	P	P
4.0	PD	P	P	—	—	—	—	—	—	—	PO	E	P/I

PD: Pre-data Collection PO: Post-data Collection
P: Planning E: Evaluation
I: Implementation

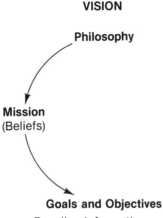

FIGURE 2.3

Planning staff should also recognize that many of those who resist are not doing so because of the specific change being recommended as much as from fear of something different. Asking a long-term teacher who has taught college-bound students for a number of years to take on hard-to-teach students will often bring howls of protest. Regardless of the amount of hard data available (dropout rates, dismal test scores, lack of skills of newer staff members in handling these students), such a suggestion is likely to be greeted with strong resistance. While a quick answer to dealing with such a problem will not be provided in these pages, options are available that should be identified prior to making such a recommendation—for example, contractual incentives, team teaching opportunities, and curriculum development programs.

Evaluating Progress and Repeating the Cycle

Educators hate failing to meet goals and objectives. They believe such failure implies that the teacher or administrator or board member has done a less than adequate job. However, literature from business, such as *In Search of Excellence*,[8] makes the point that failure can often be viewed productively, particularly when those involved are able to learn from the failure.

VISION

FIGURE 2.4

A number of obstacles hinder good evaluation. For one, an activity is often conducted "in house" by the same people who will ultimately be evaluated on its success. Consequently, even the most honest person is likely to have difficulty being objective when variables such as security, annual raises, or board and community impressions are involved.

Second, often the goals and objectives that have been established are unrealistic. For instance, one new elementary principal determined with a reading teacher that all Chapter 1 students would show a growth of one year in reading between September and June. Previously, many of these same students had gained only a half to two-thirds of a year's growth, even with extensive remediation. Critics of this goal said that projecting this kind of increase was unrealistic. On the other hand, proponents of the principal's effort argued that the goal was noble, regardless of success or failure.

The final result was mixed. Some students were able to achieve one year's progress, but the majority did not. Were those who were unable to achieve one year's growth considered to be failures? Did the principal and reading specialist fail? In this case, no. The superintendent was able to point out that when looking at the results in another way, in overall gain, in-dividually and collectively, the group performed better than it had in preceding years. Fortunately, this administrator judged from another, more positive perspective.

This story points out the need for evaluation efforts that take all pertinent information into consideration, including factors such as the population served, approach used, previous performance, and resources. A rational frame of reference will provide a great deal of help to those examining data to determine the effectiveness of practices.

— A CASE STUDY —

The following case study is related to an instructional concern in one high school; it illustrates a number of the points described.

CASE STUDY—LOW SOCIAL STUDIES RESULTS

CONCERN: Social studies final examination results for Mr. Jones's classes on the state test were below average compared to neighboring schools, as well as in relation to other schools in the state. Many of the same students scored well on their other final examinations, but they did poorly in social studies. The principal conducted a review of results from Mr. Jones's students and found they had been consistently low over the years.

BACKGROUND: Conversations were held with Mr. Jones, who did not agree that a problem existed. He argued that the students actually knew social studies, and that he just refused to "teach to the test." The principal rejected this argument and collected the following data: (a) a survey of graduates over the last three years to assess overall school offerings, with results indicating a concern by past graduates with their social studies preparation; (b) final examination grades in social studies from his school for the last three years; (c) final examination grades for the last three years for the same students in English 11 from his school; (d) final examination grades from neighboring schools in social studies and English 11.

Once data were compiled, the principal spoke with a professor from a nearby college and had a statistical analysis of the results conducted. Quantitative findings included a correlation between social studies and English 11 grades for students in each of the three neighboring schools. Students who did well in social studies also tended to do well in English 11. Students who did poorly on the social studies examination tended to do poorly on the English 11 examination.

RESULT: The principal shared the information with Mr. Jones, who finally agreed that a problem did exist and agreed to work out a corrective action plan. Based on their collaboration, the following was determined:

NEED: Over the last three years, an average of 55 percent of the students taking the state examination in social studies passed.

GOAL: To better prepare students to handle college-level social studies/history and improve final examination results.

OBJECTIVE: By June 30, 199__, at least 85 percent of the students taking the social studies examination will pass it.

ACTION PLAN: The following plan was developed:

Activities	Person(s) Responsible	Dates	Resources Needed
Teacher and Dept. Chair will analyze exam results for last three years.	Teacher	6/9__	
Representative from State Ed Bureau of Social Studies will review program and make recommendations.	Principal	7/9__ –8/9__	
Teacher will rewrite social studies curriculum.	Teacher	7/9__	$500 (stipend)
Teacher will be in-serviced in teaching methodologies.	Principal	9/9__ –10/9__	$500
Teacher will observe and meet with "master teachers" from two other high schools identified by Principal and Chair.	Teacher/ Chair	9/9__ –10/9__	$100 (subs)
Teacher will use in-service days to visit members of history depts from two local colleges.	Teacher	11/9__	
Teacher will implement curriculum changes and teaching methodologies.	Teacher	9/9__	
Weekly observations will occur; team teaching will occur.	Chair	9/9__ –12/9__	
Bi-weekly observations will be conducted.	Chair	1/9__ –6/9__	

EVALUATION: Based on an average of final examination results from June 199__ and June 199__.

— IMPLEMENTING PLANNING ACTIVITIES —

Planning activities are often the responsibility of the district's personnel director. However, many districts do not have an individual specifically designated to handle personnel matters, and consequently those responsibilities are often handled by members of the administrative staff. Exactly who will handle a particular problem will vary, depending on the issue. For instance, year-to-year staffing questions are often the primary responsibility of the school administrator, who then makes recommendations to the superintendent. Likewise, a single-school project may be the responsibility of the district's business administrator. Advantages to using internal personnel include: loyalty to district, an awareness of local "politics," knowledge of the district to help expedite the completion of tasks, and less expense.

At times, districts will opt to use an outside consultant. This is often due to the inability of staff to handle a major planning activity, because of time restrictions or the need for special skills. Advantages to using outside consultants include their lack of involvement in internal politics; outsiders can often pose questions that need to be asked but that local administrators would hesitate to ask. Other advantages are objectivity, ability to see options that inside staff may not, knowledge of activities going on in other districts, specific expertise, broader experiential background on which to draw, and finally, the ability to draw conclusions and make public statements that would be difficult for local administrators.

— SUMMARY —

This chapter outlines key components in the planning process, beginning with a description of demographic changes that must be considered by schools as they prepare for the next century. The importance of planning components, including philosophy, mission, vision, goal, and objective statements, is emphasized. A number of recommendations for conducting planning efforts are provided, including development of mission statements at both the district and local school levels. The importance of baseline information as a standard for future measurement is also discussed. Another factor that should be considered in planning is the role of the school board in providing support for facility, personnel, and program resources. The chapter concludes with a case study illustrating a planning effort made at the school level.

— REFERENCES —

1. "The 21st Century Family." *Newsweek* (Winter/Spring, 1990), p. 16.
2. Ibid.
3. Bennis, Warren. "Leadership Transforms Vision into Action." *Industry Week,* Vol. 213, No. 5 (May 31, 1982), pp. 54–56.
4. Roman, Mark B. "The Mission—Setting Your Vision in Words Is the Crucial Executive Act." *Success* (June 1987), pp. 54–55.
5. Lipham, James M., and Fruth, Marvin J. *The Principal and Individually Guided Education.* Reading, MA: Addison-Wesley, 1976.
6. Bennis, Warren, and Nanus, Burt. *Leaders—The Strategies for Taking Charge.* New York: Harper & Row, 1985.
7. Gallup, Alec M., and Clark, David L. "The 21st Annual Gallup Poll of the Public's Attitude toward the Public Schools." *Phi Delta Kappan* (Sept. 1989), pp. 41–54.
8. Peters, Thomas J., and Waterman, Robert H., Jr. *In Search of Excellence.* New York: Harper & Row, 1982.

CHAPTER

— 3 —

Recruitment

What bonds a particular group of people into an identifiable organization is how that group functions, how group members conduct themselves together, and how they structure themselves to carry out their mission. In other words, selected people, whether employed in school districts, corporations, medical associations, or other types of organizations, decide that certain mutually agreed-upon tasks should be completed so their organization can function appropriately. They define who will do what, when, where, how, and how well. To accomplish these tasks, effective organizations use job descriptions, regularly determined goals and objectives, and job performance evaluations. They identify rewards and sanctions by using salaries, promotions, demotions, and severance, and also use unspoken means such as allowing or disallowing an individual into the social structure of the work group.

— EFFECTIVE RECRUITING —

For organizations to operate in an effective manner, people must be identified who can function in harmony with their goals and leadership. An effort must be made to keep a constant watch for people who would be likely to perform well in a school district. This defines the recruitment process.

Schools are often characterized as fishbowls for two reasons. First, laws in most states require that boards of education conduct the majority of their business before the public. As a result, school and community members have the opportunity to hear their boards deliberate, argue, and come to agreement on concerns affecting them. Second, virtually all of the people who subsidize the schools were once students themselves. As a result, many consider themselves to be experts and to know what is best for the education of their children, regardless of what professionals or elected officials might say.

In addition to all this, schools service the most fragile and cherished possession of any community: its children. Theoretically, there should never be room for a "weak" teacher or administrator. Ineffective individuals may continue in school systems because of time-consuming and costly processes for termination, but superintendents and school board members will regularly hear concerns raised over staff members perceived as poor performers.

To fill vacant positions when opportunities arise, effective school administrators constantly keep abreast of employment trends, potential openings in their district, and talented persons who might be recruited if an opening does occur. This process may be hindered due to practical or contractual restrictions, but good administrators make a point of keeping an eye out for talent in case a vacancy arises.

Recruitment Procedures

To attract competent people, school districts should organize and implement specific and detailed employee recruitment procedures. The ongoing process combines both formal (newspaper advertising, college placement services) and informal (word of mouth, old boy/girl networks) means.

Formal recruitment procedures must include at least the following:

Foundation activities
Roles and responsibilities
Candidate sources
Materials and literature

— FOUNDATION ACTIVITIES —

The recruitment program is centered on matching a position with the best candidate. Demand is continually changing because people and positions change. Neither the organization nor the individuals who comprise the organization stand still, and the needs of both fluctuate. To serve the interests of each, certain elements must be part of every recruitment program. These elements should be planned and structured before initiating the recruitment process.

Determining Need

The first foundation activity involves confirming the need to fill a position. People in organizations often assume that when a job is vacated, it will be filled again and life will go on as normal. In actuality, the vacancy provides an opportunity to examine how the position functions in relation to the rest of the organization, in terms of both contributions and drawbacks. It also provides the chance to determine whether the position is needed as it exists or might be made more effective through a modification of duties. In some cases, particularly in business and industry, close examination is given to determine whether the job needs to be filled at all, or if it might simply be eliminated.

Another factor should also enter into this process. Quite often a job becomes the person in it. In other words, while a position description may exist, the individual who fills the position really defines the job. Because of special talents, time in the position, knowledge of the organization, respect given the individual by colleagues, and other related factors, the job description may differ from the job being done. After a number of years pass, administrators may look at the job description and discover that it does not relate to the duties the person in the position actually performs.

Administrators often fail to take time to review the needs of the school in relation to the jobs presently being performed. Often the jobs employees are presently performing have changed from the positions for which they were originally hired. This happens at all levels. The individual employed as an elementary principal may slowly take more and more responsibility for administering the special education program. The social studies teacher who has an interest in computers may take responsibility for a single computer course, and three or four years later will be spending half of his or her teaching time instructing computer education courses. To keep current, administrators should conduct an annual audit of student needs, staffing requirements, and district records. If staffing changes are necessary, they should be recommended by administration for board of education approval prior to the start of each school year.

Each time a position becomes available, the school administration at both the local and district levels should review the need for the position. Using a teaching position as an example, several questions are appropriate to investigate:

Does the person presently in this position have a full teaching load?
Does everyone in the department have a full teaching load?
If some department members have light loads, could sections be shifted to allow for more efficient use of staff?

Does the department provide all of the course offerings which the district has mandated?

Are there teachers in other departments who are also certified in this content area and who might be better utilized by being shared between departments?

What enrollment trends are foreseen for the immediate future?

School administrators should take the opportunity to review position vacancies regularly and determine their need or modification. As in other sectors, changes could make the position more valuable and offer more to the schools. A regular process for such review should be in place, and its implementation should be standard operating procedure. One aid to such a procedure is the use of a form to be completed each time a vacancy occurs. Completing the form will act as a reminder to the personnel administrator to conduct a review of the position.

REQUEST FOR CREATING A POSITION

Part I

(To be completed by the School or Program Administrator)

Date of request	_____
Division	_____
Effective date for position	_____
Department or program	_____
Position title	_____
Supervisor of position	_____
School district location assignment	_____
Budget code	_____
Estimated salary	_____

Attachments:

1. Rationale for creating position (if appropriate)
2. Job description or duties statement
3. Statement of qualifications for position

---

4. Civil Service forms (if required)

_____
SIGNATURE OF ADMINISTRATOR

Part II

(To be completed by Assistant Superintendent for Business)

Funds budgeted in the code   _____

Funds already encumbered   _____

Funds available   _____

Authorization for additional expenditures
(if required):   _____

   Date authorization received   _____

   Authorization signed by   _____

     Recommended approval   _____

     Recommended disapproval   _____

Transfer of funds required
_____
SIGNATURE OF ASSISTANT
SUPERINTENDENT OF BUSINESS

Part III

(To be completed by Superintendent)

Approved   _____

Disapproved   _____

_____
SIGNATURE OF SUPERINTENDENT

_____
DATE

Source: Oneida-Madison Board of Cooperative Educational Services, New Hartford, New York.

The next foundation activity requires the regular examination of all employee contracts, applicable laws and regulations, court decisions, regulatory agency rules, compliance requirements, and commissioner and state board of education decisions. Administrative staff should be involved in this review, assure familiarity with controls that might impinge on the recruitment process. In addition, team collaboration also helps ensure more consistency in the way the process is enacted on a day-to-day basis. An annual full-day seminar, or at least part of a day during an annual administrative staff retreat, on recruitment practices can provide valuable training. Such seminars are usually presented by school attorneys or labor relations officers who specialize in labor law and are able to provide updates on findings from recent court cases and legislation.

The Recruitment Policy

Following these regular reviews, a district should develop or modify its recruitment policy and regulations, as appropriate. The policy should define what is expected of recruiters and stress strict compliance by all staff with its provisions. A comprehensive recruitment policy might include the following topics:

1   *How policy is implemented.* The role of the board of education, administration, and any other involved personnel, such as screening and interviewing committees, should be included.

2   *Responsibility for implementing policy.* The duties of contact persons for each of the various activities should be clearly outlined so that all individuals involved know their responsibilities. Additionally, everyone connected with the process, either internal or external, and particularly staff and candidates, should have a clear understanding of whom to contact with questions and concerns.

3   *Centralized/decentralized/regional recruitment programs.* States differ in the organization of their school districts. Some have active regional educational agencies that assist local districts in various activities, from providing educational services such as occupational and special education programs to other services such as assisting with personnel matters. Where smaller-sized districts operate, a regional service providing assistance in advertising, collecting, and reviewing personnel applications may be utilized. In such instances, candidates may have the option of actually applying for positions in more than one district if a common application is used. Likewise, such agencies often will hold job fairs where representatives from various constituent districts may interview applicants for positions.

Affirmative action/no discrimination provisions. Unless required by an external agency or the courts, school districts are not required to be affirmative action employers. If a district practices affirmative action, their recruitment policy should include a statement of its commitment.

Nepotism. A statement regarding nepotism and whether it is an acceptable practice should be included. If acceptable, but within restricted guidelines, the written policy should specify those guidelines. If unacceptable, specific relationships to be considered as nepotism should be noted.

SAMPLE BOARD OF EDUCATION POLICY ON NEPOTISM

The Board of Education of the Applewood School District is committed to hiring the best qualified candidates to fill available positions.

I. Statement of Policy

The Board of Education will employ relatives of staff members already employed by the school district if they are the most qualified candidates for available positions and have completed the recruitment and selection process in the same manner expected of other applicants. These relatives will not be employed in positions in which they will either directly supervise or be under the direct supervision of their family members.

II. Definition of Family Member

A family member, for this policy, shall be defined as any one of the following:

Wife or husband	Grandparent
Son or daughter	Father-in-law
Grandchild	Mother-in-law
Mother	Son-in-law
Father	Daughter-in-law
Brother	Sister

III. Exceptions to Policy

The Board of Education recognizes that specific child, school, or legal demands may call for exceptions to this policy to meet needs adequately. If this occurs, the Superintendent of Schools will be responsible for administering those situations and will communicate those situations to the Board of Education at a reasonable time after such decisions have been made.

Residency requirements. A district should decide whether it will require residency by staff members if it can legally do so, and should make this information available early in the employment process. This mandate should be included in the recruitment and selection policy. Specific mandates such as residency should also appear on recruiting literature. Such a requirement could make a difference in whether a candidate decides to apply for a position, and prevents unnecessary paperwork and time consideration for candidates who are not willing to move.

Posting and advertising positions. Policies should outline where positions will be advertised and posted. Often school offices are designated, and sometimes faculty rooms are also used. In addition, many states require the school district to designate a local newspaper as its official source for posting notices. A district's official newspaper may be a required source for advertising outside of the district.

Preparation and professional qualifications. Competencies related to knowledge of subject matter, expected knowledge of trends and programs, understanding of child development, understanding of learning and instruction, interest, commitment, and other related criteria should be outlined.

Personal and professional experiences. Desired educational and professional experiences should be noted. For instance, if only experienced individuals will be considered for positions, this requirement should be noted in the recruitment and selection policy.

Information requested from candidates. Since variations exist between different school districts, this information should be specified in the policy.

Standard types of information might include a letter of interest, application, reference letters, resume, and transcripts.

(11) *Penalties for information that is not truthful.* A clear statement should be included to specify how an individual will be treated who knowingly falsifies an application.

(12) *Handling job inquiries.* Many districts prefer that all inquiries regarding positions should be made in writing to the contact person specified in the advertising information. However, some provide a phone number, implying that personal contact is acceptable. A standard procedure should be adopted, included in the policy, and reflected in recruiting literature.

SAMPLE BOARD OF EDUCATION POLICY
POLICY FOR RECRUITMENT AND
SELECTION OF INSTRUCTIONAL STAFF

The board desires an active recruitment policy to attract the best possible candidates. The screening of these candidates should result in the improvement of professional staff and a balance in experience, geographical background, etc.

I. Recruitment

    A. Determination of vacancies shall be made at the earliest possible moment.

    B. Recruitment of candidates

        1. The successful candidate will be the person with the best qualifications for the position.

        2. A recruitment brochure will be prepared and widely distributed.

        3. Individuals known to our staff (former employees, professional contacts, friends, etc.) should be used as sources for the recommendation of candidates.

        4. When desirable, advertisements in professional magazines and city newspapers may be placed to attract candidates.

        5. Selected college placement offices may be used to interview candidates on those campuses.

6. Finalists may be invited to the district for an interview.
7. Recommendations of candidates by present school personnel will be given consideration.
8. Present and former employees will be considered as candidates for openings.

II. Screening

A. Candidates will be screened by administrators.
B. Visits to selected universities may be conducted for the purpose of interviewing prospective candidates. The interviewer(s) will bring back the credentials of candidates they believe we should consider.
C. All inquiries regarding applications or vacancies should be forwarded to the superintendent, who will respond with a letter indicating whether the position is presently vacant. Upon receipt of the application, the superintendent will review the application and if it is acceptable, will request that credentials be forwarded to us.
D. All applications will be filed by the superintendent's secretary; the location of each application should be noted when it is out of the central file.
E. Interviews will be given by the principal(s) in every case. The interviewing principal will have the responsibility of sending a post-interview letter to the applicant.

After every interview, each interviewer will complete an Interview Rating Sheet [see Chapter 4] and attach the rating sheet to the candidate's application.

III. Competencies

A. Knowledge of subject matter and of new developments in that subject area.
B. Knowledge of new ideas and developments in education and efforts to implement them.
C. Knowledge of children and their patterns of behavior, growth, and learning.
D. Interest in and commitment to public education and to children.
E. Understanding of instructional responsibilities, including establishment of objectives; levels of student performance; teaching through a variety of media and materials to allow for individualized attention and encourage individual progress; proper use of special personnel; evaluation of both the curricular program and student progress.

F. Willingness to accept professional responsibilities such as supervising student teachers; working with interns, aides, or volunteers; participation in experimentation, research and continued self-development.

G. Ability to work with staff members, to take constructive criticism and act upon it, to see oneself as a member of a team, to establish positive relationships with parents and the community.

IV. Employment

A. The superintendent will have an opportunity to interview all candidates. Prior to hiring, each finalist should visit the district.

B. Prior to offering a position, the superintendent, principal(s) and, if appropriate, the department chairperson will meet to discuss the merits of the candidates. Final selection will be made by the superintendent.

C. The superintendent will offer the position and establish the salary with the finalist; salary will not be discussed specifically by principals, although they may wish to show the candidate the salary schedule.

D. Following board approval, the appointment notice will be prepared in duplicate for the signature of the clerk of the board. The original and copy will be sent to the teacher, who will sign one copy and return it to the superintendent. This will be placed in the teacher's folder.

E. Types of appointments—Every person hired for an instructional position will receive one of the following types of appointments: probationary, regular, substitute, or part-time.

V. Information and Background Data to be Collected

A. Letter of intent
B. Application
C. Recruitment control card—to be completed by the on-campus interviewer or superintendent's secretary when the application is received.
D. Interview rating sheet—to be completed by each interviewer and placed in the folder of each candidate who visits the district.
E. Credentials

> **F.** Reference checks—the principal who invites the candidate will contact references and place reference sheets in the folder.
> **G.** Miscellaneous—any other information regarding the candidate's qualifications will also be placed in the folder.
>
>
> Source: Vernon-Verona Central School District, Vernon, New York. Reprinted by permission of the Superintendent, Dr. Albert Kouba.

Activities and Information

Once a policy has been adopted, specific foundation activities must be developed. These activities should be position-oriented and include the following:

A current list of all job titles in the school district;
Current job descriptions for all positions—administrative, instructional and support;
A summary of educational qualifications and experience requirements;
Specific information on authority structures—who reports to whom;
Location where work will be performed;
Work and vacation schedules;
Salary and fringe benefits;
Relationship of the union to each position;
Other expectations, such as PTA and committee memberships.

These position-specific foundation activities and accompanying information are essential to the recruitment program and should be clearly understood by those who will carry out the process.

— ROLES AND RESPONSIBILITIES —

Regardless of the recruitment policy adopted by a school district—regionally centralized or decentralized, large or small—a number of people at various levels of authority will always become involved. Some recruitment duties will differ between school districts, but common overall responsibilities will have to be assigned and activities completed. To avoid confusion, accountability problems, and favoritism, the recruitment policy must define authority and responsibilities, and how and when these will be exercised.

The process should begin with an agreement that the conduct of a recruitment program is the responsibility of the entire management team—board of education members and administrators. In larger districts, various administrative levels will be assigned specific duties, in smaller districts a particular administrator may be accountable for a number of duties.

The first step in the development of policies and practices involves the board of education, which takes final responsibility for the operation of a school district. Ethics and prudence dictate that individual board members refrain from intervening in the conduct of recruitment activities and limit their involvement to their designated role.

The Board's Responsibilities

The primary role of boards of education is to develop policies. The role of administration is to implement those policies. Often the line between policy-making and administration becomes blurred, and board of education members become involved in the administration of activities. Personnel functions must be clearly defined so that the roles and involvement of individuals in a school district are understood. Virtually every seasoned school administrator can share a story of a board of education member asking for help with the candidacy of a friend, neighbor, or relative who is looking for a position. Clear policies, on the employment process and on the duties of board members, should be emphasized. School administrators should develop these policies in conjunction with their board members prior to, rather than during or after, a recruitment effort.

Evaluating the recruitment program. The success of the recruitment activity should be periodically reviewed. Board members should be involved in identifying questions that must be answered: What percentage of new recruits stay in the district and for how long? How many receive tenure? How many are denied? What is the staff turnover rate? What reasons do people give for leaving? How does administration follow up on staff concerns?

Financing for recruitment activities. Adequately describing the fiscal needs of the recruitment process is the role of administration; supporting the recruitment effort is the responsibility of the board of education. All major costs should be outlined for the board: printing, mailing, advertising, travel for staff and for candidates, and telephone expenses. These costs will vary depending on the type of positions being posted; a superintendent search will be more costly than recruitment for a teaching position. The personnel administrator needs to look ahead and budget annually for possible vacancies.

The Superintendent's Responsibilities

As the chief school officer, the superintendent's responsibility is to see that policies are carried out in both fact and spirit. The superintendent should provide the board with information regarding the effectiveness of recruitment efforts and guide them in maintaining and changing practices.

The superintendent is the most important person in the conduct of a recruitment program. He or she is accountable for implementing the board's decisions and satisfying the personnel needs of the district. The superintendent must advise the board of the status of recruitment activities, make final recommendations, and monitor the performance of all management team members involved in the process. To fulfill these responsibilities the superintendent must:

Provide the board with accurate data for use in establishing policies;
Set up an ongoing process for determining the personnel needs of the district;
Establish the personal and professional qualifications that candidates must possess to gain employment in the district;
Identify candidate sources that provide the personal and professional qualifications acceptable to the district;
Develop an adequate budget to sustain the recruitment program;
Coordinate staff involved in recruitment activities;
Notify the board of any instance that suggests unfairness in the recruitment process.

The superintendent often delegates responsibility to central office and school unit administrators for the implementation of many of these activities. Central office administration should manage activities that have district-wide implications, to ensure that practices affecting the district as a whole are executed in a consistent manner. Examples of these activities include:

Developing an annual plan for recruitment, at the direction of the board of education and superintendent;

Ensuring the involvement of all administrators and supervisors in the development and implementation of the annual recruitment plan;

Reviewing recommendations of staff who will be affected by the employment of a new individual;

Developing, printing, and distributing literature to be used in the recruitment process;

Maintaining a list of potential candidate sources;

Gathering and distributing all candidate information to staff involved in search activities;

Responding to inquiries of candidates in a consistent and timely manner;

Coordinating activities, visits, interviews, and follow-ups;

Monitoring compliance with relevant laws and regulations, to insure that all candidates are treated equitably;

Notifying candidates who were unsuccessful in the process.

The School Administrator's Responsibilities

The school or unit administrator is the first line of contact and ensures that:

The number of vacancies to be filled is accurately identified and reported to the central office;

The skills and competencies needed for the position are identified;

Curriculum and inservice needs of staff are continuously monitored and become part of the recruitment plan;

Results gathered from staff evaluation are incorporated in the recruitment program;

Appropriate people from various parts of the school are involved with candidates during visits, interviews, etc.;

Information on candidates' qualifications correlates with position needs;

Information gathered from candidates is carefully screened and evaluated to facilitate the selection process.

– CANDIDATE SOURCES –

If a recruitment program is to be effective, it must attract people who have a strong chance of success. Thus, a district should exert every effort to identify sources of qualified candidates. Districts vary as to how widely they will recruit. Many school districts will only solicit teacher applications within their own state. This may result from the personnel administrator's knowledge that an ample supply of teachers qualified for the vacancy are in the state; in this case, the administrator would not want to go through the work involved in recruiting someone who might not have the necessary state certification. On the other hand, when attempting to fill a vacancy for which it is more difficult to attract qualified candidates, out-of-state applicants may be actively solicited through colleges and universities with teacher education programs.

Districts may also vary in recruiting for administrative positions. Often, districts actively recruit from out of state, since board members feel going outside state boundaries will significantly broaden the pool of potential candidates. Typically, two concerns accompany out-of-state solicitations. The first is financial, and relates to the reality that transportation and lodging costs for out-of-state candidates are often the responsibility of the school board. If a candidate makes a good impression and second or third interviews are required, the costs will be even greater, especially if spouses are also invited for the return visits. The other concern that sometimes arises with out-of-state candidates is their understandable lack of knowledge of state laws and labor relations procedures. Some board members may feel that the daily operations of an administrative position are challenging enough without a new employee having to take time to become educated in law-related procedures.

The Internal versus External Dilemma

A question often arises in educational administration whether appointments should come from inside or outside of a district. There is no single answer to this question. Invariably, the perceptions of the superintendent and the board of education as to district needs will determine where to look.

Arguments to promote from within rest on the perception that if good things are going on in the district, an inside candidate would be more likely to ensure continuity. Another argument for hiring from within is that people will be more motivated if they know that a chance for promotion exists. Finally, the perception that well-qualified people within the district have a chance at positions may keep such individuals working for the district rather than moving to jobs elsewhere.

When inside candidates are probably not going to be considered, either all or none of them should be interviewed. The reason for this is simple: if these people are going to continue in their present positions, they should feel they have been treated fairly. All should be given a legitimate interview and know they were given the same consideration as other candidates. However, if an insider is _absolutely_ not going to be considered, and the administration and board have decided that they do not wish to take the time to interview inside staff, or perhaps believe that doing so would be unethical, then it is best to avoid interviewing any current staff members.

The decision to look outside may be made because decision makers perceive a need for new, fresh ideas. Likewise, they may feel that inside candidates are not well qualified or may bring with them a history of experiences known to the staff, or other factors that would affect their ability to function effectively.

Internal Transfer

Hiring from within can provide staff members with a chance to try new challenges that might be refreshing and stimulating. Internal hiring also may provide for a better program, when a staff member who is well regarded takes on a different position. Schools should regularly examine the skills and competencies of current staff to ensure the maximum use of their talents. Some staff members may be inclined to work in less-challenging positions, to avoid new and unknown situations. This could disrupt staff balance and leave some students with less-than-adequate services. A simple transfer and/or promotion could add significant productivity to an area, correct staffing needs, and repair less-than-adequate services. Often employees are interested in seeking new situations, transfers, or promotions. If the needs of both the employee and the district are satisfied, internal hiring should be considered. To identify interested and qualified employees, an administrator might consider a number of sources.

Original job application. An original application may contain information about a present staff member's willingness to teach at different grade levels or cover different subject matter.

Resume. A resume often outlines past experiences and competencies of which an administrator is unaware. This is especially true of new administrators who have not taken the time to review the personnel records of their staff members.

Annual evaluations. While certification, interest and willingness are important, ability is also crucial. A review of an individual's evaluations might provide a strong indicator of that person's ability to handle the challenges of a new position.

Dual certification. Resumes may reveal some staff members to be certified to teach in two different content areas or at two different levels, such as elementary and secondary. Checking the certification status of all staff members can sometimes provide a pleasant surprise.

Record of committee and extracurricular membership.   An individual's involvement in professional activities will provide an idea of the person's interests and capabilities. For instance, the science teacher who advises the school newspaper may have the ability and interest to teach a journalism elective.

Specific recommendations.   Reference letters, as well as word-of-mouth recommendations, are strong indicators of a staff member's ability to fill a position, especially when these references are made for a specific available position.

Creativity.   Sometimes administrators must learn to capitalize on talents and opportunities. For example, a junior-senior high school principal who felt "overloaded" with bureaucratic requirements received permission from the superintendent and school board to have a consultant conduct an organizational review. After looking at the demands on his time, the principal and consultant reviewed staff folders. One of the school's guidance counselors had done an outstanding job and had indicated an interest in school administration. While the role of guidance counselor/vice principal is often a contradiction, the counselor was so highly regarded that the principal felt she could handle the combined role. Working in conjunction with the coordinator of the educational administration program at the local college, a program was developed to meet the needs of all involved. The principal was pleased to have some much-needed help; the board and superintendent were happy to assist the principal (especially at no extra cost); and the counselor was able to enter the field of administration without having to move her family or give up income.

Recruitment Sources

Outside sources for recruiting candidates are numerous and varied. These sources need to be cultivated, nurtured, and developed. Some of the more common sources used for locating prospective candidates include:

- College placement services
- Private placement firms
- Unsolicited inquiries
- Regional education agencies
- Newspaper advertising
- Conferences
- Business
- Local media
- Government agencies
- Journal advertising

- State education departments
- Regulatory agencies
- Community organizations
- Colleague organizations

- Open houses
- Job fairs
- Job postings
- Regional recruitment

Posting the Position

The personnel administrator is usually responsible for advertising vacancies (also known as "posting") in the system. These position notices are brief abstracts that contain basic information about the position and its responsibilities. A notice will usually contain:

Job title
Effective date of the position (when the position starts)
Work year: ten, eleven, or twelve months*
Salary
Certification requirements
Experience requirements
Responsibilities and qualifications
Statement of authority structure: who reports to whom
Deadline for applications
Person to whom applications should be sent

Unless required by law or contract, it is not necessary for schools to post all position openings. Where posting is a local requirement, contracts often stipulate where vacancies will be posted (usually on bulletin boards in the district office and faculty rooms of each school), and the time the notice must be posted before a determination will be made, usually seven to fourteen days.

These contractual agreements may require that all positions that become available in the district be posted. More often, the teachers' organization agreement will only cover instructional positions. In this case, the district has the option, barring agreements in administrative or support staff contracts, to post or not post vacancy notices for support staff positions. As a result, if the board of education feels favorably toward a present employee, they can have someone appointed to a position (usually administrative) without going through the process of posting the position.

*Unless otherwise noted by law or contract, a ten-month position is equal to that of regular teaching staff (in some states, these are considered nine-month employees). Eleven-month positions require the same amount of working time from teaching staff, plus an additional month sometime during the year. A twelve-month position is year-long, with the agreed-upon number of vacation days.

Awkward Situations

Although their intentions are almost always good, school administrators and boards of education often find themselves in difficult situations when it comes to hiring. As a result, they may find themselves having to decide whether or not to grant interviews to candidates unlikely to be given serious consideration when a final decision is to be made.

Courtesy interviews. As noted in the earlier discussion of inside candidates, those responsible for the recruiting process are sometimes put in the awkward position of determining whether they will interview a certain individual, such as a local resident or someone related to a district employee or board member. Such interviews are known as courtesy interviews and are loaded with ethical questions. Boards and administrators who conduct them, knowing that the candidate will not be hired, may be considered unethical. Refusal to give an interview may be seen as callous. Perhaps the only right answer to this issue is for the administrator and board members to reject the concept of courtesy interviews and take the attitude that all candidates will be honestly considered. Boards may also adopt nepotism policies that bar the employment of relatives of employees or board members. Such a policy might eliminate some of the problem, but it can also cause others, such as eliminating the employment of a legitimately strong candidate.

Red herrings. In many cases a search will have to take place, even though those doing the hiring have a good idea that an inside candidate will be chosen. This may be necessary due to legal or contractual provisions or because those doing the hiring feel that the board or community needs to believe that the hiring is being conducted objectively. The ethical ramifications differ—candidates may have to take time off or travel, and false hopes may be raised. Those who are the pawns in such scenarios are often referred to as "red herrings."

It is best to avoid such a process, if at all possible. Many applicants will ask if there is an inside candidate. Insiders may indeed be given interviews, but this does not necessarily mean that one of them has an advantage. This should be pointed out if candidates ask about it.

For those who are victims, a good interview experience is always worthwhile. In addition, such a candidate at least has the opportunity to make a strong impression. Funny things happen in the employment process; if the primary candidate suddenly decides that he or she does not want the job, an unanticipated need to reconsider outside candidates may arise. Also, another position may open up at a future date, and the "red herring" who made a good impression may become the primary candidate.

Using committees. One of the most effective means of handling such problems is to use committees in the hiring process instead of placing total responsibility on one or two individuals. Committee involvement in hiring, particularly when teachers in applicable content areas can be involved, provides a number of advantages. First, having people in similar jobs involved in the hiring of a new teacher is logical and justified. An awareness of the necessary content knowledge, unless one of the interviewers has taught in the same district as the applicant, is a great advantage. Staff members are able to ask content-related questions to determine a candidate's understanding. In addition, a group of individuals may ask a number of pertinent questions that one interviewer might fail to ask. These questions and shared impressions provide a richer picture of candidates. Finally, and perhaps most important, by being involved in the hiring process, department members are more likely to take responsibility to help the new staff member be successful. This responsibility will surface in terms of providing assistance and moral support.

Letters of Acknowledgment

The job hunt can be a stressful, tiring process. While many veterans in the business of education can reminisce about never even having had to interview for a position ("They called me!"), the competition for positions today is keen. People applying for positions deserve to be treated professionally and with dignity. Letting candidates know their status, from the scheduling of the initial interview to the selection of a candidate, is always appreciated.

Such courtesy requires relatively little work on the part of the personnel administrator, and could make a lasting impression on applicants. Most of us can recall hearing someone talk about applying for a job and never even getting a letter of rejection. On the other hand, someone will occasionally mention that although he or she did not receive the job, "It was the nicest rejection letter I ever received!"

Education is renowned for being a small, tightly knit community. In any state, and often nationally, teachers will know fellow teachers and administrators will know fellow administrators, through professional organizations and conferences. As a result, treating individuals poorly in either the application or interview process will undoubtedly come back to haunt the person or district responsible and should be avoided, for reasons of courtesy as well as practicality.

The communication process with prospective candidates begins with the receipt of their inquiry. A standard letter should be sent to applicants, thanking them for taking the time to inquire. This letter should also request

---

LETTER OF ACKNOWLEDGMENT

June 20, 199__

Dear

On behalf of the Applewood Schools, I thank you for your interest in the position of secondary mathematics teacher.

At this time we are in the process of compiling all application material for review. Once completed, an initial group of candidates will be identified for first-round interviews. If you are selected to be invited for an interview, contact will be made near the end of July.

Please see that all application materials, including your resume, transcripts, letters of reference, a copy of your teaching certification, and the enclosed application, are forwarded to my office no later than July 10th.

We thank you for your interest in this position.

Sincerely,

Mary Jones, Ed.D.
Personnel Director

LETTER OF REJECTION

August 10, 199__

Dear

Thank you for your interest in the mathematics position that was available with the Applewood Schools.

After a careful review of the letters and resumes received, we have selected a candidate whose background and qualifications closely parallel our current needs.

Please be assured that we will keep your application materials on file for twenty-four months in case of a further opening.

Sincerely,

Mary Jones, Ed.D.
Personnel Director

(Author's note: Retaining of records for a period of time is always wise in case further openings should occur. The reference to a specific period of time, in this example, twenty-four months, may be based on state laws. Administrators should check with their respective state education departments to determine whether a records retention provision applies.)

any additional data that may not have been included with the applicant's initial inquiry. A resume, an official transcript, and letters of reference may be requested. If appropriate, the communication might inform the applicants that there are no current openings for the positions in which they have an interest. If openings do exist, applicants should be told that their interest is appreciated and that they will be notified by a particular date if they are going to be invited for an interview.

– MATERIALS AND LITERATURE –

Although the materials and literature used by a district in the conduct of its recruitment will not guarantee the hiring of the best individual, such material should at least aid in the process, by helping narrow down the field of potential candidates. Most important, all information should be checked by the school attorney for compliance with the law, regulations, and employee contracts, prior to being used in the district's recruitment activities.

The materials and literature will be numerous and varied, but should at least include the following:

- Vacancy notices
- Job descriptions
- Response letters
- Journal ads
- Marketing letters
- Community brochures

- Application forms
- Salary program
- Fringe benefits program
- Work calendars
- Newspaper ads

- Recruitment brochures
- District brochures
- Policies
- Regulations
- Employee contracts

— SUMMARY —

This chapter outlines the need for a district to plan and implement an aggressive and energetic recruitment program. It discusses the importance of an effective recruitment program and the many constraints which boards of education and administrators may confront in the process. The four major factors in the recruitment process are introduced and described: foundation activities, roles and responsibilities, candidate sources, and materials and literature.

Foundation activities begin with confirming the need to continue or create a position, and the development of a policy which outlines the recruitment process. The section on roles and responsibilities describes the missions of various groups, such as boards of education and individuals who play a role in recruiting. These responsibilities include efforts to develop policy, finance, plan, and evaluate what will occur. Discussion of candidate sources involves the identification of potential applicants, from within and outside of the system. It also lists important types for information that should be reviewed for current staff, such as job applications, resumes, evaluations, certifications, and recommendations. This section concludes with a review of awkward situations administrators may face, such as courtesy and "red herring" interviews, and discusses approaches which help avoid some of these problems. The materials and literature section lists types of recruitment literature to be used in the process, from initial vacancy notices through advertising to employee contracts.

CHAPTER

— 4 —

Selection

Selection of the right person to fill a position is the focal point of the personnel function. Selection initiates and interrelates with all other personnel activities. For example, successful hiring tests the adequacy of recruitment activities. It begins the individual employee's personnel record, initiates the employee orientation program, puts into motion the employee evaluation system, and performs other related procedures until the departure of the employee from the district. The selection process should identify people who meet the qualifications and standards set by the organization and ensure that they are in positions that will allow the organization to operate with maximum success. In addition, the process aims to ensure that employees possess the skills, competencies, and potential for continued productive employment.

A number of influences, described later in this chapter, impinge upon the selection process. The selection approach must reduce or eliminate the effects of these influences and enhance the prospects of hiring the right person for the job.

— IDENTIFYING APPLICANTS —

Number of applicants available. In the best of all worlds, the applicant pool would be ample to provide a number of qualified candidates. In reality, this is not always true. Small, rural districts often find themselves searching for good, qualified applicants. As a result, administrators are not always able to find candidates about whom they feel extremely positive. At times, administrators will select alternatives such as recommending someone as a long-term substitute. By doing so, administrators have a chance to observe the individual for a period of time. If the initial doubts are confirmed, the substitute status allows administrators the time to conduct a further search. Another positive aspect of such a decision is that it allows the substitute to save face. Since the person was not hired in a regular, tenure-line position, he or she will not have to go through the stress of a formal termination.

Legal considerations. Often constraints are placed on school districts from sources such as local contracts, state and federal statutes, and court judgments. District personnel must be aware of these constraints and be careful to satisfy them. For instance, some local teacher contracts will require that all open positions must be posted in the school. Failure to observe what may appear to be a minor obligation could result in a costly legal procedure against a board of education.

Affirmative action. As discussed further in Chapter 5, school districts are not required to be affirmative action employers under normal circumstances. However, districts that advertise themselves as such create an obligation to take positive steps to identify, hire, and support individuals from underrepresented groups. Districts advertising themselves as affirmative action employers may be called upon to prove they have taken these steps.

Accuracy of information gathered. States vary regarding the "sensitive" questions that can be used by prospective employers. For instance, in some states it is possible to gather information on individuals who have been convicted of child abuse or molestation. In other states this information is not available. As a result, administrators must thoroughly check all references on potential candidates, including professional contacts who may have not been listed on the application form, such as colleagues, supervisors, and members of the board of education.

Interpretation of information gathered. Those reviewing employment information must have a clear idea of needs and priorities. A candidate should not be allowed to spend over half of a one-hour interview talking about sailing, even if an administrator involved in the interview process happens to be an avid fan of sailing. Unfortunately, such situations are common, and the job-related skills, abilities, and beliefs of a candidate may never come out during the interview.

Political pressure. Often referred to but ill-defined, "political pressure" to consider a particular candidate is nevertheless common in the employment process. Seasoned administrators have experienced this in any number of forms, from the subtle "She's the daughter of my minister and I've known her since she was a youngster" to the more direct "If you hire him, I'd really appreciate it." Political pressure becomes extremely difficult when a candidate is related to a board member or staff member in a district. By using committees in the hiring process, some of this stress can be removed or at least reduced.

Nepotism. Nepotism laws vary in different states. As with political pressure, nepotism often places those involved in hiring in awkward positions. Nepotism occurs in virtually all types of districts. Rural districts are often the most vulnerable to this problem, since the candidate pool may be limited by geography, and the individuals who have the required education and certification are often members of the same family. The best approach to nepotism is a clear board policy, as outlined in Chapter 3.

Organizational traditions. Too often, school districts conduct the employment process by using the same steps and forms they have always used. Unfortunately, failure to examine and improve can be costly. Allowing a single individual to make decisions or using recruitment materials that fail to solicit valuable information will place the school district at a disadvantage.

Community expectations. The often-used quip that everyone has an opinion is appropriate to community expectations about hiring. For example, it is a common belief that people who grew up or live in the school district automatically should be given preference in hiring. In addition, some community members might be aghast at the idea of hiring a member of an underrepresented or nontraditional group, such as a female industrial arts instructor.

To ensure that children receive the best education possible, regardless of political pressures or community concerns, the selection process should be conducted in a well-structured manner. Activities should be clearly defined and performed in a consistent fashion by all involved, to ensure that those who merit employment are hired. The steps in the employee selection process should include at least the following:

Establishment of a selection policy
Examination of all candidate information
Reference checks
Interviews

– SELECTION POLICY –

A board of education should inform applicants, residents, and staff of employment practices. Regardless of the size of a school district, the selection process should begin with a board-adopted policy for recruitment. (See the sample policy in Chapter 3.) The policy should identify the people to be involved in the selection of individuals who will be employed by the district. The selection policy should also address at least the following provisions:

Statement of philosophy: A broad statement providing an overview of the purpose and beliefs of the district.

Policy implementation: An outline of the roles of the board, administration, committees, and any other units involved in the implementation of policy.

Equal opportunity employment: A statement that the board observes and practices equal opportunity employment, if applicable.

Employment of relatives: Clarification as to whether employment of relatives is acceptable, and if so, under what conditions. For instance, requiring that a greater percentage of those voting in favor of a related candidate be required, such as two-thirds instead of a simple majority vote, or disallowing relations on the board from voting altogether.

Legal constraints: A statement regarding any laws or regulations affecting the selection process.

Steps in the selection process: An outline showing each step in the process and the order in which they will occur.

Qualifications acceptable to the district: Specific criteria for selection, to reduce the potential for later misunderstanding of why a particular candidate was chosen.

Techniques used in the selection process: A statement of the specific tests, interviews, or other techniques used in making the selection.

Screening applications: A statement of how screening will take place, what criteria, if any, will be given special weighting, and the time line that will be followed.

Process for making the final recommendation: An outline of what channels will be followed, for instance:

> 1. Screening of applications by principal →
> 2. Interviewing committee recommends semifinalists to principal →
> 3. Principal recommends selected candidate to superintendent →
> 4. Superintendent recommends selected candidate to board of education

— CANDIDATE INFORMATION —

The first step is to determine the data to be given priority in the final selection decision. According to a number of studies, the most useful evidence of future success is past success in a similar position. In addition, attention should be given to appropriate professional characteristics that relate to a candidate's ability to perform the job.

The initial phase of the review process is the verification of all information accumulated about a candidate being considered for employment in the district. The application form itself becomes the starting point for collecting information on each interested individual. A well-structured application form provides a uniform method for collecting pertinent data. Many districts go the extent of noting in their recruitment materials that applications *must* be completed, even if the information requested is included in a candidate's resume and cover letter. It should be stated whether official certificates and transcripts will be immediately required or whether unofficial ones will be sufficient for initial screening. Official transcripts *must* be provided before final hiring occurs and should be sent directly from the educational institution, not from the candidate.

All past employers should be contacted to verify a candidate's past performance and professional characteristics—strengths, weaknesses, and reason for leaving the previous job. If this information is favorable, character references should be verified next. Of interest are the personal and interpersonal behaviors of a potential employee. The length of time known and the relationship of the reference should determine the weight given to this evidence. Finally, academic references should be checked and verified, particularly to ascertain certification and establish salary eligibility.

Several key questions should be resolved before collecting information:

How will data be verified? Telephone, mail, or direct personal contact?

Will all prior employers be verified? Or just the last two, or the last employer and one character reference, or some other combination?

What should be done when the verification process results in conflicting testimony? What weight should be given to conflicting information? Should more recent information be given stronger consideration? Who should be informed of these conflicts?

How should verified data be organized? How should it be reduced to a summary? What should be included and in what format?

The above list should be tempered, based on whether candidates are just entering the job market or have been in the profession for a number of years. The items may be weighted depending on whether candidates are applying for a position in their prior experience area or switching to a new one—classroom to administration, custodian to head custodian. Verified data recorded should reveal information related to each of the above questions.

– CHECKING REFERENCES –

Failure to check references thoroughly can create a problem in the selection process. Prior to inviting a candidate for an interview, an exhaustive check of references should be conducted. Unless this is accomplished in a uniform manner, results may be confusing, and inconsistency could result in legal consequences.

A number of methods can be used to check references, but a district should include at least the following in its process:

Development of a format for checking references.
Reference checks by prospective supervisors.
Contact with former employers (personal, written, or by telephone). Final checks should be made by telephone, especially when districts rely heavily on paper references for initial contacts.
Use of a prepared form to record comments made by each reference.
Informing references of the reason for calls and the organization represented.
Checks of educational credentials to verify institutions attended, graduation dates, major field(s) of study, and certification status.
Contact with character references made, but given less weight.
Determination on handling requests by candidates that their present employers not be contacted.

The most important part of the reference check process is the questions a reference is asked. Questions such as the following should be included in checking with present and former employers.

How does this candidate get along with staff? Students? Parents?
How does this candidate respond to criticism?
What are this candidate's strengths?
What are this candidate's weaknesses?
What are this candidate's outstanding accomplishments?
Why is this candidate leaving your employ?
What is the candidate's potential for growth?
Is the candidate conscientious and responsible?
Would you employ this candidate again if he or she applied to you for
   a position?

APPLICANT REFERENCE RECORD

Teaching and/or Student Teaching Check

Name of candidate _____ Date of call _____

Applying for _____ Person called _____

Title and address of person called _____

Telephone number(s) _____

   1. Rapport?
   2. Discipline?
   3. Open-mindedness?
   4. Reaction to criticism?
   5. Fluency?
   6. Ability to plan?
   7. Knowledgeable about teaching methods?
   8. Ability to evaluate student work?
   9. How would you rate this person as a teacher?
   10. Ability to work with superiors?
   11. Character?
   12. Would you hire or rehire this person?

Additional comments:

APPLICANT REFERENCE RECORD

Dear _____ :

_____ is being considered for the

position of _____ in the Nowhere Central

School District and has listed you as a reference.

Please complete the following checklist and return it to us in the enclosed envelope. Please contact me at XXX-XXXX if you wish to make additional comments.

Thank you for your assistance. *All information will be kept in confidence.*

Sincerely,

_____

SUPERINTENDENT OF SCHOOLS

Compared to other teachers you have known, please rate this candidate:

	Upper 10%	Upper 25%	Upper 50%	Lower 50%	Don't Know
1. Initiative					
2. Creativity					
3. Enthusiasm					
4. Ability to work with supervisors					
5. Ability to work with peers					
6. Rapport with pupils					
7. Rapport with parents					
8. Classroom planning					
9. Ability to maintain discipline					
10. Willingness to improve professionally					

11. Contribution to the school outside of regular hours	
12. Overall teaching success	

General comments:

_____

_____	_____
SIGNATURE	TITLE

Reference Checks and Liability

Persons new to the selection process often view it as a simple set of procedures. This is a misconception that has resulted in a number of administrators finding themselves in court. Falsified information has often been provided about matters such as certification status and past legal entanglements. For these to become public *after* an individual has been hired will be embarrassing for the administration and costly to reconcile.

Telephone checks. Candidates for positions in school districts are often local, from in the geographic region, or at least the same state. Because of this, telephone calls are the most common form of employment verification. If a candidate is already employed locally, chances are good that the administrator interested in hiring will know the administrator for whom the candidate works.

Besides being convenient, telephone calls are also the best way of getting valuable information on candidates. The large number of lawsuits against employers has resulted in employers becoming cautious about the written comments they are willing to make about candidates. In one case, a state supreme court indicated the personal liability of a superintendent and ruled that an administrator could be held personally liable for slanderous remarks, even though his reference to a fellow superintendent was made in his official capacity.[1] State laws vary, but as a result of such cases, many school attorneys have advised their clients to limit their comments, even positive ones, and only provide the dates and position title of a candidate's employment. If this practice becomes widely adopted, it will have a significant effect on the employment process.

Telephones also provide a security risk for users. An administrator receiving a phone call from an alleged administrator does not know whether the caller is in fact an administrator, or may perhaps be an acquaintance of a staff member or even a private detective working for a candidate. All of these situations have occurred, and an administrator receiving a call should be certain about the identity of the person at the other end of the telephone line. If in doubt, the administrator receiving the telephone request for information is advised to say that he or she is busy and will call back. This gives the administrator the opportunity to check the telephone book or directory assistance, to verify that the telephone number given was indeed the number of the correct school administrator.

Written. Many districts have adopted the use of a printed reference form. A set form makes it possible for employers to survey a broad cross section of references more efficiently. It also provides clear reason for not hiring an individual if several recommendations are weak. If written recommendations are solicited, they should be followed up with telephone contacts.

Confidentiality. Most recommendation forms from universities and colleges provide applicants with the option of retaining or forfeiting their right to access. Many candidates have been counseled to give up access to letters of recommendation, on the assumption that doing so will increase their credibility with those giving them consideration. Written recommendations are usually strongly positive, as candidates will not ask someone to write a letter if they are not confident that the writer will be positive. Veteran administrators have learned to look for certain factors in reviewing recommendation files. First, does the file contain all of the letters that would logically be included? If the file belongs to a teacher who has recently graduated from college, letters from professors and from supervising teachers who monitored the candidate's student teaching should be included. Obviously, such letters should be read carefully. Often, the principals of the schools where the candidate student-taught will also send a letter. If such letters are not included, administrators should find out where the candidate taught and make contact with the appropriate persons in those schools. If the teacher is experienced, letters from supervising school personnel such as department or grade level chairs, principals, and superintendents should be included.

In either case, letters should be recent, from within the last few years.

A number of factors can result in different perspectives on a candidate's performance, so information from recent supervisors is essential.

When asked to write a letter, school administrators should always assume that the candidates will eventually see, directly or indirectly, their letters of recommendation. Though not always the case, access to files occurs commonly enough that such a presumption is legitimate. Teachers and administrators get such access in any number of ways. For instance, a principal conducting an interview with a teacher candidate, or a superintendent or board member interviewing an administrative candidate, might say, "According to Dr. Jones, you had some trouble getting along with a few parents when you first started teaching." In another situation, the teachers' union negotiated into the labor contract language that was interpreted as allowing staff members access to all information included in their individual personnel files. The administration at the time had not intended to allow teachers access to their letters of recommendation, but the union interpreted the agreement differently and argued that teachers did have such access. In cases where staff members move up and become administrators, they have access to all personnel files, including their own. The net effect is that one should be cautious in writing recommendation letters.

Release from liability. There are no guarantees regarding the protection of management from potential actions involving employment procedures. The best action that any board and administrative staff can take is to maximize their protection from lawsuits. One method of doing this is by requiring that prospective candidates for positions sign a form releasing

---

CONSENT AND RELEASE

I authorize the Nowhere School District to inquire, at their discretion, into my professional background and professional experiences, and I hereby release any member or agent of the district from any liability regarding me, regardless whether said information is in my application or not. I further understand that the information gathered, in part or whole, may be shared with school district members involved in the employment process. I further understand that all information gathered regarding my application will be the property of the school district and will not be released to me.

_____   _____
APPLICANT'S SIGNATURE   DATE

the district from liability for actions that occur during employment checks. Such a statement may provide some protection, but there is still no guarantee that an action will be prevented. The sample release included here is only an example. Any district that adopts the use of a release form should have its attorney review its hiring process and develop an appropriate form.

Networking. Professional networking is a standard activity for many educators. Networking includes activities such as membership in professional organizations, attending conferences and meetings, and taking courses. Networking is important so that school administrators can locate colleagues with whom they can interact both personally and professionally. On a personal level, it allows for interaction with people who share similar experiences and can empathize with the problems and stresses related to the life style of school administrators. On a professional level, it provides important contacts who can be extremely valuable resources. The personnel process is one place where networking can be extremely useful. By knowing other administrators, both locally as well as statewide, administrators can more easily gain useful information on job candidates. Although an administrator may not be personally acquainted with the principal for whom a teacher candidate has worked, he or she may know another administrator located in a neighboring district. A call to the nearby colleague will often provide access to the candidate's principal.

– INTERVIEWS –

Most school districts conduct two sets of interviews—preliminary and final. Preliminary interviews are sometimes referred to as "get-acquainted" interviews. They allow candidates a chance to see the school and district where the position is and to learn something about the personality and expectations of their potential supervisor. When a team approach is used in hiring, candidates may also have the chance to meet potential fellow teachers, other district administrators, and possibly even parents, board members, and students.

Based on impressions made in the preliminary interview, finalists are invited back for in-depth interviews, usually with the immediate supervisor and central office personnel such as an assistant superintendent or superintendent.

Obviously, size of district plays a large part in the hiring process. In smaller districts, the superintendent may be involved in the hiring process from the start, including the checking of references. In larger districts, the superintendent may play no role in the screening and interview process, leaving such decisions to others. Whatever the process, the administrator or secretary who contacts candidates to invite them for interviews should make a point of letting the candidates know who will be seeing them.

Implementing the Interview Plan

The district's interview plan should be comprehensive and exact. Prior to conducting interviews, a district must settle several questions.

Who decides which candidates will be interviewed? The district's policy may answer this question by stating that either the personnel director, or individual school administrator will have the final word in the identification of the best teacher candidates. The district's business administrator might have the responsibility for identifying support staff candidates. Many districts do not have a formal policy, and leave the choice to either tradition or the wishes of the district's superintendent or board of education.

Specification of who makes the decision on job candidates should be included in a board policy, and not left vulnerable to changes in superintendents or board members. Location of the position, hiring criteria, and authority structure should influence the decision on who selects the candidates to be interviewed.

How many interviews will be conducted? The number of candidates to be interviewed may be specified in a district's policy, but may vary according to the principle of supply and demand and certain political realities. Elementary teaching positions have long been popular, so openings for such positions have resulted in a large number of applicants. A larger pool is likely to provide a greater number of strong candidates. In this case the persons deciding who will be interviewed may want to invite as many as eight to ten candidates for preliminary interviews. In job categories that are more difficult to fill, administrators may find that few certified candidates are available.

Law or regulation may specify the number of those to be invited for interviews. Apart from legal constraints, no definite number exists to answer this question, although six to eight preliminary interviews seem to be most common. Commonly, two to three finalists are asked to come back for final interviews, to go into greater depth and discuss more detailed topics such as those reviewed in Chapter 5 (Orientation).

In some situations, every candidate applying for a position may be given an interview. In one case a new principal actually interviewed over thirty applicants for a vice principalship. While the principal doing the interviewing patted himself on the back for a thorough job, he did little more than waste time, as the possibility of actually remembering the responses of each candidate would be minimal. On the other side, some of the candidates felt cheated and would not have gone to the expense of traveling and taking time off if they had known that their chance was one in thirty.

In this case the principal had the authority to conduct preliminary interviews on his own; perhaps the fact that he was new to his position had something to do with his zeal. However, he could have saved himself and many of the applicants a great deal of time if he had carefully reviewed the job criteria and applications *before* conducting his interview marathon.

What information will be supplied to those being interviewed? In order to provide all candidates the fairest opportunity, interviews must be conducted in a consistent manner. Prior to the interview process, a determination should be made about what information will be provided to all candidates before their interview visits. Teacher candidates might wish to see information on curricular programs being used, a copy of the labor contract, or test score data. Administrative candidates might be interested in enrollment trends; the organizational chart; budget, curricular, and testing information; and copies of labor contracts. The information to be provided should be sent to all candidates. If additional information is requested, all candidates or none should be provided with that information.

What information will be supplied to those conducting the interview? This question can be a sensitive one, especially when a group representing various aspects of the school community is involved. With regard to confidentiality, the larger the number of individuals involved in the interview process, the more difficult it is to maintain confidentiality.

If a group is going to be involved in the screening and interview process, that fact should be included on the job vacancy announcement and in the application material sent to potential candidates. Since vulnerability to breaches in confidentiality and potential lawsuits resulting from inappropriate questioning are increased by the use of a group, the administration should provide training for all members who will be involved in interviewing.

Involvement of teacher representatives in the employment of administrators has become popular in some school districts. In such cases, administrators and board members should recognize the fact that union representatives often make calls to teachers from the districts of candidates who are being interviewed. Unfortunately, these contacts are sometimes made without the knowledge or direction of the personnel office in the hiring district. As a result, confidentiality may be breached, the word of one person may be taken as absolute, and candidates may sometimes be unfairly labeled. With responsible union leadership, such instances can be avoided by providing legitimate involvement in the process.

How will conflicting and/or adverse comments gathered during the interview be handled? If the interview process, including initial screenings, is handled properly, every candidate will have some strengths and weaknesses identified. Weaknesses do not mean that an individual is incompetent or has such poor human relations skills that he or she would not be able to perform in an acceptable manner. However, a dilemma could easily arise if one highly regarded teacher candidate has relevant experience that another highly regarded candidate lacks. When narrowing the field of mechanic candidates, interviewers in a district that owns all diesel buses might learn that one good candidate has several years experience working with diesel engines and that an otherwise excellent candidate has no experience with diesels.

By determining priorities ahead of time, such dilemmas can be minimized. For instance, mandating certain experiences, skills, or accomplishments and making these explicit in the job description may immediately eliminate some potential applicants. Additionally, weighting each of the criteria to be used in the screening and interview process will allow for a numerical rating.

Laws and Regulations

Interviewers should become knowledgeable about what is acceptable in interviews and applications. A district is wise to conduct annual training dealing with the laws and their impact on the selection process. The persons conducting the interviews should know about equal employment laws and regulations that guarantee a person's rights to fair treatment in employment.

During the past twenty-five years, Congress has enacted into law several statutes that protect prospective and current employees from employment discrimination. Each statute affects employers in different ways. Collectively the statutes proscribe a wide range of conduct that would differentiate job applicants on the basis of race, ethnic or national origin, sex, handicap or disability, religion, sexual preference, and age. The statutes are directed toward the provision of equal opportunity for employment and non-discrimination in the compensation, promotion opportunities, and benefits for a particular position.

In addition to the statutes enacted within the past twenty-five years, a number of claims have emerged based on the civil rights legislation enacted following the Civil War and the constitutional claims derived from the

Fourteenth Amendment to the United States Constitution. The following is not intended to describe in detail the federal laws pertaining to the civil rights of individuals and the prohibitions against discrimination. What follows is merely a brief description of several of the more important statutes that apply in the employment selection process.

Title VII of the Civil Rights Act of 1964. The Civil Rights Act of 1964[2] proscribes discrimination on the basis of race, color, religion, sex, or national origin. Title VII, as originally enacted, did not apply to public employers such as school districts. However, in 1972 the statute was amended by Congress to include public employers. As a result of Title VII and other employment statutes, school districts are obligated not to discriminate in employment practices.

Pregnancy Discrimination Act. On October 31, 1978, President Carter signed Public Law 95-555, a pregnancy disability amendment to Title VII of the 1964 Civil Rights Act. The Pregnancy Disability act was a separate piece of legislation, but is now an integral part of Title VII. The amendment to Title VII was necessary because of the decisions of the United States Supreme Court in *Geduldig v. Arello,* 417 U.S. 484, 8 FEP Cases 97 (1974), and *General Electric Company v. Gilbert,* 429 U.S. 125, 13 FEP Cases 1657 (1976). In *Gilbert,* the Court ruled that employers who exclude pregnancy-related disabilities from coverage under otherwise comprehensive income protection plans do not discriminate on the basis of sex in violation of Title VII. In reaction to these decisions, Congress enacted the amendment to specify pregnancy as a disability that should be treated in the same manner as any other disability for other employees. Thus, the sex discrimination prohibitions contained in Title VII were expanded to cover a medical disability unique to one sex.

Districts have different titles for leaves related to child-bearing and child-rearing. Various popular terms include pregnancy leave, child-bearing leave, and maternity and/or paternity leave. "Unpaid leave of absence" is the most appropriate.

Civil Rights Act of 1968. The Civil Rights Act of 1968[3] provides criminal penalties for interference with an individual's employment rights on the basis of race, color, religion, or national origin. The Act has not been utilized to a great extent, but it is an available remedy for discrimination by employers.

Equal Pay Act. The Equal Pay Act[4] was an amendment to the Fair Labor Standards Act of 1963, and makes it unlawful to discriminate on the basis of sex in the payment of wages for equal work on jobs that require equal effort and responsibility under similar working conditions. As part of the Fair Labor Standards Act, the Equal Pay Act is now administered by the Equal Employment Opportunity Commission.

Age Discrimination and Employment Act of 1967. Employers, both public and private, are prohibited by the Age Discrimination and Employment Act[5] from discriminating in hiring or firing against workers who are forty years of age or older. The purpose of the ADEA is to promote the employment of older persons based on ability rather than age, and to prohibit arbitrary age discrimination in employment.

Vietnam Era Veterans Readjustment Act of 1974. This statute[6] applies to employers that have single contracts or subcontracts with the federal government in the amount of $10,000 or more. These employers are required to take affirmative action to hire and advance in employment disabled veterans and veterans of the Vietnam era. Under most circumstances this particular statute is of limited application to school districts that do not have direct federal contracts (as opposed to federal grants and aid).

Civil Rights Act of 1866 (1870). Following the Civil War, Congress enacted the Thirteenth, Fourteenth and Fifteenth Amendments to the Constitution of the United States. In addition, in an attempt to protect the constitutional rights of blacks following the Civil War, Congress enacted several statutes to provide a remedy for blacks suffering racial discrimination. The 1866 Act[7] provides a federal remedy against racial discrimination, not only in public employment but in private employment as well. In most instances, Section 1981 claims are made together with claims under the Civil Rights Act of 1871 (see below) and Title VII of the Civil Rights Act of 1964. Section 1981 provides that:

> All persons within the jurisdiction of the United States shall have the same right . . . to make and enforce contracts, to sue, be parties, give evidence, and to the full and equal benefit of all laws and proceedings for the security of persons and property as is enjoyed by white citizens, and shall be subject to like punishments, pains, penalties, taxes, licenses, and exactions of every kind, and to no other.

In order to make a claim under Section 1981 a timely charge would have to be filed with the Equal Employment Opportunity Commission under Title VII.

Civil Rights Act of 1871. In addition to Section 1981, Congress enacted a series of statutes, beginning in 1871, to protect the rights of blacks from state action and to protect the rights guaranteed by the Fourteenth Amendment. The statutes, which include Section 1983, are also known collectively as the Ku Klux Klan Act.[8] Since the advent of the civil rights movement of the 1960s and the enactment of an attorney's fees statute in 1976, the statute has been one of the primary sources for litigation in the area of employment discrimination.

Section 1983 provides that:

> Every person who, under color of any statute, ordinance, regulation, custom or usage, of any State or Territory, subjects, or causes to be subject, any citizen of the United States or other person within the jurisdiction thereof to the deprivation of any rights, privileges or immunities secured by the Constitution and laws, shall be liable to the party injured in an action at law, suit in equity, or other proper proceeding for redress.

Title IX of the Education Amendments of 1972. Title IX[9] provides that no person shall be subject to sex discrimination under any educational program or activity receiving federal financial assistance. In 1982, the United States Supreme Court in *North Haven Board of Education v. Bell,* 456 U.S. 512, 28 FEP Cases 1393 (1982), held that Title IX coverage was limited to specific programs within an institution that receives federal funds. In 1987, Congress enacted the Civil Rights Restoration Act of 1987[10] and overturned the *North Haven* decision and a subsequent decision of the United States Supreme Court in *Grove City College v. Bell,* 465 U.S. 555 (1984). The Civil Rights Restoration Act expanded the coverage of Title IX so that the entire institution that receives federal funds is now subject to the requirements. The Civil Rights Restoration Act of 1987 applies not only to Title IX but to other civil rights laws, including the Rehabilitation Act of 1973.

Rehabilitation Act of 1973. The Rehabilitation Act of 1973[11] contains two sections that apply to employers with respect to their hiring of employees who are deemed to be handicapped. Section 503 requires employers with federal contracts over $2,500 to take affirmative action to employ handicapped persons. If the contract is for $50,000 or more and a company has fifty or more employees, the contractor must prepare an affirmative action program and make it available to all employees. In most instances, Section 503 of the Rehabilitation Act is not applicable to public school districts. However, Section 504 of the Rehabilitation Act prohibits discrimination against handicapped persons by an employer receiving federal financial assistance. This statute is directly applicable to most public school districts and thus is a prohibition of employment discrimination against handicapped persons.

The Interview

The next step involves the preparation and conduct of interviews. In preparing, those who will be involved should be thoroughly familiar with the following:

Position responsibilities/job description;
Educational and experience qualifications required for the position;
Salary and fringe benefit programs applicable to the position;
Supervisor of the position;
Supervisory responsibilities of the individual in the position;
Location where the job will be performed;
Relationship of the position to the union;
Candidate information and background;
Questions to be asked of candidates;
Information to be given to candidates during the interview;
Which members of the interview team are responsible for making the selection recommendation.

Once the preliminary activities are completed, the interviews can take place. Well-constructed interviews should provide decision makers with evidence relevant to the candidates and their qualifications. Unfortunately, a job candidate is sometimes ushered into an administrator's office and spends the next hour listening to the administrator talk about topics ranging from who won Sunday's football game to the administrator's Christmas vacation plans; candidates may leave without ever being asked questions about their abilities or experiences. In such cases no criteria exist, or at least none are systematically applied, an interview guide is lacking, and ultimately the decision is based on whatever vague personal impressions the administrator has received. The result is obvious: any effective staff members will be hired more by chance than by design.

Constructing the Interview Protocol

A logical connection should exist between job requirements, job description, and the interview questions.

Needs → Vacancy Announcement → Job Description → Interview

Determining need. A preliminary assessment of need for a position which has been vacated should have already taken place. Assuming that the need is justified and has been accepted by central office administration, the next step should be the development and posting of a vacancy announcement.

Vacancy announcement. Having justified the continuing need for the position, the personnel or other administrator in charge of the recruitment and selection process should write a vacancy announcement. The purpose of the vacancy announcement is to provide notification to interested parties that the position is open, to give them information of primary interest, and to tell them how to go about obtaining a comprehensive job description. Vacancy announcements usually include the following information:

Title of the position   Certification requirements
Approximate starting date   Salary range
Work year   Authority structure
Primary qualifications needed   Deadline date for applications
Responsibilities   Contact person

Job description. The job description should be based on the identified needs and skills. Usually a description consists of several parts and is consistent with the information outlined and requested in the vacancy announcement:

Job title
Authority structure
Basic function of the position
List of major responsibilities
Key duties for each major responsibility

Identifying necessary abilities. Once the need has been determined, competencies outlined in the current job description should be updated if necessary. Teaching skills tend to be easier to categorize, since they are more consistent within various content areas. For instance, science teachers require special organizational skills for supervising laboratories. Some elementary schools require primary teachers to have basic instrumental music skills.

VACANCY ANNOUNCEMENT
(TEACHING POSITION)

Position: High School Social Studies Teacher
Subject Areas: American History and Global Studies
Starting Date: September 4, 199___
Qualifications: The candidate must show demonstrated success in planning, managing, organizing, instructing and evaluating students in secondary social studies.
Certification: The candidate must possess or be eligible to hold a valid (as appropriate) certificate as a secondary social studies teacher.
Salary: Per negotiated contract.
Filing Deadline: August 1, 199___
Contact Person: Interested applicants should send a letter of application, resume, transcript, and placement file to:

Dr. Mary Jones
Personnel Director
Applewood Schools
1 Applewood Ave.
Applewood, State

VACANCY ANNOUNCEMENT
(ADMINISTRATIVE POSITION)

The Applewood School District is seeking certified and qualified candidates for the position of High School Principal, to succeed Mr. John Smith who has announced his retirement after serving the district for the past twenty-eight years.

The following information is provided for the benefit of interested parties:

Position: High School Principal
Starting Date: July 1, 199___
Qualifications: Interested candidates must be highly motivated and capable of providing creative leadership for a secondary school (grades 9–12) of 1,200 students. Prior secondary school teaching experience and at least five years of administrative experience are required.

Certification:	The candidate must possess or be eligible to hold a valid (as appropriate) state certificate as a school administrator.
Salary:	(As appropriate)
Filing Deadline:	March 1, 199___
Contact Person:	Interested applicants should send a letter of application, resume, transcript, and placement file to:

Dr. Mary Jones,
Personnel Director
Applewood Schools
1 Applewood Ave.
Applewood, State Zip

Support and administrative staff are often required to show evidence of specific skills. A secretary may be asked to demonstrate typing and shorthand ability. An administrator may be asked to have experience in constructing a master schedule or in athletic directing. Two methods provide the simplest means of determining position competencies: asking the person who holds the job and observing that person as he/she actually performs the work. The request often surprises people, and they may have difficulty accurately describing exactly what it is they do each day. One strategy for gathering this information is to ask an employee to keep a log for a few days, during which time they stop each half hour and write down exactly what they have been doing.

Observation is another useful method, and systematic observation is preferable. Few administrators have the time to stop what they are doing every half hour to find out what their secretary is doing. If the administrator trusts the secretary, who has already been asked to do a self-observation, observation by the administrator may be unnecessary. However, an administrator should informally watch and note particular tasks he or she observes. Secretaries may not realize how much or exactly what they actually do in the course of the year. Consider the many different tasks that a good school secretary does throughout the entire school year, not just over a period of a few weeks: bookkeeping for the school budget and school clubs, inventory control, organization of purchase orders, word processing, and liaison to vendors, parents, and staff, to name just a few.

To determine the abilities of candidates, interviewers should decide how they might evaluate a candidate's qualifications to perform each of the important functions outlined in the vacancy announcement and job description. For an administrative position, evidence of programs might be used, through curriculum guides or descriptions of how particular situations were handled. For a teaching candidate, a plan book, descriptions, and copies of instructional materials might be appropriate. A support staff member might be asked to show evidence from a civil service or locally administered test, as appropriate.

Interview questions. Once job competencies have been determined, actual questions should be developed. The content of questions falls into three categories: ice breakers, personal/factual, and professional.

Ice-breaker questions are asked at the start of the interview, and are aimed at helping the candidate feel at ease.

How was your trip?
Did you have trouble finding us?
Tell us a little bit about your present school.

These might even take place in conjunction with a tour of the school, as physical activity helps relieve stress and may make people feel more comfortable.

Personal/factual questions are concerned with personal information, such as specific dates of past work experiences, names and addresses of references, and confirmation of citizenship. Typically, one question is all that needs to be asked to get responses on each topic. These questions are normally asked near the start of the interview, following the ice breakers.

Professional questions focus on specific job-related tasks, and provide the responses interviewers should use to determine the qualifications of each applicant. Professional questions should be based on the specific competencies that have been determined and listed in the job description. Two to three questions should be coded and asked for each competency. The order of the questions should be random, and responses for each competency should be compared after the interview has been completed to check on reliability to confirm that the candidate is consistent in his or her responses.

Various types of questions should be asked during an interview. This variation provides an opportunity to observe a candidate's ability to respond in different situations:

Experiential: "Tell us about the most difficult discipline situation you ever ran into with a student, and how it was handled."

Situational: "The principal asks you to raise the grade of a student you failed, so the student can pass and graduate. How would you deal with this type of situation?"

Opinion: "What do you see as the most effective method of grouping children for reading instruction, and why?"

Dilemma: "Which is more important, teaching skills or content?" (Whichever answer the respondent gives, the interviewer argues the other, to determine the candidate's ability to articulate responses in a stressful situation).

Variations of these types of questions will occur. Using all four approaches will prevent an interview from becoming static; interviewers and candidates will be more alert, and interviewers will be able to observe how a candidate might respond to various types of situations.

Probes. While a number of pre-planned questions should be developed to solicit a candidate's responses, interviewers should also be prepared to ask follow-up questions. These are also known as "probes" and are usually not pre-planned, since they are situational, based on how a candidate responds to a particular question. For instance, the principal candidate who is asked, "Tell us about your professional experiences up to this point," might say, "I was a fourth-grade classroom teacher for five years. My administrative internship was in my own district, where I worked under the principal of my school." Probes from interviewers might include questions such as, "What grades are included in your school?" "What were your specific responsibilities during your internship?" "How long did you intern?" "Did you have teaching responsibilities during the time when you were interning?"

Since personnel administrators will have less control over the probes that will be asked, they must stress with those interviewing that probe questions, like all others, should deal only with professional concerns and not include information of a personal nature and unrelated to the position.

Pilot interviews. Many administrators will conduct a pilot interview prior to actual interviews. A pilot is conducted with someone who is not a candidate for the job, and is a simulation that allows interviewers the opportunity to check on various aspects of the planned interview situation. Clarity of questions, responsibility for asking specific questions, probes that might be asked, and an approximate idea of the length of time needed to complete the actual interviews can be ascertained through a pilot interview. In addition, the rating form used to evaluate the impressions made by candidates can also be checked to determine its validity. To make the pilot useful to all involved, the person who serves as the interviewee should be given feedback on his or her performance.

Starting the interview. Good interviews are active experiences involving a group of at least two people. A number of dynamics come into play when a group convenes. In addition to the substance of the questions and answers discussed, personal and interpersonal observations and relationships take place. A person interviewing for a teaching position, who answers questions exactly the way the interviewers would hope, may still not get a position if he or she attends the interview wearing blue jeans and a T-shirt. Conversely, a maintenance candidate attired in jeans and a T-shirt may be offered a position. Research on interviewing tells us that the first minutes of the interview are the most important and make the most lasting impression. Skilled interviewers should be aware of their own perceptual screens and be able to deal with their biases objectively.

Evaluating candidates. Many exchanges take place during the course of an interview. Although most are verbal, others occur as well. As noted above, manner of dress will often make an impression. Tone of voice, eye contact, and even posture will make lasting impressions. The individuals who are evaluating candidates must gather final observations that will take into consideration all of the factors that have been determined as important for success in the job being considered.

The fairest way of coming to these conclusions is through an interview rating form that asks interviewers to grade each candidate objectively. This tool should be a logical outgrowth of the job description and list of questions developed for the interview. The form should provide a rating scale and space for comments. Some organizations prefer a numeric scale, and others prefer ranges such as Unacceptable, Satisfactory, Excellent. The most important job of the rating form is to allow interviewers to discriminate legitimately. In other words, once the process has been completed, interviewers should be able to tell candidates why they were offered or not offered the position. This is not to imply that candidates who were not offered the job were "bad," although some might have been judged so, but that one candidate was rated as stronger than others.

One question that many interviewers ask is whether it is appropriate for them to take notes during an interview. With the large number of exchanges that occur, it would be unfair not to take notes. To place candidates more at ease, interviewers might wish to explain at the start of the interview that they will be taking notes and that no disrespect is intended if they are looking down to write periodically.

Another answer to notetaking is taping, through either audio or video

APPLICANT REFERENCE RECORD
INTERVIEW RATING SHEET FOR
TEACHER APPLICANTS

Applicant _____ Date _____

Interviewed by _____

Please circle the appropriate number below:
(1) Superior (2) Excellent, (3) Above average, (4) Average, (5) Below average.

Personal appearance (grooming, posture)	1	2	3	4	5
Voice (pleasing, well-modulated, easily heard)	1	2	3	4	5
Communication (conveys ideas clearly, extensive vocabulary, excellent command of English)	1	2	3	4	5
Personal attributes (self-confident, tolerant, friendly, well-integrated mature personality)	1	2	3	4	5
Physical limitations affecting teaching	1	2	3	4	5
Alertness and comprehension	1	2	3	4	5
Enthusiasm for teaching	1	2	3	4	5
Breadth of interests, including community activities	1	2	3	4	5
Knowledge of new materials and approaches	1	2	3	4	5
Creativity	1	2	3	4	5
Rapport with children	1	2	3	4	5
Awareness of individual needs and capabilities	1	2	3	4	5
Special abilities useful to school (cultural, recreational, etc.)	1	2	3	4	5
Awareness of own teaching effectiveness	1	2	3	4	5

Summary

Suitability	1	2	3	4	5
Education	1	2	3	4	5
Experience	1	2	3	4	5
Final rating	1	2	3	4	5

Appointment recommended? _____

Comments: _____

_____

_____

_____

technology. Although not used in the majority of schools at this time, taping has gained great acceptance. One advantage includes the ability to go back and check a candidate's responses to specific questions. This is particularly useful when a number of candidates have been interviewed and some of their comments begin to become confused in the minds of the interviewers. If taping is going to take place, security (maintaining the tapes during the interview process and erasing them afterward) should be considered. In addition, candidates should be given the courtesy of knowing that they are going to be taped prior to the interview, and given the opportunity to decline the interview if they so desire.

Conducting the interview. In the course of an interview, a number of interactions and exchanges take place. A skillful interviewer will consider the following:

Putting the candidate at ease in the beginning of the interview by using ice-breaker questions;

Asking appropriate personal/factual questions to obtain information regarding the candidate's background, credentials, and other areas of concern;

Asking questions without editorializing;

Taking notes on a rating form;

Occasionally summarizing or clarifying what the candidate has said, to give the applicant the opportunity to correct, expand upon, or reaffirm responses;

Encouraging candidates to ask questions;

Terminating at the appointed time by explaining the planned time for completing the selection process, and thanking the candidate for participating in the interview.

– INTERVIEWS AND APPLICATIONS –

School administrators have difficulty keeping up with changes in state and federal laws relating to the rights of candidates. The following quiz is intended to determine how much administrators know about the kinds of questions appropriate to ask on a job application or in an interview. Answers and explanations are included later in the chapter.

Job Applications and Interviewing: What's Legal and What's Not?

Place an "L" next to those questions or requests you believe to be legal and an "I" next to those you believe to be illegal:

_____I_____ 1. What is your maiden name?

_____I_____ 2. What is your previous married name?

_____L I_____ 3. Have you ever worked under another name?

_____I_____ 4. What do you prefer—Mr., Ms., Miss, or Mrs.?

_____I_____ 5. What is your marital status?

_____I_____ 6. Where were you born?

_____I_____ 7. What is the birthplace of your parents, spouse, other relatives?

_____I_____ 8. Submit proof of your age.

_____I_____ 9. What is your religious denomination or affiliation? (Or, What religious holidays do you observe? What church do you attend?)

_____L I_____ 10. Are you available for Saturday and/or Sunday work?

_____L_____ 11. Are you a citizen of the United States?

_____L_____ 12. If you are not a citizen of the United States, do you intend to become one?

_____I_____ 13. Require applicant to submit naturalization papers.

_____L_____ 14. List past work experiences.

_____L I_____ 15. List organizations, clubs, societies, lodges to which you belong.

_____I_____ 16. (For men) What is your spouse's maiden name?

_____L_____ 17. Submit names of persons willing to provide professional and/or character references.

_____I_____ 18. Supply names of three relatives other than father/mother, husband/wife, or dependent children.

_____L_____ 19. List related work experiences that would help you with this job.

_____I_____ 20. What relative can we notify in case of accident or emergency?

_____L___ 21. What foreign languages can you read, write, or speak?

_____I___ 22. How did you acquire the ability to read, write, or speak a foreign language?

_____I___ 23. Have you ever been arrested for any crime? If so, stipulate when and where.

_____I___ 24. List the names of dependent children under age eighteen.

_____I___ 25. What arrangements have you made for the care of your children?

_____I___ 26. What is the lowest salary you would accept?

_____I___ 27. What is your height and weight?

_____I___ 28. Have you ever had your wages garnished?

_____I___ 29. What is the general condition of your health?

_____I___ 30. Do you have any impairments (physical, mental, or medical) that would prevent you from performing in the position for which you have applied?

_____I___ 31. Have you ever been refused a fidelity bond?

_____I___ 32. What kind of work does your spouse do?

_____I___ 33. Attach a photograph to the application form.

_____I___ 34. Provide the *option* of putting a photo on the job application.

_____LI__ 35. List the names of relatives employed here.

_____I___ 36. Color of eyes and hair.

_____L___ 37. Have you served in the Armed Forces of the United States or in a state militia?

_____L___ 38. Did you receive a dishonorable discharge?

_____L___ 39. What public and private schools did you attend?

_____L___ 40. Are you eighteen years of age or older? If not, state your age.

Question Bank

The preceding section provides examples of inquiries or requests that are on sensitive matters. Interviewers should have a bank of potential and appropriate questions that can be used. The following section provides examples of questions that may be useful with prospective teaching and administrative candidates.

Questions/requests for information — teaching candidates:

1. Tell us a little about your academic preparation.
2. Describe your student (or previous) teaching experiences.
3. When teaching, would you prefer to instruct children with high, average, or low ability?
4. What advantages and disadvantages do you see to the individualized instruction approach?
5. What advantages and disadvantages do you see to whole-group instruction?
6. In a heterogeneously grouped classroom, you might have reading levels spanning five or more grade levels. How do you meet the needs of such a varied group within the same class?
7. Do you prefer teaching in a homogeneously or heterogeneously grouped classroom, and why?
8. In which do you see the most value, teaching skills or teaching content?
9. If we walked into your classroom and opened your plan book, how would we find your plans laid out?
10. How do you evaluate student progress?
11. How often do you test?
12. Do you see the final examination as a test of what was learned in class?
13. If we looked at your students' report cards, would grades be in the shape of a bell curve? Please explain.
14. In your last grading experience, what percentage of students received A's? B's? C's? D's? F's?
15. When a student gets a failing grade, how do you determine whether the student failed or the teacher?
16. A low achiever works hard and earns an average of 60 percent. An average achiever works little and earns an average of 85 percent. What grade do you put on their respective report cards?
17. What would you like to see students be able to do by the time they reach the end of your course?
18. What do you see as your greatest professional strength?
19. What do you see as your greatest professional weakness?
20. On a scale of 1 to 10, 10 being high, where would you place yourself as a disciplinarian and why?

21. Tell us about the most difficult discipline situation you have had to handle.
22. Have you ever hit a student? If so, describe the situation.
23. What do you see as the school's role in disciplining children?
24. What do you see as the role of the home in disciplining children?
25. How many children did you send to the office in the last month of school? For what reasons?
26. What steps would you take in a disciplinary situation? Please indicate who you would involve.
27. How do you see the role of the school administrator in relation to the teacher?
28. What should the administration expect from you?
29. Have the recommendations made to you in observations been useful? If so, how?
30. Why do you want to teach here?
31. Describe your most significant teaching experience.
32. A number of educational programs are the subject of staff development programs. Which recent initiatives are you most familiar with and what do you see as their positives and negatives?
33. What skills and interests would you be able to bring with you to our school?
34. Within the grade/subject you would be teaching, which sub-areas are you most comfortable teaching? Least comfortable?
35. Have you ever taught in a team-teaching situation? If so, please describe it and indicate what you felt were the advantages and disadvantages.
36. Which is more important in teaching, the means or the ends?
37. What are your professional plans for the next five years?
38. What can you bring to our district over other candidates we interview?

Questions/requests for information—administrative candidates:

1. What do you feel are your greatest accomplishments as an educator?
2. What do you believe are the most important duties of a (position title)?
3. What do you believe are the least important duties of a (position title)?
4. Why should we hire you over other candidates?
5. Where do you see yourself five years from now?
6. A number of staff development programs have recently received

attention in education; which do you believe hold the most promise and why?

7. How do you keep your supervisor informed of sensitive situations occurring in your (school/program)?
8. What do you see as the relationship between your administrative position and the (principals/superintendent/board/community)?
9. How would you like your work evaluated?
10. Given the choice, how would you go about evaluating staff?
11. How would you deal with a situation in which your supervisor denied a request that you felt was important?
12. How would you handle a staff member who was performing below your level of expectation?
13. Describe any experiences you have had with negotiations.
14. Describe any experiences you have had with teacher empowerment efforts.
15. What do you see as the advantages and disadvantages of merit pay systems?
16. How would you go about evaluating the present status of the (program/school) you are interested in leading?
17. How would you implement a public relations program?
18. What kinds of committees do you think should exist in a district?
19. What kind of decision-making power should each committee be given?
20. How would you go about building a budget?
21. If budget cuts are required, how would you make decisions?
22. What are your views concerning the *Nation at Risk* report?
23. How do children learn?
24. How do you feel about the gifted versus enrichment argument?
25. How would you implement a program for at-risk children?
26. If test scores in your program were low, how would you determine the problem?
27. Teachers you supervise are complaining about class sizes, and you have been asked to present a report to the superintendent. How would you approach this task?

Following the interview. Just as the face-to-face interview is important and should be conducted in an appropriate manner, what takes place immediately afterward is also important. During this time, summaries and selection decisions are formulated. The interviewers should follow a step-by-step plan that concludes with a selection recommendation. The plan should include at least the following:

Rewriting of notes taken during the interview—recalling and expanding on key points;
Comparing notes with the job description and the educational and personal qualifications required for the position;
Comparing completed notes with reference statements;
Rating each applicant according to the standard developed on the interview rating form;
Discussing all of the above with members of the interview team and reaching consensus on the ranking of candidates

Taping Sample Lessons

Many districts have adopted the strategy of having candidates teach sample lessons to classes of students. In some cases these sample lessons are observed, in others they are videotaped, and in some cases, both are done. Tapes are provided to evaluators, usually teaching and administrative staff members, who review the lesson. This evaluative information is added to other information gained from references and interviews to make a final decision.

Candidate Selection

The conclusion of the selection process comes about when an offer is made to, and accepted by, the chosen candidate. The individual responsible for making the selection should inform the superintendent of the first, second and third rankings of applicants. If the superintendent approves of the rankings, the highest-ranked candidate should be called and offered the position, based on the approval of the board. Should the first candidate decline, the superintendent should again be asked for approval, and the number two candidate contacted.

When the job is accepted by a candidate, acceptance should immediately be confirmed in writing, and the candidate notified that his or her name will be given to the board of education at its next meeting. The superintendent will usually know whether board approval is probable and whether it is safe to contact those candidates who will not be considered. In this case, written notification should be made to unsuccessful candidates. If board confirmation is in doubt, the superintendent should refrain from sending letters until the board acts.

The chosen candidate, once approved by the board of education, should be sent a letter that offers the job and includes the following kinds of information:

Position title
Type of appointment
Salary
Date to begin work
Work schedule (calendar)
Work station (school)
Pre-employment forms, literature, requirements to be completed
Requirement that the candidate immediately notify the district of job
    acceptance in writing
Offer to help candidate relocate (housing, etc.)

The rejection letter sent to those who were not chosen should be brief, courteous, and complimentary. It should also state the title of the position for which the person applied. Administrators should not provide commentary on why the person was not chosen. Administrators are not required to provide such information, and by doing so could conceivably open themselves and their districts to unnecessary lawsuits. If pressured to give a response, any comments should first be reviewed with legal counsel and should be made orally rather than on paper.

Following approval by the board of education, the new candidate, if already employed in another district, may be held for a period of time before being allowed to leave. An understanding of whether this is the case should be reached as soon as possible so that appropriate interim staffing may be arranged. Additionally, many administrators believe it is ethical to contact the school principal who supervises the candidate to make him or her aware of the hiring as soon as possible.

— REVIEW OF LEGAL QUIZ —

I 1. What is your maiden name?

> *This question is not relevant to a person's ability to perform a job and could be used for a discriminatory purpose. For example, a woman's maiden name might indicate her religion or national origin. It also constitutes an inquiry into marital status, which is listed separately.*

I 2. What is your previous married name?

> *Asks, in effect, whether an individual has been widowed or divorced. By its nature it is discriminatory because it is only asked of women.*

L/I **3.** Have you ever worked under another name?

Same as #1. However, when necessary to obtain information for reference checks or transcript release forms, such a question is not improper.

I **4.** What do you prefer—Mr., Ms., Miss, or Mrs.?

Simply another way of asking an applicant's sex and marital status. Even asking for a first name serves no preemployment purpose other than to indicate the applicant's sex.

I **5.** What is your marital status?

Refusal to employ a married woman has been held to violate Title VII of the Civil Rights Act of 1974 and also statutes in several states.

I **6.** Where were you born?

Attempts to determine national origin.

I **7.** What is the birthplace of parents, spouse, other relatives?

Attempts to determine national origin.

I **8.** Submit proof of age.

The Age Discrimination in Employment Act prohibits discrimination on the basis of age against individuals who are forty years of age and over. After hiring, proof of age may be requested. Many states have their own human rights laws that prohibit discrimination against persons aged eighteen and over.

Additionally, a number of states no longer have a mandatory retirement age. As a result, an employer may request an age limit be set by the state's individual civil rights or human rights agency if they believe they have a valid justification for doing so.

You may not request someone's date of graduation from elementary or high school. You may request the date of their graduation from a technical school or university in order to get proof of attendance.

I **9.** What is your religious denomination or affiliation?

Title VII of the 1964 Civil Rights Act prohibits discrimination on the basis of religion.

L/I **10.** Are you available for Saturday and/or Sunday work?

This may serve to discourage applications from persons who are prohibited for religious reasons from working on weekends. On the other hand, the district may need to know whether an applicant can work these days. Because Title VII prohibits discrimination on the basis of religion, an employer must demonstrate an inability to reasonably accommodate a prospective employee's religious observance or practice without undue hardship on the conduct of the employer's business. If this kind of question is asked, the district should indicate that a reasonable effort has been made to accommodate the religious needs of employees.

L **11.** Are you a citizen of the United States?

Candidates may also be asked whether they can prove that they are legally entitled to work in the United States and to provide a Social Security number. As of November 11, 1986 employers may be fined for employing individuals not legally entitled to work in the United States.

L **12.** If you are not a citizen of the United States, do you intend to become one?

I **13.** Submit naturalization papers.

L **14.** List past work experience.

L/I **15.** List organizations, clubs, societies & lodges you belong to.

Questions 12 through 15 are legal if relevant to candidate's ability to perform the job and illegal if not relevant to the job. They may be seen as an attempt to determine religion, race, or national origin. Schools might want to include a statement such as, "Exclude organizations whose identity would indicate race, creed, color, or national origin," or might also want to reword the question to: "List professional organizations."

I **16.** (For men) What is your spouse's maiden name?

This would have no bearing on a candidate's ability to perform the job.

L **17.** Submit names of persons willing to provide professional and/or character references.

I **18.** Supply names of three relatives other than father/mother, husband/wife, or dependent children.

This could provide information on national origin.

L **19.** What related work experiences would help you with this job?

I **20.** What relative can we notify in case of emergency?

This inquiry may be asked only after *a person has been hired.*

L **21.** What foreign languages can you read, write, or speak?

This is legal as long as it refers to a job requirement.

I **22.** How did you acquire the ability to read, write, speak a foreign language?

This may be seen as an attempt to determine religion, race, or national origin.

I **23.** Have you ever been arrested for any crime? If so, stipulate when and where.

Consideration of arrest records may be illegal, since an arrest record is not an indication of guilt. Some states have also determined that the discharge of or the refusal to hire or promote any individual because of a conviction record is illegal, unless it can be shown to prohibit that person from satisfactorily performing the job in question or that the prohibition is necessary to the safe and efficient operation of the business, or that a state or local licensing law or regulation prohibits the employment of such individuals. In some states it is unlawful to discriminate because of a former criminal record (ex-offender status).

I **24.** List names of dependent children under age eighteen.

Explores what many employers believe to be a common source of absenteeism and tardiness.

I **25.** What arrangements have you made for the care of your children?

Same as #24.

I **26.** What is the lowest salary you would accept?

Because in the past, women have worked in lower-paying jobs than men or have been paid less for the same work, a woman might be willing to work for less.

I **27.** What is your height and weight?

Some employers have imposed minimum height or weight requirements that are not related to job performance and that might discriminate against women and certain nationalities. Unless directly related to the job, this question should not be asked. Although some positions, such as those with police and fire departments, may require candidates to pass physical fitness tests, in most instances employers cannot predict present or future abilities based on physical size or potential physical difficulties.

I **28.** Have you ever had your wages garnished?

This has no bearing on the ability to perform work effectively.

I **29.** What is the general condition of your health?

Employers are prohibited from asking questions concerning the present or past health status of an applicant or of an employee being considered for promotion.

I **30.** Do you have any impairments (physical, mental, or medical) that would prevent you from performing in the position for which you have applied?

Questions that elicit general information about a handicapping condition should be avoided. Any question asked must be directly job-related. For instance, "Would your [epileptic] condition threaten the safety of your fellow employees?" Logically, candidates would not apply for a position in which their handicap would prevent them from being able to handle job-related duties. That being the case, such a question is best omitted altogether.

I **31.** Have you ever been refused a fidelity bond?

This could be an indirect effort to find flaws in a person's past. A bond may be denied without an individual knowing it.

I **32.** What kind of work does your spouse do?

Asks for marital status and is irrelevant to job performance. Also, some employers may be reluctant to hire a woman if she would then be the second breadwinner in the family.

I **33.** Attach a photograph to the application.

I **34.** Attach a photograph (optional).

Either requiring or providing the option of a photograph is illegal since it might indicate race.

L/I **35.** List names of relatives employed here.

May reflect a preference for relatives of present employees. Illegal if it has the effect of reducing employment opportunities for minorities. May reflect a rule that only one partner in a marriage can work for an employer; such a rule hurts women more than men and serves no necessary business purpose. In education, employment of close relatives of board members is treated differently in different states.

Boards also have the option of adopting nepotism policies that prohibit members of the same family from working in the same school. When a marriage occurs after employees have worked together, findings have varied.

I **36.** Color of eyes and hair.

Not related to job performance; could serve as an indication of race.

L **37.** Have you served in the Armed Forces of the United States or in a state militia?

L **38.** Did you receive a dishonorable discharge?

Inquiries should be accompanied by a statement that a dishonorable discharge is not an absolute bar to employment and that other factors will affect a final decision.

L **39.** What public and private schools did you attend?

L **40.** Are you eighteen years of age or older? If not, state your age.

Effective January 1, 1985 for public employers and January 1, 1986 for private employers, the maximum age limit for age discrimination has been removed.

The answers provided are in reference to education, and their legality may differ in other fields. To be legal, the question must be relevant to the individual's ability to perform the responsibilities of the position. Because interpretations of laws and regulations vary, administrators should contact their legal counsel to verify whether specific questions and requests can lawfully be included in their hiring process. State and federal human rights offices and civil rights offices may also be useful sources of assistance.

— APPOINTMENT —

Procedures vary, but in many states a recommendation must be made by the superintendent of schools before the board of education may act to approve or disapprove an appointment. Typically, appointments include at least the following:

1. The *name* of the appointee.
2. The *tenure area* or *areas* in which the professional educator will devote a substantial amount* of his or her time.
3. The *date of commencement* of probationary service or service in tenure in each such area.
4. The *expiration date of the appointment,* if made on a probationary basis.
5. The *certification status* of the appointee in reference to the position to which the individual is appointed.
6. Other information required by specific state law should also be included.

— SUMMARY —

This chapter reviews key components of the selection process. It discusses affirmative action, the review and interpretation of information collected for candidate reviews, the types of pressure often put on school administrators to hire a particular individual because of personal contacts or nepotism, and the inherent pressures based on organizational traditions and community pressure. The selection policy and its components are also presented and described. Methods for checking references and who should be contacted are listed, along with a number of potential questions that might be asked of those contacted. A brief discussion of liability is also provided, with cautions for administrators.

A description of the interview process includes determination of who will be interviewed, how many interviews will be conducted, what information will be supplied to those doing the interviews, and how conflicting or adverse comments that arise during the process will be handled.

Various federal laws affecting the selection process are outlined, including Title VII of the Civil Rights Act of 1964, the Pregnancy Discrimination Act, the Civil Rights Act of 1968, the Age Discrimination and Employment Act of 1967, the Equal Pay Act, the Vietnam Era Veterans Readjustment Act of 1974, the Civil Rights Act of 1866, the Civil Rights Act of 1871, Title IX, and the Rehabilitation Act of 1973.

The interview process itself is described, including a method for developing an interview format based on need, vacancy announcement, and review and development of the job description. Various types of interview questions

---

*Exactly what amount of time a professional staff member must spend working in a specific tenure area in order to receive credit for tenure is determined by state laws. In some states, people who spend a substantial period of time in more than one tenure area may receive tenure in the appropriate areas.

such as experiential, situational, opinion, dilemmas, and probes are described. In addition, methods for rating candidates and sample rating scales are provided. A quiz on which questions are legal or illegal in interviews or on job applications is also provided. Suggestions are made for activities following the interview, such as rewriting notes, making the final selection, and contacting candidates who were not selected.

— REFERENCES —

1. True v. Ladner, 213 A.2d 257 (Me. 1986).
2. Civil Rights Act of 1964, 42 U.S.C. Section 2000(e) et seq.
3. 18 U.S.C. Sections 245 et seq.
4. 29 U.S.C. Section 206(d) (1976).
5. 29 U.S.C. Sections 621–634 (1976 & Supp. III 1979).
6. 38 U.S.C. Section 2012 (1976 & Supp. III 1979).
7. 42 U.S.C. Section 1981.
8. 42 U.S.C. Section 1983.
9. 20 U.S.C., Sections 1681 et seq.
10. P.L. 100-259, 102 Stat 28 (1988).
11. 29 U.S.C., Sections 701–796i (1976 & Supp. III 1979).

CHAPTER

— 5 —

Orientation

Various studies indicate that a large percentage of people who enter the teaching profession leave it within their first few years. Those who leave are often the most competent and able. Any number of reasons may exist for changing jobs, but the phenomenon of beginning teachers leaving the teaching field supports the need for orientation to the profession, as well as to a particular school, to allow for a smooth transition from life as a student to life as a teacher. Undoubtedly, some individuals new to the educational profession will still determine that teaching is not what they want to do for the rest of their working lives. However, it would be unfortunate to think that some may leave for an avoidable cause such as a poor introduction to their profession.

Orientation may be viewed as a school district's effort to assist employees adjusting to a new community, school district, school, and job. It may also be viewed as a method by which a school district educates employees about the work to be performed and the relationship between this work and the school and community. Orientation deals with supplying information, giving direction, extending a welcome, and making new employees aware of what the district expects and can offer.

The district must ensure that its orientation program is well-planned to accomplish its goals. An orientation effort should begin with identifying program goals, then be developed to meet those goals.

— PROGRAM GOALS —

Several goals should be included in an orientation program. Each district must decide what it wishes to accomplish and who is to be included in the efforts. However, certain basic goals should be met in communicating with all new employees. The following sections describe content goals and process goals.

Sharing general information. New staff members will always have general concerns that should be addressed as soon as possible, starting with the interview process. Information regarding the community and its makeup, housing availability, employment trends, support for the schools, and what the community can offer residents are all of interest to new staff members. A copy of the local newspaper would probably be appreciated, and should be provided to each candidate.

Further information about the district, such as size, number of schools, grade-level configurations, support assistance from personnel services staff, program offerings, and curriculum, would also be of interest to new professional staff members. Specific information about the position, such as expectations, student-to-teacher ratio, daily schedule, and the number of other professionals on the grade-level or subject-matter team would also be valuable.

New staff are also likely to be interested in knowing specific information on staffing procedures. For instance, elementary teachers might want to know if they might be moved from one school or grade level to another. For many, seniority is a concern, so they might want to know if there is any chance they might be victims of a reduction in force. A list of staff and their respective number of years of service might be worth sharing.

Supplying assignment data. In addition to the general information provided, candidates will want to know about the specific duties and responsibilities of their new position. The teachers' role in counseling, testing, contacting parents, and supervisory functions (playground monitoring, after-school activities, coaching, advising, monitoring detention, bus duty, and study-hall duty) should be outlined beforehand so that teachers are not surprised when they report for their first day of work.

Another matter of importance to most staff members involves their evaluations. Teachers understandably want to know how their performance will be judged. Orientation should answer concerns regarding criteria, standards, and instruments used to make evaluations.

Identifying program activities. The personnel administrator and other staff members involved in the orientation process should determine how information will be provided to new employees—through presentations, bus tours, visits, speakers, and/or film or videotape. Scheduling time for events, both initial and throughout the school year, must also be addressed. Orientation may take place on the day before the start of the school year, and may also use release time and after-school times. However, administrators should be aware that many unions have filed grievances on the use of times such as the day before the start of school, based on the position that this time is outside of the contract and that teachers cannot be required to attend.

Allocating program responsibilities. A decision must also be made about responsibility for planning the orientation program and controlling its overall management. Many districts have included staff from various school areas in orientation activities. For instance, peer teachers, supervisors, business office staff, administrators, parents, and community members may all play some part in the presentation phase. Overall control usually rests with the district's personnel administrator, or with someone from the central office staff if a full-time personnel administrator is not employed by the district.

– PROGRAM DEVELOPMENT –

Development of the orientation program should determine what content will be included, how the content will be divided into individual presentations and activities, who will attend sessions and activities, when sessions will be held, and who will conduct them. While a great deal of information may be included in an orientation program, the district must decide what is appropriate for its new employees. At the least, each district should include the following in its program:

> *The community:* Its organizations and facilities, economy, history, agencies, residents, parents, customs, and values;
> *The school system:* Its philosophy, policies, programs, procedures, expectations, staff, customs, and values;
> *The positions:* Job descriptions, school locations, courses of study, textbooks, supplies, materials, pupil support services, expectations, and authority structure;
> *The individual:* Housing, recreational activities, union membership, and financial institutions.

An orientation program should begin with a set agenda, divided into scheduled sessions but flexible enough to permit change as the need arises during the program for a given year. Initially, content should be divided into individual presentation sessions based on the four topics listed above. However, enough flexibility should be allowed to permit separate sessions for subtopics, combination sessions linking topics and subtopics, and private sessions to satisfy specific individual concerns.

The specific sessions and who attends them should relate directly to the background of the new employees. An individual already employed in the district and recently promoted to a new position may need considerable information on the new position, particularly if the change involves a move into an administrative role; some reiteration of information about the school system and some exposure to the community may also be appropriate. The content should be based on factors related to the individual's in-district employment history, including types of jobs held, length of time employed in the district, and whether the individual resides in the district. Certain in-district jobs require more exposure to specific kinds of information than others. For instance, an individual employed in the district for the first time, who has held a job in a neighboring district, is likely to need more information about the position and individual concerns and less about to the community and the school system. Depending on resources and opportunity, a set of sessions on each area (community, school system, position, and individual) may be necessary, with emphasis on the ones that best suit the needs of the greater number of new employees.

Scheduling. One important decision involves deciding when sessions will be held. New employees have needs that begin when they formally accept a position. These needs may continue through the period before reporting to the district, through their first semester on the job, and through their first year or two. Presentation sessions and activities should be scheduled during all of these periods, based on the needs of new staff. The best method may be to schedule a day with a number of sessions and activities just before students begin classes. A luncheon together on this day would provide a chance for socializing. Additional sessions might be scheduled during the first semester. Sessions and activities for the individual could be scheduled on a regular basis during the first year or two, as needed.

One question with regard to orientation is whether participants get paid for time spent attending. As noted previously, unions in some districts have made an issue of this, contending that staff members should be remunerated for any extra time required for orientation. In other districts, teachers understand orientation to be a professional responsibility. School administrators new to a district should consider, in planning an orientation program, whether this question has been addressed by the union contract or through past practice. The accompanying box provides a sample first-day orientation program.

Conducting program evaluations. Determining the effectiveness of an orientation effort is crucial if the program is to meet its goals. A method of evaluation should be determined and implemented on a formative,

---

**SAMPLE AGENDA FOR NEW STAFF ORIENTATION
DAY 1: TUESDAY, AUGUST 24, 199__**

8:00–9:00   **Coffee and donuts with school principal**

- Position description, expectations
- Evaluations
- Extracurricular opportunities
- Tour of building

9:15–10:00   **Formal welcome by superintendent**

    — *Board office*

- District philosophy and future plans
- District policies and goals
- Background and organizational structure

10:15–10:45   **Paperwork**

    — *Business office*

- Review and signing of contract
- W-4 forms
- Certification check
- Payroll/deductions information

11:00–12:00   **Meet with your supervisor and/or mentor teacher**

    — *In your classroom*

- Expectations
- Department policies, goals
- Program/test review
- Trouble-shooting

---

ongoing basis, to ensure the needs of new staff are being met. Means for doing this might include paper surveys, interviews, or some combination. Questions should focus on how new employees feel about the orientation process and how the needs of the district are served by the orientation process, and should examine selected characteristics of new employees, such as performance, retention, and, satisfaction.

— ENTRY —

The most critical period, and the one that generates many lasting impressions for new staff, begins with job acceptance and initial reporting to the district. Activities should be planned and executed with care and efficiency. The district should supply information and schedule a number of entry activities.

A formal welcome to the district. Because entry to a district leaves a lasting impression, administrators should make contact with new employees in a way that will help ease their way into their new positions. Taking time for a cup of coffee and offering assistance will let new staff members know that the administrator has a sincere interest in the employees' transition. The importance of this early contact and offer of support cannot be overstated.

Contact with colleagues. Early contact with new colleagues should provide a chance to get acquainted before everyone becomes involved in the day-to-day rigors that accompany most teaching jobs. The importance of informal organizations in schools is well documented. Allowing new staff to become familiar with and accepted by colleagues on a personal level will facilitate the conduct of professional activities.

Financial and contractual benefits. Of interest to all employees is how their salary will be paid and what benefits are provided. An opportunity should be taken to review the district's contract with all employees, to explain salary schedules; pay periods; medical, dental, and optical coverage, and other contractual benefits—sick leave, personal time, sick bank options, early retirement provisions, and so on.

Presentation Sessions

Formal presentation sessions scheduled after employees report to the district should address topics such as:

Job expectations
Job performance
Behavior on and off the job
Relationship with supervisors, co-workers, parents, and students
Potential adjustment difficulties recognized by co-workers and supervisors as well as by new staff.

All of the above lead to the critical consideration of who will be involved in planning and conducting the orientation program. To control, organize, and evaluate, a number of individuals with a variety of backgrounds should be included. An opportunity can thus be provided for a number of residents and employees of the district to participate in an important school function. They may be asked to take responsibility for decisions about content, format of presentation, scheduling of sessions, and decisions on who will cover what content; this is an excellent tool for generating support for the schools. Consideration should be given to involving representatives from various school constituencies.

– INVOLVEMENT BY SCHOOL CONSTITUENTS –

Individuals and groups in the school community have a stake in the success of the schools. Providing these representatives with the opportunity to become involved in the orientation process can enhance their commitment to the school and improve the quality of orientation for new staff members.

Advisory committees. Most districts have a number of advisory committees made up of staff members. An introduction to the various committees and their goals and methods of operation should be provided to new staff, who are likely to be asked to sit on committees during the course of their careers.

Local organizations. A common concern in many school districts is the perceived division between school and community. The orientation program is an excellent opportunity for the district to overcome such perceptions by inviting representatives from organizations to visit the school, to share information regarding their groups and how the groups might support efforts made by the schools. This introduction might also be used as an opportunity for community organizations to identify potential members.

Employee units. Representatives from departments such as curriculum and personnel, and employee organizations and unions, will appreciate the opportunity to discuss the services their department or association can provide. The orientation period is most appropriate for this introduction, since most of these services are of immediate value and interest to new employees.

Government agencies. A number of governmental offices may be useful to staff in schools. Human rights and child welfare offices are often utilized by professional educators. Civil service agencies offer a variety of services of value to support staff members. Explanations of how to contact such services should be provided to new staff members through representatives or literature.

To ensure the usefulness of orientation, the process of scheduling speakers and programs should be closely coordinated and monitored by the central administration, and a well-qualified individual should be assigned to serve as orientation chairperson.

— THE COMMUNITY —

As noted, four major components of the orientation program will be of importance to new staff: community, school system, position, and the individual. All should be introduced early in the employment of a staff member.

Because the schools belong to the people of the community, the schools should certainly reflect community expectations. Thus, new employees should understand the relationship between the school and its community. Points that might be covered include:

History of the area
Business, industry, and service institutions
Educational opportunities
Government and political structure
Socioeconomics of the community
Educational profile of the community
Demographics, including information on racial, minority, and non-English-speaking components
Family service agencies
Health-related services
Construction, particularly residential
Predicted growth or decline
Transportation services
Shopping
Social opportunities
Weather

Presentation of information to new employeee may be delivered through various means, including:

- Open houses
- Panel discussions
- Visits
- Conferences
- Movies
- Slides
- Letters
- Brochures
- Event calendars
- Service organizations

- PTO/PTA groups
- Buddy system
- Newspapers
- Newsletters
- Coffee hours
- Meetings with politicians
- Meetings with business leaders
- Mini-tours
- Welcome wagon

– THE SCHOOL SYSTEM –

The school system should inform new employees about how the district operates, what it expects, and how they fit into this design. This information may best be shared through discussion of:

District goals
District policies
District procedures
District organizational structure
District expectations
Student assessment and performance results
Income sources and expenditures
Special support facilities and personnel
Support staff
Staff discipline
Academic freedom
Future directions
Growth/decline
Problems/concerns
Tracking/grouping of students
Support services
New district programs
Money spent per child

A district may wish to use some of the following to develop presentations and activities:

- Handbooks
- Brochures

- Breakfast with . . .
- Lunch with . . .

- Manuals
- Charts
- Meetings with the board
- Receptions
- Cookouts
- Visits
- Board minutes

- Slides
- Movies and tapes
- Forums
- Curriculum guides
- Annual reports
- Regional school education reports

— THE POSITION —

To a new staff member, the most important phase of an orientation program concerns his or her new position. A complete and detailed understanding of their jobs and all that affects them contributes to the success of new employees. Problems that arise on the job are usually related to a lack of knowledge about the position, especially about expectations and desired outcomes. Thus, new employees must know:

Physical layout of district (size, number of schools, student population, class sizes)
District goals
School program/department/unit goals
Certification requirements
Evaluation procedures
Student special services
Employee special services
Co-workers
Parental relationships
District policies and procedures

Districts may use some of the following presentations and activities in this aspect of employee orientation:

- Handbooks
- Brochures
- Forms
- Mentors

- Conferences
- Visits
- Meetings with parents
- Meetings with other teachers

— THE INDIVIDUAL —

New employees continually adjust as they become accustomed to their jobs. Age, health, marital status, and financial, sibling, and parental obligations change through the years and influence performance and attitudes. One employee may have an easy time making adjustments; another may need greater support. People do not come to the job as equals. Skills, talents, and personal problems differ dramatically and affect the success or failure of each employee.

The nature of such personal issues dictates that presentations and activities be ongoing. A defined program for all new employees should be conducted during the first semester and for some should go beyond the first year. Sample components can include:

Mentors
Conferences with immediate supervisors
Hotline availability
Employee assistance program
I-have-a-question meetings
School visits
Congratulatory notes
Round-table meetings
Availability of information committee

Once initial contacts have been made, a checklist to be completed by the personnel director is one means of monitoring orientation activities. (See the accompanying box.)

PERSONNEL ORIENTATION CHECKLIST

Employee name _____ Position _____

School _____ Starting date _____

Date

_____ Request for position

_____ Posting and advertising

_____ Employment application received

_____ Letters of recommendation received

_____ Copy of certification received

_____ Transcripts received

_____ Interview
_____ Notice of job offer
_____ Contract and salary notice signed
_____ W-4 form completed
_____ Health insurance (sign-up or decline)
_____ Retirement (apply or decline)
_____ Oath of allegiance
_____ Pre-employment physical
_____ I.D. photo
_____ Civil service application (classified positions only)
_____ Personnel data card
_____ Information packet provided:

- Job description
- Telephone directory
- School calendar
- Performance review form
- Conference request form
- Request for approval of study form

- Union agreement
- Payroll schedule
- Credit union information
- Absence report form
- Travel regulations
- Expense voucher
- Mileage reimbursement

Source: Oneida-Madison Board of Cooperative Educational Services, New Hartford, New York.

— PRESENTERS —

Four areas to be addressed in an orientation program have been outlined: community, school system, position, and the individual. Those developing the orientation program should identify the individuals best suited to presenting information. It might be appropriate to have an elected community official, such as the mayor or a city council member, speak about the community. A member of the parents' association might also be involved in such presentations. School administrators, particularly the school superintendent and assistant superintendent, might discuss districtwide concerns and practices. School, administrators, department or grade-level chairs, the school librarian, fellow teachers, guidance staff, teacher-center representatives, and others involved with instructional program concerns might discuss matters related to the position. The district's business manager, payroll/benefits clerk, teachers' union president, teacher colleagues, and a "buddy" or mentor teacher might be involved in the component designed to orient the individual.

The last area discussed, the individual, should be considered as more important than the other three. The entry period into the school district is the most crucial in determining a staff member's attitude toward the school. The wise administrator will make every effort to provide a great deal of personal support during a new staff member's entry into the system. If the person is from outside of the area, offers of assistance in locating housing, child care, and financial, legal, and other services should be made. Regular contact and concern during this period can pay off in the long run, in terms of ensuring job satisfaction among employees.

— SUMMARY —

This chapter discusses the importance of the orientation process in retaining effective teachers and the important components of such a process. Program goals include sharing general information, supplying specific assignment data, allocating program responsibilities, and conducting program evaluations. Program development involves communicating information about community, school system, position, and the individual. In addition to the content to be covered in a orientation program, session schedules and persons presenting information are also important. The process provides an opportunity to involve a broad cross-section of school community members in welcoming new staff members.

— 6 —

Staff Development

— BY WILLIAM D. SILKY, ED.D. —

Most formal organizations today recognize that once they have hired an employee, they have an obligation to ensure the continuing education of that individual. This ongoing training is necessary not only for the personal benefit of staff members, but also for constant adjustment to external and internal changes and for improvement in the organization. Futurists such as Nalsbitt and Aburdene,[1] and business management experts like Peters,[2] remind us that change is a constant and that rapid adjustment to change will continue to be demanded of people and organizations as the millenium approaches. In a recent *New York Times* article by Fowler,[3] a report from the American Society of Training and Development was quoted as saying, "In the 1990s, American corporations must do much more training of their workers." Schools and school districts also find themselves in this situation.

Training of employees is not a new phenomenon, particularly in the private sector. For years, organizations have trained new employees in specific job skills. The supervisor taught the foremen, who in turn instructed the workers. What is new is the amount of money being spent on formal education by organizations. An artricle in *U.S. News and World Report*[4] stated that formal training in the private sector was costing $30 billion per year in 1986. The figure is even higher today. This imperative for constant training and retraining is present in the public sector and in public schools. As Fielding and Schalock[5] state:

> In at least one important way education is like any other business or profession: the quality of personnel is of central importance. No matter how sophisticated or extensive a school's resources or how carefully developed its policies, without the skill and commitment of teachers and administrators,

127

a school cannot succeed. Effective education depends on effective professionals.*

One might ask then, "How do we ensure that we have effective professionals in our schools?" Clearly, the initial step is to hire competent professionals at the outset. A second and perhaps equally important means is to work with both new and present staff in the constant pursuit of higher levels of skill. In education today, this is called "staff development." The choices are not mutually exclusive. Obviously, even the most able staff will need continuing training and support to maintain and improve their instructional effectiveness.

– DEFINING STAFF DEVELOPMENT –

"Personnel development," "training," "inservice education," and "staff development" are all terms that might be found in the literature associated with the ongoing learning that organizations, schools in this case, provide their employees. "Personnel development" is the term usually applied to the process by people employed in the personnel management or human resource field, in both the private and public sector. Included under this phrase can be a variety of activities, including individual development, group development, system development, and board member development.[6] This usage has a much broader connotation than the discussion in this chapter. "Training" usually has a much narrower meaning. Training implies that skills will be taught by those performing the training and learned by the trainees. Little provision is made for other kinds of knowledge than skill or procedural knowledge.

In the 1970s, the term "inservice education" was popularly used to imply ongoing teaching of and learning by teachers who were already in the classroom. This was to distinguish it from "preservice education," which referred to students studying to become teachers. Inservice education usually consisted of workshops or non-credit-bearing college courses focusing on the improvement of teaching strategies. It was not until the mid-1970s that the term "staff development" became popular to describe what school districts hoped to do for the continuing education of their professional employees.

---

*This is not to imply that the continuing development of other school employees such as secretaries, bus drivers, and custodians is not important. Chapter 12 (Administering Support Staff) discusses the need for such training of non-instructional employees.

The National Education Association[7] defines staff development as "education mandated for practicing professionals," but here a preference is given to the broader definition used by the Regional Laboratory for Educational Improvement of the Northeast and Islands.[8] This broader meaning of staff development encompasses all those activities in which professional staff members engage that are intended to enhance their ability to perform their jobs and/or make them more productive employees. This can include such activities as college course work, district-sponsored staff development training sessions, activities supported by teacher centers, mentoring, peer coaching, clinical supervision, action research involving the professional, institutes, seminars, and individually determined professional or personal development plans. Therefore, in accordance with the work of Howey,[9] teacher staff development includes six major functions: improvement of teaching (pedagogical skills); understanding and discovery of oneself; cognitive development; development of theories of teaching; development of the profession through research; and career development.

— ADULT DEVELOPMENT THEORY —

Until recently, schools structured their staff development offerings based on the familiar pedagogy of working with K–12 students. Since the mid-1970s, those who provide staff development have begun to recognize that the adult learner is different in many ways from the younger student. A number of researchers have written about stages of adult life. Cross[10] summarized many of these views and assigned a name to each of the adult development stages. The paragraphs that follow are derived from her synthesis.

During the ages from eighteen to twenty-two, the individual is primarily concerned with leaving home. Major events include establishing a new living arrangement, entering college, and starting a first full-time job. People are concerned with establishing their own autonomy from the family and developing new peer relationships. Young adults are caught between being in and moving out of the family. On the one hand, they want to be adults and on the other have a fear of their ability to fill that role. Between twenty-three and twenty-eight years old, the individual is moving into the adult world. Important events will usually include marrying and establishing a new home, perhaps becoming a parent, and getting hired (and perhaps fired). During this period, people actually consider themselves as adults. They will also begin building a dream, perhaps around their career, and will look for a mentor to guide them.

The ages from twenty-nine to thirty-four include a search for stability. Singles may wish to marry and the childless to start a family. For those with children, during this time the children enter school. Individuals are progressing in their careers or considering changing careers, and they may consider returning to school. Separation, divorce, and remarriage may occur. These five years are a time when most adults strive for success. Women who have stayed in the home may decide to emerge, and want their husbands to take over some of the household responsibilities so that they can have a chance at a career. Meanwhile, men are concerned with being successful, which often means they spend more time away from home. Long-range goals are usually set, in a search for stability, security, and control. The individual accepts the needs of growing children, yet desires to reappraise current relationships. There is a tremendous concern for being successful, particularly in one's work life. This stage of life has been found to be a difficult time for many teachers, because of the conflict between wanting to break out and the need for security.

Between thirty-seven and forty-two an adult is becoming his or her own person. Priorities begin to change; men want to nurture and women may want to achieve something outside the family. Important events during this time might include a crucial promotion, development of a sense of responsibility for a three-generation family including growing children and aging parents, and perhaps a break with one's mentor. Adults usually realize during this time that they must face reality. The reality that they are aging and must confront their own mortality may strike them. Frequently, adults in this age group will want to reduce dependent ties to their spouse, mentor, and boss. A reassessment of marriage, personal priorities, and values is undertaken. Questions asked by adults in this stage are often, "Have I done the right thing?" and "Is there still time to change?"

Careers usually peak between ages of forty-five to fifty-five, best characterized as a period of settling down. Quite often individuals will find that they have become mentors to younger employees. They may become grandparents, as their own children are leaving home. The community may benefit as individuals often strive to become more actively involved. New hobbies and interests emerge. Emotionally, this period finds individuals with an increased feeling of self-awareness and competence. They begin to enjoy their choices in life and lifestyle. This is frequently considered the best time of life, despite the nagging question of whether it may be too late to do some of the things people want to do in life. People in this stage of life can have the potential to be our greatest teachers and administrators.

The mellowing years are from ages fifty-seven to sixty-four. In this time period people prepare for retirement. Health problems frequently appear, and spouses may die. Individuals accept and adjust to the aging process and become concerned with accomplishing goals in the time remaining to them. Individuals find greater comfort with themselves, and their spouses become increasingly important to them. Overall, there is a mellowing of feelings and relationships.

Finally, ages of sixty-five and after become a period of life review, during the retirement years. Health often begins to decline, new living arrangements appear, daily routines shift, personal finances change, and friends begin to die. Most people prepare themselves for the death of their spouses. Individuals are concerned with their search for integrity. There is an acceptance of self and a gradual disengagement from life's activities. Individuals review the accomplishments of their lives and often exhibit eagerness to share everyday human joys and sorrows. Family becomes extremely important as death becomes a new presence in people's lives.

Krupp[11] has recognized these developmental stages and has drawn from them implications for working with aging teachers. She contrasts how over-forty and under-forty teachers view time, life priorities, mortality, their careers, mentoring, destructiveness, nurturing, and aloneness. Krupp notes that how individuals feel about time and priorities is influenced by their adult developmental sage. Persons over forty have their priorities ordered, do not want to waste time in meetings, and may not be open to new ideas. Many insights about adult employees can be found in this work and must be understood by personnel administrators as they engage in staff development activity.

For many years, adult education, in-service education, and other attempts to teach the adult learner were modeled on the pedagogy used for teaching children. Knowles[12] is credited with developing one of the first paradigms that distinguished pedagogy from "andragogy." Although andragogy, or the method of teaching adults, was popularized by Knowles, the word itself is traced back to Germany as early as 1833.[13] Regardless of derivation, the definition of the characteristics of adult learners and methods of teaching adults received their greatest contributions from Knowles.

Dalellew and Martinez[14] have summarized the major concepts that Knowles and others have identified about adult learners. A summary of the major understandings includes:

Motivation: Adult learners are motivated to learn by internal forces. Therefore, forcing them to engage in staff development is not only unproductive, but may even create animosity.

Concept of themselves as learners: Adults are self-directed learners; they do not necessarily need a "teacher" to guide their learning, as is usually the case with children.

Orientation to learning: Adults want to take the new learning and immediately apply it to their own situation. Although most adults will engage in learning for learning's sake, staff development planners should be cognizant that adult participants will want to make immediate application of their learning.

Role of the learner: Adults have had numerous life experiences that they bring to learning situations. As a result, they are less likely to alter their world view than are children. Adults' world view has become rigid.

Understanding adult learning better will help personnel administrators begin to explore planning and engage in staff development initiatives.

– EFFECTIVE STAFF DEVELOPMENT PRACTICES –

The poor quality of staff development in many schools has been lamented for a number of years. Too often districts have decided what their staff members need, planned an activity to address the need, implemented the planned activity, and evaluated it for effectiveness, only to find that the effort had little or no impact. The impact may even have been a negative reaction by the employees to having to participate in what they perceived as a meaningless, time-wasting exercise. The past fifteen to twenty years have revealed much about effective staff development practices, and as a result, many schools have altered their approach to this process.

The Rand Corporation[15] studied four cases of staff development efforts initiated between 1973 and 1978. The study showed that a clear relationship existed between the reason a staff development project was started and success in its implementation and incorporation. A project motivated by a need that had been identified by committed staff was likely to be successfully implemented later. On the other hand, when a project was used as an opportunity to collect federal money, as is sometimes the case, later success was less likely.

A commitment from school district leadership is essential. Administrators at the school and central office levels must communicate to district professionals that staff development is a priority. This commitment can be shown in a variety of ways, including allocation of adequate funding to support high-quality programming, participation in specific staff development activities, making time available for staff development, and publicly announcing the importance of and the administration's commitment to high-quality staff development.

Successful staff development should be planned cooperatively by the district administration, staff development professionals, and targeted participants. High-quality staff development is something done *with* teachers, not *to* them. Consequently, including teacher involvement in the planning phase will help ensure that the participants' views are represented and will build commitment to the resulting staff development plan.

Content selected for staff development efforts must reflect the needs of the participants. Even if the intended offerings are to advance organizational goals, the needs of individual teachers must also be considered and addressed. This is perhaps the most important understanding derived from the research. Unless and until individual needs are identified and addressed, little change will take place in organizations. Organizations do not change; people do!

For staff development programs that intend to alter attitudes and behaviors of participants, a long-term commitment to change is required. Too often such efforts have been of the one-shot variety; the planners hoped that one workshop session would change the way teachers teach and the beliefs they hold. Most researchers today indicate that such change will only take place through a sustained three-to-five-year staff development program. Joyce and Showers[16] have discovered four elements that are essential in staff development programs if teachers are to internalize information and transfer new skills to their classrooms: theory must be presented; the trainers must provide modes of the new behaviors; practice opportunities should be followed by immediate and specific feedback; and on-the-job site coaching must occur after the initial training.

Individuals undergoing change in behaviors as a result of staff development efforts will be operating at varying levels of concern and use, and staff developers should be cognizant of these levels. Hall and Loucks[17] have provided a model to understand teachers' concerns as they approach staff development. An employee operating at the lowest level of concern, which they referred to as "awareness," will show little interest for or involvement in the change that is the focus of the staff development effort. Once persons have developed a general interest in and awareness of a specific desired change, they are said to be operating at the "informational" level of concern. The "personal" level of concern finds individuals struggling with the demands of the staff development program and their perceived inadequacy to "do it right." Following the initial staff development training, participants struggle with their ability to "manage" the new skills, to fit the new behaviors into the way they normally behave. Having mastered the management of the new behaviors, the teachers then develop a concern for the "consequence" of their new behaviors on their students. Once proficiency is reached, the concern level is with "collaborating" with colleagues. Finally, and at the highest level of concern, is the individual's interest in "refocusing." This level of concern deals with improving the innovation that was the focus of the initial staff development effort.

7 levels of concern

Knowledge of effective staff development practices is necessary but not sufficient for high-quality programming. Effective planning that *utilizes* this knowledge is also essential.

— PLANNING FOR STAFF DEVELOPMENT —

As discussed in Chapter 2, long-range planning is not new to public school personnel administrators. Identification of potential retirees and needed replacements, recruitment plans, and preparation for contract negotiations are all examples of how planning has affected the personnel administrator. Planning for staff development, by contrast, has usually had a minor role for the personnel office, although this role has become increasingly important in recent years.

The planning team. Several steps have been found useful in planning high-quality staff development. A districtwide long-range planning team should be developed, including representatives of all professional staff groups in the school district—teachers (elementary, middle, and high school), teacher assistants, guidance counselors, social workers, psychologists, and administrators. The personnel administrator should be a key member of this long-range planning committee. Within fixed parameters, decisions by this staff development planning committee are best made by consensus. Selection of the right people to serve on this committee is critical. Staff members who are well-intentioned and committed to the idea of working together for the betterment of individuals and the organization should be sought.

The long-range planning team must understand its purpose within the context of the overall mission of the school. Therefore, one of the first activities the committee should undertake is a review of the district mission and goals. All resultant planning should be consistent with the mission and goals, while at the same time attempting to address individual needs. Once the review is completed, a comprehensive needs assessment must be conducted.

The needs assessment. Identifying what individuals need in relation to the district's goals has often taken the form of a pencil-and-paper self-report survey for each staff member to complete and return. Utilizing this approach as the total needs assessment has several flaws. First, the planning committee frequently spends an inordinate amount of time designing the staff survey, thus shifting the purpose from needs identification to survey design. Second, through the structuring of the survey questions, the respondents may give feedback *only* on those suggested needs listed on the survey. Finally, such a survey may assume that what people list as their needs are indeed their needs, which is not always the case, since many people feel they must report *something*. While needs assessment surveys have their place in the planning process, identification of needs must take a much broader approach.

Multiple data sources should be used to create a needs assessment landscape for staff development planning. These data sources might include self-report surveys, but could also include recommendations from reviewing personnel supervision/evaluation reports, student achievement indicators (standardized test results, attendance patterns, etc.), instructional program evaluations, and personal interviews. From a compilation of the data yielded by these efforts, planning of staff development options can begin.

The long-range planning team should summarize the results of the needs assessment in terms of district and school goals. Based on this summary, a multi-year plan should be outlined. For instance, a five-year planning model might be laid out so that in the first year of the plan, fairly detailed specific activities and their costs should be described. For the remaining four years, only a sketch of the staff development activities should be described, for two reasons. First, considerable change may be needed after the implementation of the first-year plans; second, continuing modification of the plan assures the entire staff of their continued involvement in the planning process. The final plan should be circulated to the entire school staff for review and comment. Once the planning team has received feedback from the faculty and made any adjustments, the plan should be forwarded to the local board of education for adoption. Each subsequent school year should begin with review of the implementation of the plan.

The planning team's role does not end with needs identification and plan development. Careful monitoring of plan implementation will necessitate the planning team's meeting several times throughout each school year, to discuss any difficulties and make minor adjustments. The planning team should also engage in continuous, systematic evaluation so that ongoing improvements can be incorporated into the staff development program design.

– EVALUATION OF STAFF DEVELOPMENT –

If little attention has been paid to effective staff development over the years, even less has been directed toward the evaluation of staff development programs. A typical approach to assessing staff development activity has included self-report surveys from those who participated. Although the importance of participants' perceptions of the quality and usefulness of staff development should not be minimized, these should never constitute the total evaluation.

Understanding the purposes of the staff development program from the outset will help guide the evaluation design. For example, was the program intended to change individual employees, the organization, students, or all of these? Clearly, knowing the answer to this question will assist in determining how to collect data and assess it. Loucks-Horsley and others[8] have provided a constructive approach to collecting meaningful data.

If the intended staff development effort is to change the knowledge base of participants, pre- and post-tests of this knowledge should be administered, and/or participants should be surveyed about their learning. On the other hand, if the intention of the program is to alter skill level and use of skills by participants, direct observation of the participants in their work settings would be the best evaluation method. If observation is not possible, data sources might include interviews with the individuals, surveys, analysis of work documents (products), or other data collection methods. If the staff development program has as its goal the altering of the attitudes, opinions, or feelings of participants, then surveys, interviews, and other means of data collection would be most productive.

Staff development can have the individual teachers as its focus, and it also may sometimes be appropriate to alter the school or school district (organization) or students. To evaluate whether a staff development initiative aimed at changing the school is effective, surveys of all groups concerned, coupled with interviews, observations and informal data collection, will prove most effective. Data from pre- and post-testing, surveys, observations, interviews, and document analysis should also provide useful feedback.

Summative and Formative Evaluation

Once the evaluation data are collected and analyzed, they can serve either a summative or formative purpose. To measure project impact to justify initial funding, the data will assist the evaluator in determining whether the money, time, and effort was well spent. If no additional use of the data is intended, the process is considered summative evaluation. Data analysis leading to changes and improvements in existing or future staff development efforts is referred to as formative. In this case, the intent of the evaluation is to provide the planners with insight for later staff development activity.

– SUMMARY –

This chapter has provided an overview of staff development administered as a personnel function. All indications point to the need for continuing training and retraining of employees as a means to maintain the viability of schools. However, understanding and accepting this need is not enough. Personnel administrators involved in such planning must have a clear understanding of what staff development is and how adult learners are different from other learners, as well as knowing the attributes of effective staff development programming and ways to evaluate staff development efforts.

– REFERENCES –

1. Naisbitt, J. and Aburdene, P. *Megatrends 2000*. New York: William Morrow, 1990.
2. Peters, T. *Thriving on Chaos*. New York: 1988.
3. Fowler, E. "Companies Urged to Add to Training." *New York Times*, June 27, 1989, p. 87.
4. "Why Business Spends Billions Educating Workers." *U.S. News and World Report*, 1986. February 10, 1986.
5. Fielding, G.D., and Schalock, H.D. *Promoting the Professional Development of Teachers and Administrators*. ERIC/CEM EA 017 747, 1985.
6. Castetter, W.B. *The Personnel Function in Educational Administration*. New York: Macmillan, 1986.
7. *Excellence in our Schools. Professional and Staff Development: An Action Plan.* Washington, DC: National Education Association, 1985.
8. Regional Laboratory for Educational Improvement of the Northeast and Islands. *Continuing to Learn: A Guidebook for Teacher Development*. Washington, DC: Office of Educational Research and Improvement, U.S. Department of Education, 1987.
9. Howey, K.R. "Six Major Functions of Staff Development: An Expanded Imperative." *Journal of Teacher Education* (Jan.–Feb. 1985), pp. 58–63.
10. Cross, P. *Adults as Learners*. San Francisco: Jossey-Bass, 1981.
11. Krupp, J.A. "Sparking an Aging Staff through Increased Awareness of Adult-Developmental Changes." *School Administrators Association of New York State Journal* (Winter 1982–1983), pp. 9–13.
12. Knowles, Malcolm. *The Adult Learner: A Neglected Species*. Houston: Gulf Publishing, 1973.
13. Feuer, D., and Geber, B. "Uh-Oh . . . Second Thoughts about Adult Learning Theory." *Training* (Dec. 1988), pp. 31–39. Clearinghouse on Educational Management. 1988.

14. Dalellew, T., and Martinez, Y. "Androgogy and Development: A Search for the Meaning of Staff Development." *Journal of Staff Development*, vol. 9, no. 3 (Summer 1988), pp. 28–31.
15. Berman, P., and McLaughlin, M. *Federal Programs Supporting Educational Change*, vol. III: *Implementing and Sustaining Innovations*. Santa Monica, CA: Rand Corporation, 1978.
16. Joyce, B., and Showers B. "The Coaching of Teaching." *Educational Leadership*, vol. 40, no. 1 (October 1982), pp. 4–10.
17. Hall, G., and Loucks, S. "Teacher Concerns as a Basis for Facilitating and Personalizing Staff Development." In *Staff Development: New Demands, New Realities, New Perspectives* (A. Lieberman and L. Miller, Eds.). New York: Teachers College Press, 1979, pp. 36–53.

— 7 —

Personnel Procedures

Usually the two entities involved in hiring teachers and administrators for school systems are the school superintendent and the district's board of education. The process is designed to provide checks and balances on power. Each entity must give approval before an offer of employment can be made. Once the decision to hire is made, a series of procedures that afford a number of protections are required.

— PROBATION —

In most circumstances, teachers are initially employed on probationary status. Probationary staff members have limited rights to their positions, although these rights will vary depending on whether protection is provided by local contracts. (Just-cause provisions that may require judgment by a neutral third party are discussed later in this chapter.) Most states require that probationary teachers being dismissed should be given prior notice of the board of education's intentions. A primary purpose of this notice is to provide individuals with the opportunity to plan for further employment, but the notification may also give those employees an opportunity to request reasons for their dismissal from the administration or board of education. Although probationary staff members may have no statutory right to hearings, inappropriate dismissal reasons could result in giving employees such rights. Examples of such grounds might include charges of dishonesty, prejudice, and immorality. Such comments can be reframed and rephrased in front of a hearing officer so that the burden of proof placed on the administration becomes much more difficult. As a result, administrators should be extremely careful about any information they put in a letter or give orally, since they may be required at some future date to provide convincing evidence to justify their statements. The best advice would be to consult with the school district's attorney before any such communication with an employee.

Evaluating. One of the most prevalent problems faced by the legal counsel of administrators involves the dismissal of staff members, both probationary and tenured. Lawyers and labor relations officers are often called into a school district to prepare a dismissal case against a staff member, only to find that the individual has received consistently satisfactory performance evaluations. The counsel is then told to develop a case. If a neutral third party is to hear the case, advocates know that they are entering into a process likely to have an unsatisfactory conclusion for the school district.

Probably the most common failure of school administrators in dealing with probationary staff members involves the confusing messages often given these individuals. The new, inexperienced teacher entering the classroom for the first time needs a great deal of support and direction regarding expectations. The recent empowerment movement, which encourages mentoring by veteran teachers, directly addresses this concern. An experienced staff member can help someone new to the profession learn about critical job security concerns such as evaluation by explaining from the classroom teacher's perspective how evaluation really takes place. Anyone who has worked in a classroom environment and has been evaluated by administrators can share stories of the kinds of behaviors evaluators look for during the observation-evaluation process. Although educators are concerned with valid observation procedures, ultimately human beings are making the final judgments, and personal leanings and beliefs will enter into those judgments.

In fairness to instructional or support staff members, every school administration should have a clear outline of evaluation criteria available, to define exactly what the criteria used in the evaluation process mean. These criteria should be jointly decided upon by the group that will be evaluated and those who will conduct the evaluations. Finally, the criteria should become part of the orientation process, to be reviewed with all new staff members prior to the conduct of the first evaluation. A review of the criteria should also be conducted with veteran staff members, either in a faculty meeting or in pre-observation conferences.

Observing contractual obligations. Standard advice for any new administrator includes, "Read the contract and when you're done, read it again!" This may be followed by, ". . . and read it at least once a month during the first years you are on the job." Unfortunately, many administrators assume that contract language is logical, reasonable, and constructed to promote the welfare of the individuals who work within the contract. Not so. Many unions have negotiated contractual provisions that limit the ability of administration to observe and evaluate staff members effectively, thus making the administrator's role much more difficult in important decisions regarding feedback to staff members and, in some cases, staff retention or termination. For instance, some contracts state that administrators are only allowed to enter classrooms with the prior knowledge of teachers concerned, and that teachers must be notified when class visits are for evaluation purposes. Such provisions may cause difficulties for administrators, particularly those who believe it essential for them to visit classrooms regularly on a walk-through basis and observe problems during these visits. Take for instance the administrators who reported finding a teacher sleeping at his desk. The absurdity of waking the teacher and announcing "Here I am!" shocks the reasonableness of anyone. Methods for handling such situations should be in place in the district. For instance, the administrator might write a memo to the staff member, to be included in the staff member's personnel file. All administrators should have a clear understanding of how to handle such situations.

Tenure. Tenure is provided to staff members in almost every state, and gives great protection to staff members by the statutory rights that guarantee they cannot be relieved of their duties at the sole discretion of a school board or administration. The time necessary to acquire tenure varies from state to state, but commonly ranges from three to five years of continuous service. Credit for part-time and substitute service *may* be provided, but this must be ascertained by specific state. In some states, substitute teachers who work for a full year in place of teachers who have been ill may be given credit for that full year if they are then appointed to regular, tenure-track positions. Adjustments in accruing credit toward tenure also may exist for part-time staff. For instance, a teacher who works on a half-time basis in a kindergarten class *may* use that service to receive a full year's credit toward tenure and seniority in some states. The time required to receive tenure in a district may be less for teachers who were previously tenured.

Tenure status provides teachers with due-process rights as a result of provisions of the Fourteenth Amendment. As the law was originally conceived, teachers should be insulated from arbitrary and capricious decisions by school board members or administrators.

Tenure protection does not necessarily extend to positions that require yearly appointments, such as coaching and advising positions. The termination of people in such positions provides tenure advocates with arguments for the need of such protection. An example might be the termination of the coach whose team does not have an acceptable won-lost record, or who fails to place the board of education president's son on the basketball team. Another is an athletic director who was not reappointed because she recommended that the football team be dropped, as an insufficient number of students tried out; her recommendation threatened the chosen activity of those who did want to play.

Arguments against the tenure concept are also convincing. Teachers and administrators who fail to plan, abuse children, are incompetent, or fail to follow school curriculum are in many schools. The costs and time needed to remove such staff are often beyond the reach of some schools, particularly when the process may still result in the district losing the cases. As a result, many poor performers are allowed to continue. Steps for removal of individuals are discussed later in this chapter.

While states have the right to modify tenure laws, changes that have occurred have usually resulted in strengthening rather than weakening such protections. These changes have been the result of strong lobbying by teacher unions, as shown by the fact that commensurate protections have not usually resulted for administrators.

Tenure by estoppel.   Although tenure can only be granted by a school board, failure to act on a tenure recommendation, either for or against, can also result in a person receiving tenure. If a board of education fails to complete termination proceedings prior to the conclusion of a probationary period, the board may be estopped (prevented) from denying tenure.

This phenomenon is frequent in some school districts and is usually the result of sloppy recordkeeping. It can particularly affect smaller school districts that do not have regular full-time personnel directors and experience a frequent turnover of other administrators. As a result, unless accurate, up-to-date files are kept on *all* employees, a new administrator may not be aware of staff appointment and tenure dates. Personnel offices have various means of keeping track of staff members, and many have backup methods. For instance, some use a master sheet that lists employees' names, appointment dates, employment status, and the dates and types of any actions by the board of education. In addition, color coding of personnel files (based on probationary or tenure status) allows administrators to scan the appointment notices of individual staff members quickly to ascertain important dates.

Administrators.   Administrators are usually afforded less employment protection than teaching staff members. The ability to acquire tenure varies from state to state. Some administrators are employed through appointments and others are afforded tenure. Variations may even occur within states, based on the type of administrative position. Ordinarily, superintendent positions are the least protected; the only security provided to persons in

EMPLOYEE PROBATION AND TENURE STATUS

Name	Date Appointed	Probationary Period From	To	Date of Action	Type of Action Approved	Denied

Source: Oneida-Madison Board of Cooperative Educational Services, New Hartford, New York.

these positions comes through individual employment contracts or limited statutory protections based on conditions of appointment.

- PROMOTION -

The process of promotion for instructional staff usually involves the opportunity for teachers to obtain administrative positions in their own school district. However, the concept of career ladders within teacher ranks has become popular in the 1980s, so chances for advancement by remaining in teaching exist.

Employees are usually supportive of the practice of promotion from within, since this may provide them with the opportunity to move into a new and more rewarding position. Promoting from within also holds one major advantage for employers. Teachers who sees the potential for promotion may be willing to work a little harder, take on extra assignments, and conduct themselves in a manner that they believe will make them more valued to those who supervise and evaluate them.

There are also disadvantages to promoting from within. Many administrators believe that the promotion of internal candidates may be uncomfortable for school personnel. Board members and existing administrators might wonder whether promoted staff members would be able to deal in a fair and impartial manner with people who were recently their colleagues.

Another negative often attributed to promoting an internal candidate deals with the idea of "bringing in new blood." Those hiring often believe it wise to hire an outside candidate, because someone from a different district may have fresh ideas and different experiences on which they can draw.

Sometimes an inside candidate is rejected in favor of an outsider because of other inside candidates. Candidates from within the district may be told that they were not selected for a position because other capable inside people also applied, and rather than hurt someone's feelings, the decision was to choose an outsider.

Probably the best advice for potential administrators is to do the best job they can in their present positions. This may impress district decision makers that an inside person is a candidate worth promoting. If the district does decide to hire an outside candidate, diligence should at least produce a positive recommendation when one is ready to look for a position elsewhere.

– TRANSFER –

The concept of transfer in education law involves the movement of an employee from one tenure area to another. However, local contracts sometimes broaden that definition and consider that transfer also includes a change within the same tenure area, or even between schools in the same district. Administrators are best advised to avoid discussion of transfer in a bargaining agreement.

Transfer of teaching staff falls into one of two categories: voluntary and involuntary. Voluntary transfers commonly occur when a vacancy becomes available in a district and a staff member requests the position. Such requests are usually made and completed with little fuss. Problems related to transfer usually occur in the involuntary transfers.

Boards of education usually have the right to transfer teachers, after consultation with the superintendent. However, such transfers should not take place because of an arbitrary decision by a board or administrator. In cases when a transfer is the result of acts the school board does not favor, or is seen as punitive, the transfer may be judged to be unconstitutional. Since the right to transfer teachers is usually held by the superintendent of schools with approval by the board of education, many teacher contracts have attempted to include language to provide some protection to teachers. Contract language will outline procedures to be followed if vacancies occur in the district. These procedures involve application guidelines and designated periods of time for posting positions.

Union proposals may ask that contract provisions for involuntary transfers be changed to require consent by the teacher affected. District representatives are likely to resist contract language that provides any guarantees to staff. While labor will argue that a teacher working in an area by choice is likely to be more effective, management may counter by stating that administrators are better qualified to make assignments, based on their broader view of school needs and their observation of the performance of staff members. If language in a local contract does discuss transfers, boards and administrators must observe all procedural steps outlined in the document.

Reasons for involuntary transfers vary. In some cases, a person may be transferred because the administrator making the decision believes that the teacher may be more effective working with students in another grade level or with different subject matter. In other cases, teachers may be seen as ineffective in their present positions, but not so ineffective that they may be brought up on charges for dismissal. In the latter circumstance, the administrator making the transfer may believe that the change will put the individual in a place where ineffectiveness will be minimized.

In instances when school boards have been extremely dissatisfied, teachers have sometimes been given full-time student supervision responsibilities, such as six periods of study hall or hall duty. This has usually occurred after the district was unable to convince the person to resign or was unable to obtain a termination through dismissal proceedings. A word of warning is appropriate here; contract language in some districts could use the term "transfer" with different definitions; in some districts it might mean a grade-level change, as from third to fourth grade.

— DEMOTION/REDUCTION IN RANK —

The terms "demotion" and "reduction in rank" are sometimes referred to in local contracts; their meaning may vary from district to district. Loss of professional rank, salary, or prestige are generally considered to be characteristics of demotion. One example of a demotion would be the transfer of a department chairperson to a teaching position. A reduction from a full-time to a part-time position might also qualify as a demotion. The definition of demotion varies from state to state and may even vary on a case-to-case basis.

Demotion decisions are the responsibility of the board of education and cannot be delegated to administration, although the administration can be directed to carry out the board's decision. Demotions may be instituted for two reasons: to make more effective and efficient use of available resources, and as disciplinary actions. If appointments to department chair positions are made on a yearly basis, and rights to such positions are not covered by contract, the board has the right to make and change such appointments. If the board believes that a person has not done the job satisfactorily, a new appointment may be made. Examples of this are not uncommon, particularly in highly visible positions such as department chairs or athletic coaches.

— RESIGNATION —

Resignations must be voluntary and in writing. Although administrators may urge staff members to resign, the administration does not have the right to threaten staff members to do so. Any threat of consequences such as transfer, demotion, or being brought up on charges could result in a complaint against the administrator who threatened such actions.

A letter of resignation should be addressed to the board of education and should include the effective date of termination. "I intend to . . ." or

"I am planning on . . ." should be rewritten to say, "I resign my position as a (job title), effective (date)." The person submitting the resignation has probably had little training in writing such letters and may need some assistance. Some districts have gone to the extent of developing a form letter for resignation.

Resignation by an ineffective staff member has several advantages. By resigning, teachers are able to avoid what could be damaging to their professional reputations. If a person has the potential to be an effective staff member, but the match with the particular district is a bad one, the possibility of finding a job in another district exists. Administrators involved in the termination of such individuals should be objective about whether the perceived ineffectiveness is due to the individual or to community and/or organizational dynamics. Another advantage is one appreciated by the board and administration. If an individual appeals a termination decision, the time and legal costs involved may be formidable. Joint agreement to leave gracefully may be advantageous to both parties.

– DISMISSAL –

In determining a need to release a teacher, school administrators must consider a number of questions: Is the individual a nontenured or tenured employee? Is dismissal related to a professional issue such as performance, or to an external factor such as a mandated reduction in force? If nontenured, are there any contractual provisions that provide the employee with protection? If tenured, does the district have a strong case that will hold up through a lengthy and intense process?

Nontenured versus tenured employees. The process for terminating a probationary teacher is relatively simple. However, guidelines usually differ for the dismissal of probationary teachers during the probationary period and the dismissal of probationary teachers who have completed their probationary appointments but are not recommended for tenure. Each type will be outlined.

Dismissal for Just Cause

Some employee contracts provide protection to nontenured staff by including a "just-cause" provision. Since protection by tenure usually takes effect after a designated time period (usually three to five years), provisions concerning just cause take effect before the commencement of tenure, if such provisions are included in the contract.

These articles usually state that "a nontenured employee may not be dismissed, disciplined, or lowered in rank without just cause." There is no universally accepted definition of "just cause." Additionally, the test for just cause may differ from a situation in which cause is based on competence (outlined below) to one involving misconduct (generally less ambiguous). However, many labor relations specialists agree on some general tests of just cause that should be applied by administrators who may find themselves before an arbitrator in defending their decisions. These tests may be judged by the following questions:

a. Does the employee clearly understand his or her duties and responsibilities?
   − A clear job description should exist. No one can be expected to fulfill job responsibilities that have not been made clear. The description should be provided upon entry into the position, and preferably in the original posting of the position.
b. Were the criteria for evaluation made clear to the employee?
   − If a standard evaluation form is used, it should be reviewed and discussed at the beginning of the supervisor and staff member's working relationship. This should allow for explanation and clarification by both parties.
   − If a narrative is to be used, the supervisor should notify the employee of the criteria to be used. The job description and annual objectives may provide a useful frame of reference.
c. Was the employee evaluated in a manner that was fair and consistent with treatment of other employees?
   − Administrators must be able to show that they dealt equitably with an employee who has experienced difficulties, in the same way as with other employees of equal rank. If problems persist, continued additional observations or evaluations are appropriate, as long as the intent is the remediation of a problem.
d. Were concerns and recommendations provided in the evaluation?
   − Specific recommendations should be provided for any concerns raised by the supervisor.
   − Offers of assistance should be provided. This assistance may take a variety of forms, including the opportunity to observe others or receive staff development training and other appropriate programs or education that might help in overcoming the problems that concern the administrator.

e. Did a reevaluation take place in a reasonable period of time, to review the employee's progress?
   - A reasonable amount of time to make the changes should be provided. Once problems and solutions are identified, the administrator should probably observe the teacher again within a week or two, or earlier if the problem could be serious.

f. Was the employee forewarned in writing of what would happen if performance did not meet satisfactory standards?
   - The employee should clearly understand the potential ramifications of failure to meet the expected standards, especially if it may mean termination of employment.

g. Did further evaluations point out specifically that required improvement did not occur?
   - The initial concern should be reviewed, and attempts to remediate and any observations of continued unsatisfactory performance should be noted. Again, specific information should be stated.

h. Are penalties consistent with the offense?
   - Where appropriate, show that a pattern exists.
   - Administrators must be able to justify the consistency and fairness of their actions.

i. Were penalties consistent with the individual, as well as with other employees of similar rank?
   - A track record of consistency is important.

j. Is there substantial proof of the employee's wrongdoing?
   - The burden of proof is on management to show, without question, that the employee has not met job responsibilities, that students and staff have not received reasonable service, and that the district has suffered due to the poor performance.

Discipline of Employees

The ability to hire, fire, and seriously alter the way people function in their professional life will have a direct bearing on how they perceive themselves personally as well. Physical and emotional repercussions are common results of stresses that occur on the job. The source of these stresses, in the eyes of many staff members, is the school administrator. Rationalization often comes in the form of comments like, "She doesn't like me," or "He doesn't understand my methods." Administrators are often called upon to be the bearers of communications that staff members do not want to hear; this communication often comes in the form of discipline.

Disciplinary actions are taken for various reasons. Usually they are aimed at changing inappropriate behavior or attitudes, or terminating a staff member's employment.

Changing behavior. Many administrators would agree that the best way to create change in a school is through the careful employment of staff members who share a common vision. However, not all administrators have the advantage of hiring new staff members to replace those who do not share this common vision. As a result, administrators must sometimes compromise, recognizing that many teachers may be effective but in ways different from what the administrators might prefer. Compromise too has its boundaries, and administrators often find themselves dealing with concerns that are so pressing that they must be addressed. For instance, take the social studies teacher who has adopted a Learning Activities Package (LAP) program. The teacher has a cardboard box in the front of the classroom on a table, in the box is a series of learning activities for each unit to be covered in the curriculum. Students in the class complete one set of learning activities, turn them in to the teacher, then go on to the next set. The teacher has developed such a rigid process that almost no teacher-to-class interaction takes place, other than giving occasional directions. Students never discuss issues, and the teacher's expertise in providing answers to student questions is rarely witnessed.

In the ideal situation, the administrator can take the staff member aside, share the concern, explain why it is a concern, and state what should happen to rectify it. In an ideal situation, the staff member will listen carefully, weigh the points being made, smile, and agree to modify or change both in spirit and action, meaning that the change will be a permanent one, not one that just occurs when the administrator visits the classroom or makes an observation.

Such changes can be difficult, especially for a tenured teacher who has been behaving in a certain way for a number of years, but administrators are appointed to make difficult decisions that affect the lives of staff and students. When an administrator's training and knowledge, meaning *real* knowledge gained through experience and awareness of research, tells him or her that a behavior is inappropriate, the administrator's job is to respond. The welfare and education of a large number of students must come before the hurt feelings of a staff member, although the staff member is also part of an administrator's concern. The conclusion to such an effort is through follow-up and positive reinforcement. The administrator must not only be willing to confront the problem, but must take the time to follow up, to ensure that the recommendations made were really implemented and that a "pat on the back" is given, to let the staff member know that his or her efforts to change are appreciated.

Changing attitudes. Probably one of the most difficult jobs of any school administrator is trying to change the attitudes of employees toward their jobs. This topic is discussed in some depth in Chapter 13, on teacher empowerment. The compulsion approach does not work effectively in the long run, and the role of the administrator must include various means of making employees feel better about themselves and their jobs. The direct approach may produce favorable results, especially with new staff members who are concerned with becoming accepted into the social structure of the school system. For tenured, long-term employees, efforts usually should be more indirect and address opportunities for greater self-growth. Whatever the method, a positive attitude is critical to job performance.

Termination of employees. The decision to terminate the employment of a staff member usually begins with the discipline process. When faced with such situations, an administrator often finds himself or herself in a double bind. On the one hand the administrator is fully aware that the feeling of security that comes from positive reinforcement is likely to result in the teacher's repeating behaviors for which he or she was recognized and reinforced. On the other hand, if the teacher's behavior has not changed enough to warrant continued employment, making positive statements can have a backlash effect if the administrator is called before a hearing officer. As a result, the administrator must be constantly aware of the duality of his or her role.

Why Discipline?

Although termination may ultimately be required, a number of reasons exist to make effective disciplining preferable to removal.

Maintenance of staff. Most staff members are good, effective individuals who want to do their jobs well. If a disciplinary action can resolve a problem and allow a district to maintain such people, it is to everyone's advantage, and also sends a clear message throughout the school district: that people are appreciated. Not only does this serve the district well internally, but is important in building an image of the district that will attract better candidates when positions become available.

Costs. With all of the financial needs of providing better education for children, no district likes to spend money on procedures involving discipline or dismissal. If administrators can modify a concern by providing support and direction, such efforts are likely to be less expensive than the legal costs that could be involved in dismissal, particularly that of tenured staff members. Even in the case where a staff member may be probationary and dismissal is relatively inexpensive, additional costs must be considered — readvertising, interviewing, and orienting a replacement.

Prevent lost productivity. Disciplinary actions, especially extended ones, are disconcerting for almost anyone touched by them. The individuals concerned are constantly thinking about how they are perceived by colleagues, whether their job security might be threatened, and how that could affect matters such as income, maintaining a home, and the potential for further employment. The administrator involved must overcome self-doubt regarding whether the decision was just, how he or she will be perceived by staff members, whether their attitudes will affect his or her ability to function with them, and the serious consequences that might affect the individual being disciplined.

The faculty as a whole is also touched by such actions. Union representatives will be required to spend time and effort in investigating the case and building a defense, if appropriate. Some staff members may have strong feelings on whether the individual being disciplined deserves what he or she gets, and this can also cause dissension in the ranks.

Unfortunately, all of this takes away from the primary mission of the school — the education of children. Faculty room discussions will often revolve around the case rather than textbooks, curriculum, and children. A "we and they" attitude often results, with people looking at the situation as a matter of win or lose for the faculty in relation to the administration.

While all this is true, the worst mistake an administrator can make is to back off from making a decision or to allow inappropriate behaviors to continue. By being intimidated, the administrator eventually gives up all ability to supervise effectively. If indeed the needs of children are the most important determinant in the decisions that school people make, the decision should be clear.

The Chinese general Sun Tzu noted that "To win without a fight is the acme of skill." Truly skilled administrators are the individuals who are able to balance the human needs of adult staff members with the critical educational needs of the young people they are charged with educating.

Personal self-worth. Being told that your efforts are less than satisfactory can be devastating. Administrators are in positions of authority, and although a teacher receiving such news may rationalize it in a number of ways, such charges can have a damaging affect on the way the teacher views himself or herself. Administrators owe honesty to individuals, and they also owe compassion. The skilled administrator should be able to judge a failure or inadequacy within its context. For a fault that is not so great that it cannot be overcome with reasonable effort, the approach taken should resemble "I noticed that quite often when you were explaining a concept to the students, a few of them were having side conversations that you did not control. This problem could be easily handled by . . . ."

Anyone with a teaching certificate is aware that students cannot learn if they are engaged in conversations having nothing to do with the topic being taught. By focusing on the concern and how it might be handled, the administrator should use his or her own responsibility as a teacher to provide a learning experience for the staff member. Remember that the historical role of a school building administrator was to act as principal (or first) teacher. Thus, those administering schools should be able to provide such direction, or *they* are the ones who are failing.

Administrative time and energy. One of the administrator's most valuable and treasured resources is time. Administrators buy books on time management; they attend lectures and listen to tapes. Poor recruitment that ultimately leads to the dismissal of a staff member can require a significant amount of time. Investing time in aiding a teacher whose performance is questionable may be much less costly in the long run than terminating the person, and then initiating the employment process all over again.

Why Administrators Fail to Discipline

The preceding points should be seriously considered before beginning any type of disciplinary actions against school employees. However, the concerns should not be held so sacred that improper acts are ignored. Too often administrators take the view that conflict is bad, and that a grievance or other upheaval in the system is a reflection of poor administration. On the contrary, an organization must take steps to improve its functioning if it is to operate effectively. To believe that every employee is working at a satisfactory level is naive; to subscribe to the idea that every employee is able is questionable. Good administrators always hope the question of whether someone can be saved can be answered positively. However, when it cannot, school administrators must have the strength and conviction to act appropriately. A number of reasons can explain why administrators do not act.

Fear of failure. As noted, many administrators take the view that conflict is bad and destructive. However, situations involving matters such as grievances and dismissals should be viewed from a positive perspective. A grievance can provide an opportunity to clarify a confusing practice or language in a contract. Once clarified, all parties will have the opportunity to understand clearly how to operate in the future. With a dismissal, all of the human considerations already noted must be given serious thought, but if an individual is actually damaging or shortchanging the children's education, a good administrator should take a stand. To act responsibly, an administrator must document and build a case carefully. If an employee is not performing in a satisfactory manner, this should be documented. Done in conjunction with the school district's attorney or labor relations representative (usually the personnel administrator or a local or regional representative), such actions should result in successful discipline. In a worse-case scenario, in which the administration's case results in failure and the staff member is retained, the administration still wins on two counts. First, the message that the employee's performance is unacceptable has been made public. Another case may be instituted in the future and, knowing that, the employee may begin to look for other employment. Second, once the reason for the case being lost is known, the administration has the opportunity to learn from experience and build the case appropriately if the problems continue and another attempt is made to terminate the individual's employment.

Lack of skill. Another reason many administrators fail to act on employee discipline matters involves their lack of understanding of how to institute the procedure properly. Unfortunately, most schools of educational administration fail to educate prospective administrators on initiating such processes. Literature on discipline and job termination is also sparse. Most administrators learn through on-the-job experiences or possibly through the advice of the school district's attorney. While an attorney's advice should be given strong consideration, it is not necessarily sacred. Attorneys are not likely to understand the informal structure of the system, since they do not work in it on a full-time basis. Thus, while their advice is useful, it may have to be tempered, or actions timed to achieve maximum usefulness.

Probably the most useful source for such education is veteran administrators. Their experiences can help someone who is handling a sensitive matter—how to approach it, what steps they might take first, how to word a memo or letter, how to set up a power base to make sure that support for the action will be given, etc. Unfortunately, many newer administrators fail to use this source for one simple reason: ego, or the unwillingness to admit a need for help, for fear they will look bad. For some, admitting a weakness or lack of experience is often interpreted as a critical fault. In reality, most veteran administrators appreciate and enjoy the opportunity to work with colleagues new to the profession, and to serve as mentors and pass along some of the valuable skills and knowledge they have gained over the years.

Organizational dissonance. Many administrators fear that action against an employee will result in "turning the school upside down." Administrators who gain a reputation for dismissing staff could in fact have this effect. They may be seen as "terminators," aimed at eliminating individuals without due consideration. Such people have operated in the education business, and their presence can be cause for alarm. Fewer exist today, and most boards are hesitant to hire them. In reality, the concerned administrator who makes a rational, well-thought-out decision is likely to gain support from staff. However, all administrators should be aware before becoming involved in such cases that the staff is likely to side publicly with their fellow teacher, right or wrong. Most veteran administrators can recall stories of staff members coming into an administrator's office and saying something like, "Even though we have to back [this staff member], I want you to know that I think you're doing the right thing!" The first time or two that this happens, many administrators are perplexed with the fact that it has occurred and that professionals who stand in front of a classroom of children and extol the virtues of being strong and standing up for what they believe is right, lack the ability to do so themselves. However, as these administrators become more familiar with the mentality of unionism, they come to expect, if not to understand, that such actions are more the norm than the exception.

Organizational commitment. Another reason that many administrators fail to initiate disciplinary actions is because of a concern for support. While failing to win is not necessarily damaging if a case is properly handled, failing to have the support of the central office (particularly the superintendent) and board of education can be. It sends a clear message to the administrator that his or her ability to supervise effectively is in trouble. The best advice for an administrator contemplating action is to gain commitment for support ahead of time through the personnel office and superintendent, who will be responsible for informing the board, if appropriate. If sufficient work has not been completed for a firm case, the personnel officer can help make sure that proper steps occur. If the action will not be supported for some reason—such as the person in question being the board president's daughter-in-law; or the central office being aware that the person plans to hand in a resignation in the near future; or some such complication—the administrator is best advised to continue documentation without taking any action. Regular status reports to the personnel office about the case should continue.

Employment status.   One of the worst reasons for refusing to discipline is the employment status (probationary versus tenured) of an employee. A new school administrator was lamenting the drinking problem of a staff member and stated her belief that the person might even be coming to school under the influence of alcohol at times. When asked why she did not investigate the situation more closely, she responded, "I can't; he's tenured." It is sad to think that any administrator would actually believe that persons are allowed carte blanche because they hold tenure appointments. While tenure laws and protections differ in various states, no state endorses behavior such as drinking on the job or teaching while under the influence of alcohol. Administrators need to be well-versed in how to handle such situations.

– CONFRONTING PROBLEMS –

Every administrator will eventually have to deal with problems involving personnel. The best way to handle one-time personnel problems is through the most unobtrusive means possible. For instance, one example would be the teacher who spends the study hall period in the hallway, talking with colleagues instead of monitoring the students. While he or she stands in the hall, students are left unattended. The potential for injury exists, and the teacher, as well as the building administrator, could be held liable for any youngster being hurt, especially in an unsupervised classroom. In dealing with such incidents the administrator should ask the teacher to listen privately for a moment to explain legal and ethical concerns and ask that the teacher stay in the classroom. This type of request can be done with an explanation and a smile, which should result in the employee's understanding and the problem's being remedied.

In some instances, problems persist; although a clear request has been made, the employee's unacceptable behavior continues. When this happens, a stronger response by the administrator is necessary. This process is known as progressive discipline and is based on a progression of responses by the administrator.

A disciplinary system should follow a series of steps such as the following:

   a. Counseling
      – Employees should be counseled privately, concerns should be discussed in a constructive spirit, specific recommendations should be made, and a clear understanding given of what will happen if changes are not made.

b. Written warnings
  - If little progress results from verbal warnings and counseling, a written warning should be given to the employee. A statement should be included that more severe discipline may take place unless changes occur.
c. Subsequent warnings
  - Any additional warnings should depend on the gravity of the infractions, time between their occurrence, and any other relevant factors.
d. Fines or suspension
  - Decisions regarding the use of these sanctions should be based on the seriousness of the infractions and suitability of actions and their legality.

– CRITICAL COMMUNICATIONS –

As noted, perhaps one of the most stress-producing situations administrators have to deal with is employee discipline. Administrators are well aware that confronting an employee regarding inappropriate conduct often results in some response, possibly through the informal organization of the school, with actions such as not talking to an administrator or refusing to help in school programs and activities. More formal response might be felt through a litigation process that affects both the informal and formal organizations. In cases where an administrator avoids taking action in order to be seen as "the teachers' friend," other problems can result: deficiencies in the education provided to students, lower morale among staff members who resent what has been allowed to occur, and reinforcement of the message that inappropriate conduct is acceptable.

When matters do arise about which communication is necessary, administrators must be careful about what is said and who says it. States vary in what they allow and expect; administrators should contact their district's personnel administrator and/or counsel if a sensitive matter arises. According to Hogan and Sarzynski,[1] communications usually take one of two forms: a corrective admonition and a disciplinary reprimand. (See Figure 7-1.)

Corrective admonitions. Communications that are corrective admonitions usually:

a. Come from the employee's immediate supervisor;
b. Are aimed at improving the individual's performance or remedying the inappropriate conduct that occurred;

c. Are the result of a problem of a relatively minor nature;
d. Send the message that such conduct should not occur again;
e. Refer to future actions.

These communications do not use the word "reprimand."

Disciplinary reprimand. Reprimands are stronger communications. They typically:

a. Come from the board of education or superintendent;
b. Are formal reprimands for some misconduct;
c. Result from a more serious type of problem or misbehavior;
d. Point out clearly to the employee that what he or she did was unacceptable;
e. Are accusatory in nature.

A letter of reprimand should clearly point out that it is just that, and the term "reprimand" should be included. A statement including the term could very well begin the letter: "This letter of reprimand is a result of . . . ."

FIGURE 7.1   Letters of Corrective Admonition or Disciplinary Reprimand*

The Letter	*Corrective Admonition*	*Disciplinary Reprimand*
Who the letter is from	Immediate supervisor	Board of education or superintendent
Direction of letter	Improvement of performance	Formal reprimand for prior conduct
Nature of letter	Performance evaluation	Misconduct of the employee
Severity of misconduct	Not serious	Substantial
Type of admonition	Don't do in future	What was done was bad
Use of word "reprimand"	No	Yes
Thrust of letter	Reference to future activities	Accusatory

*From *Handbook of Topics and Forms Pertaining to Teachers* by John B. Hogan and Edward Sarzynski (self-published, Binghamton, NY, 1986). Adapted by permission of the authors.

Writing the Letter

As noted, any communications should be reviewed by a personnel director, attorney, or labor relations representative before being sent to a staff member if the letter might ever be used in a reference or as evidence in further proceedings against the staff member. Since any communications may be and probably will be responded to, administrators must be sure to be able to defend their actions. No guarantee will fully protect the writer of a letter, but the following suggestions might be considered.

Ascertain the facts. Nothing destroys the credibility of a critical communication more than a misstatement of fact. Any comments made in a disciplinary letter must be accurate. To ensure this accuracy, the administrator should speak to the employee in question *before* writing the letter. If other people are involved, the administrator should also speak with those individuals, to ascertain that their perceptions were accurate. Once the conversation with the employee has occurred and the decision to send the letter has been made, the employee should be told that a letter is forthcoming.

Be timely. Time distorts memory. A critical communication must be sent in a timely fashion to ensure accuracy, applicability, and impact. In addition, a lapse in time would be suspect to a hearing officer, who would probably question why administration did not respond to the incident immediately.

Be brief and to the point. Administrators sometimes add comments to reduce the sting of a disciplinary message. If misconduct is enough to warrant a letter, administrators should be brief and to the point in their communications. Added comments only provide the employee with potential points for argument. A beginning such as, "You've done a fine job except . . . ," could be interpreted by the receiver as saying that his or her overall performance is acceptable and the letter concerns a relatively insignificant matter. People do not like hearing critical remarks about themselves and are likely to interpret what has been said with a different meaning from the intent of the administrator who wrote the letter.

Cite previous discussions. If related problems have occurred previously, note these and any actions that have already been taken, such as conversations or previous communications. This substantiates the fact that the problem is a continuing one, previous assistance was provided (or at least was offered and refused), and the problem still exists. Just-cause provisions make it imperative that administrators show they went beyond reasonable expectations to provide assistance.

Specify facts. Information about who, what, why inappropriate, where, and when should result from of observations by the administrator and information he or she has received through conversations, testimony, and/or written communications. The letter should specify exactly what occurred; who was involved in the incident and the nature of their involvement; why the incident was inappropriate (violated policy, practices, civil law, interests of children and/or staff); where the misconduct occurred; and when it occurred. Specificity and accuracy heighten the credibility of the letter.

In addition, the letter should refer to the confirming conversation that occurred and should note that the facts in the letter were substantiated in that conversation. In this way the employee is less likely to claim in a future hearing that the meeting took place, but the facts were never discussed.

Once all appropriate information has been gathered and verified through conversations with involved parties, the communication should be given to the employee as soon as reasonably possible.

Type on school stationery. Any critical communication is official and should be typed on school stationery.

Verify transfer to the individual. A common practice of union representatives is to speak of alleged communications. Any disciplinary letter should be made in duplicate with a space for the recipient to sign both copies, one for personnel files and the other for the recipient. The signature should be an acknowledgment that the letter was received, not an indication of agreement to its contents. Under the signature of the administrator, the following sentence might be placed, "The following signature indicates that this letter has been received, but does not acknowledge either agreement or disagreement with its content."

Rebuttal. Administrators must always assume that, the employee will respond to a critical communication with the assistance of his or her union. By having conversations with the involved parties beforehand, not only can facts be ascertained, but arguments that might be used by the employee can possibly be identified. Accuracy, verification, timeliness, brevity, relevance, and specific facts will help to minimize the force of any arguments that may be made.

Further meetings. If a rebuttal is to be made, a meeting may be held with the employee and his or her union representative, to discuss the communication and its cause. This meeting can be used by the union representative to trap the administrator. Comments made in such meetings may later be used before a hearing officer or judge. If the misconduct may lead to further disciplinary procedures, the administrator should also have a representative in attendance. If a union representative attends with the employee, the district's personnel director should sit in with the administrator. If the union's attorney attends, the district's attorney should attend.

Administrators must keep one important point in mind: unless specified by law, regulation, or contract, an employee may not have the right to bring anyone to such a meeting. Administrators should check the restrictions pertaining to their situation and be prepared to act accordingly. If an employee surprises an administrator by showing up for a meeting with a lawyer, the administrator must know whether he or she has a right to cancel the meeting or delay it until the administrator can invite the district's legal representative.

Copy to personnel file. To avoid questions about the intent of a letter, include "cc: Personnel file" at the bottom, under the recipient's signature. Not doing so could result in the employee later stating that he or she did not think the incident was of any significance and had no idea the letter had been placed in the personnel file.

Administrators have sometimes removed material from a personnel file as a gesture of reconciliation. Such a practice is ill-advised. The importance of files is reduced when their contents are seen as transient. Administrators should give careful consideration to whether a critical communication serious enough to warrant inclusion in an employee's personnel file should be made. If so, once entered it should remain there permanently. The exception is when the employment contract states that any letters outlining misconduct are to be withdrawn after a specific period of time if no further infractions occur.

– THE DISMISSAL PROCESS –

Every state has its own set of procedures that must be followed to terminate the service of a staff member. States laws vary, but the reasons for cause for termination are similar. Reasons usually focus on problems such as disability, lack of certification, incompetence, unwillingness to perform assigned duties, cruelty, insubordination, immorality, drunkenness, and unprofessional conduct. Many of these reasons are specific and easily identifiable. The staff member who is unable to complete teaching duties because of a permanent physical incapacity resulting from a serious accident or an individual who clearly lacks the required certification can probably be released fairly simply. Other grounds, such as incompetence, unwillingness, and immorality, are often open to discussion, since they are usually dependent on perception and interpretation. Acceptability of grounds for termination differs by state and situation, so further discussion is best left to local experts in education law.

Terminating Tenured Staff Members

Regardless of the reasons for termination, it is usually to the advantage of the district to have teachers leave of their own accord rather than after a lengthy and often uncomfortable dismissal process, especially if the teachers concerned are tenured. Many administrators are unaware of how to convince tenured staff members to resign, but a number of administrators have had success at instituting procedures that result in voluntary resignation. The following outlines a procedure followed by experienced administrators to obtain the resignation of staff members without going through the cost and turmoil often associated with termination. The procedure is applicable to both probationary and tenured staff, but the focus here will be on tenured employees.

Although differences for treatment of tenured and non-tenured staff exist, similarities warrant a single discussion of how to prepare for the dismissal of staff members who have manifested behaviors that warrant their release. Figure 7.2 outlines a four-layer overview of the teacher termination process.

Identifying Cause

The first phase of the termination process is the identification of the problem or cause. As noted, certain charges are more subjective and can be more difficult to prove than others. Nonetheless, it sometimes is necessary to use such a charge if it is the reason for concern. Regardless of the charge, a strong case supported by documentation will be required, particularly if the teacher is tenured. If the charge deals with a more subjective matter, such as incompetence, documentation will probably require verification over a long period of time, usually years. An experienced education attorney should be able to tell administrators whether the quantity and quality of information they have available will be sufficient.

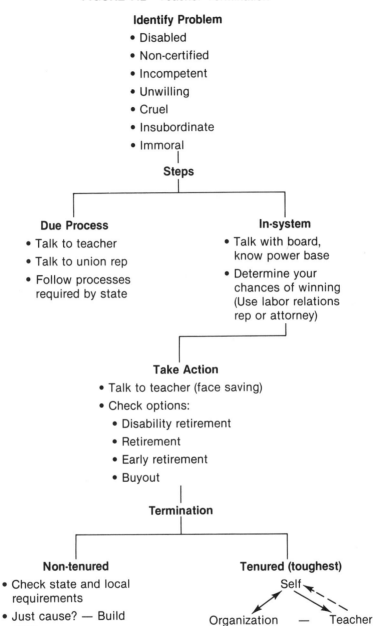

FIGURE 7.2 Teacher Termination

Identify Problem
- Disabled
- Non-certified
- Incompetent
- Unwilling
- Cruel
- Insubordinate
- Immoral

Steps

Due Process
- Talk to teacher
- Talk to union rep
- Follow processes required by state

In-system
- Talk with board, know power base
- Determine your chances of winning (Use labor relations rep or attorney)

Take Action
- Talk to teacher (face saving)
- Check options:
  - Disability retirement
  - Retirement
  - Early retirement
  - Buyout

Termination

Non-tenured
- Check state and local requirements
- Just cause? — Build case
- Talk to teacher
- Follow process

Tenured (toughest)

Self

Organization — Teacher

163

Steps

The second phase of the termination process involves steps that are due process and in-system in nature. Due process steps include the following:

Discussion with the teacher. First, the administrator should talk with the teacher and share the gravity of the concerns that exist. This discussion with the teacher should not be the first of its kind. A number of discussions resulting from the observation and evaluation process should have already taken place, so that the teacher will not be surprised by the administrator's concerns. Previous discussions should have included comments by the administrator that concerns were grave enough that potential for a dismissal recommendation existed if matters did not improve. If the teacher is working in a probationary status without just-cause protection, the administrator should make clear at this point that the district has the authority to dismiss through a relatively simple process. If the teacher is tenured and wishes to remain in the position, further steps will be required.

Although previous discussions occurred, this discussion will be the first in which the administrator informs the teacher that every reasonable allowance has been made, improvement has not taken place, and a recommendation for dismissal is going to be made. This discussion might be sufficient to move the teacher to resign on his or her own.

Discussion with a union representative. Discussion might also be held with the union representative, although the administrator should speak with the district's personnel director and superintendent first, to determine whether such discussion is contractually required or in the district's best interest. An advantage to the involvement of the union is to make clear that the district's case is strong enough to support the dismissal. In such an instance, the union president may act as an intermediary to try to find a common ground that the teacher and district could accept in terms of other alternatives. For instance, instead of pursuing termination, the district might send the teacher home for the remainder of the year with pay, if the teacher will submit a resignation to be effective June 30. Administration will benefit if the union can be convinced that the case is strong enough to work with the district rather than against it. However, the administration should not reveal information about its case that should best remain private until a hearing takes place.

Follow legal processes. Administrators *must* have a clear understanding of the legal processes to be followed in terminating a staff member. Most union representatives would acknowledge that many of their "winners" have been the result of cases that are thrown out on procedural grounds rather than on merit.

In-system steps also take place, usually at the same time as the due process steps.

Knowing your power base. An administrator must be assured of support from the central office, particularly from the personnel director and superintendent. They in turn should inform the board of education of procedures that are taking place, to make sure the board will be willing to provide the necessary support, in resources and in spirit.

Determine chances of winning. The cost of dismissing a tenured staff member is often large, not only financially but in the emotional energy spent. Additional potential cost in temporary disruption of the educational process in the school must also be considered. Consequently, before getting too far into the termination process, the administrator initiating the case should be sure the district's attorney believes that there is a reasonably good chance of winning if the case should go all the way to a hearing.

Taking Action

Steps up to this point have had a relatively low level of confrontation. They have included the identification of the problem, discussions with the staff member and possibly the union representative, and confirmation of support from the central office, board, and attorney. If these actions have not resulted in resignation of the staff member involved, the administrator must proceed to the third phase, which involves options for gaining a resignation.

Disability. In some cases, an individual's behavior may be the result of physical and emotional causes that manifest themselves on the job. Questions about a person's health may be appropriate, and an administrator should consider such a possibility. Disabilities may be of a temporary nature, and a leave of absence for medical reasons could provide an opportunity for the employee to remedy the problem. Another result of such leaves is that they may result in the employee finding other job opportunities during the time away from the school.

Disability laws vary considerably from state to state. Local statutes determine how disability is verified, its extent, and the benefits to victims. However, the concept itself is widely accepted and can be a useful alternative for employees who qualify.

Retirement. It is illegal to suggest that a relationship exists between age and performance. In fact, the most effective staff members are often veterans who bring years of experience to their jobs. However, if a staff member with problems is eligible for a regular retirement, this might be an opportune time to suggest the retirement option. Many veteran staff members who have been teaching for a number of years may find that the amount of money they are making by working is not much more than they would receive if they retired and began drawing benefits. In many cases these same teachers have a great deal to offer and might find it both financially and personally rewarding to continue their careers in parochial or private systems or to look outside the field of education.

Early retirement. Education retirement systems vary throughout the country. Some states have adopted early retirement options for employees, allowing them to choose to retire earlier than they would otherwise be entitled to. For instance, if the normal retirement age in a particular state is 60, a state's governing bodies may decide that in a particular year they will allow any individuals who have worked in the system for a specific number of years, and who have reached a specific age, to retire early. For instance, a 58-year-old who has at least 20 years in the system may be allowed to retire with the same benefits that he or she would have earned by waiting until the age of 60. The benefit to the state is that it may be able to vacate the position entirely and save the cost of that employee, or it may be able to hire a replacement at a considerably cheaper rate.

Buyout. Sometimes a school district and an employee whose services are no longer desired should consider a financial buyout, which might bring a number of advantages. Rather than spending large amounts of money on legal fees and other costs such as administrative time, a buyout might actually be cheaper in the long run. In many cases a termination includes a buyout anyway, so early agreement to this option may be advantageous.

A buyout can also eliminate a bad public relations impact that may otherwise occur. Even a problem teacher may have some supporters in the community or on the staff. A prolonged termination process is likely to bring some of these people to make public protests at board meetings and with the press.

The legality of a buyout should be explored with the school district's attorney before the subject is raised with the employee. In some states a buyout may be acceptable, but in others it might be considered a gift of public funds and therefore be questionable.

Cutting a deal. One of the most popular options for terminating a staff member involves coming to an agreement based on the specifics of the individual's situation. This usually results from attorneys meeting privately and coming to terms that are an acceptable compromise for both sides. Deals might include payment of the employee's compensation and insurance for a period of time. A deal might also provide that no negative recommendation will be given regarding the individual, and possibly that a letter of recommendation acceptable to both parties will be written before a final agreement is reached.

Initiating Termination Procedures

The final phase involves initiation of the procedures necessary to terminate the individual. In the case of probationary staff members, the process is simpler, and an administrator's primary duties include reviewing of state and local requirements and making sure that proper steps are followed within the required time. If just-cause protection exists, sufficient evidence must be available to support the recommendation for termination.

If the individual to be terminated is a tenured staff member, the administrator involved must be fully aware of the procedure he or she is going to follow and to understand its ramifications. Effects of this process are likely to touch upon many of the staff members in the school. First, the administrator should assess his or her own abilities to carry out the necessary actions. The administrator should be aware that his or her efforts will be under constant scrutiny. While the decision to terminate may be justified, friends of the individual and union representatives will be looking for any excuse to point a finger at the administrator and state that actions are less than honorable or are being done for personal vindication.

The process can also affect the organizational climate in the school. Staff may be well aware of the justification for what is being done, but sympathy for a colleague may lead to some staff members acting in hostile ways or ignoring requests for cooperation. Administrators should be sensitive to the influence their decisions have on their schools, and to the fact that school climate may be influenced against them.

Other dynamics also come into play, as interaction occurs between other staff members and the teacher being terminated. The administrator can do little about this, and should *not* engage in politicking with staff members in an attempt to alienate the terminated individual from co-workers. As noted, every move made by the administrator will come under scrutiny. Efforts at influencing opinion would be seen as manipulative and cast the administrator in a bad light.

Finally, the relationship between the administrator and the teacher will also change. The administrator has worked with the teacher up to this point to try to make changes, but the administrator has now stated the decision to terminate. The administrator's role as supporter is now gone, and the staff member should clearly understand that his or her services are no longer desired. At this point many administrators try to continue to be friendly to the staff members who are about to be terminated. Since educators usually enter the profession because they like working with people, taking on a role that requires them to act harshly can be difficult. However, the show of being the teacher's buddy is unrealistic and possibly misleading. Once the decision to terminate has been reached, an administrator should be businesslike and candid in dealing with the individual.

Strategies for Dismissal

There is no guaranteed method to ensure that a tenured staff member will leave without fuss. However, a number of administrators have found that certain approaches have been useful in convincing tenured staff to resign their jobs rather than going through legal proceedings. The following includes suggestions and descriptions of strategies actually used by school administrators to terminate tenured staff members.

Cover all bases. Administrators who decide that a tenured teacher should be terminated should try to convince the staff member to resign voluntarily, but should also document and build a strong case that can be used before a hearing panel or judge if all other efforts fail. The advice of one lawyer to districts that plan to terminate a staff member states three rules: document, document, and document.

Documenting. Advice to document is often heard in the study of management, but most training programs are not particularly specific about exactly what to document.

Good management is as much art as science. "Red flags" indicating problems on the horizon are often picked up intuitively by administrators. If asked to explain why or how a suspicion came about, many administrators would be unable to answer. However, put a group of administrators in a room to discuss such intuitive judgments, and probably everyone present would acknowledge that such intuitive leaps do occur.

Most veteran administrators, particularly those in personnel offices, schools and superintendencies, have learned a great deal about legal processes in order to survive in their jobs. Some potential problems are obvious: The maintenance employee who shows up for work obviously under the influence of alcohol is relatively easy to spot. The teacher who calls in sick on the first day of hunting season may be more difficult to handle. When suspicious circumstances arise, an administrator is best advised to note concerns in a "memo to self," to be kept in the administrator's personal file and *not* be shared with anyone else. The memo should contain the known facts and outline the administrator's concern. Such memos are best kept in a file at home rather than in the office. However, information from an administrator's personal file may not be allowable in a hearing on disciplining or dismissing an employee. Thus, such memos should be for informational purposes and only referred to in a future official communication if the content can be documented. The administrator may not need to pursue the matter if a problem does not actually exist; maybe the employee really was sick on the first day of hunting season. However, judgment may tell the administrator that the event is symptomatic of a bigger problem that may eventually be so great as to require investigation. If no further instances occur, the administrator has invested only the few minutes necessary to write the "memo to self." If related behaviors are manifested, the administrator may find the memo a useful reference.

Many administrators also find telephone logs to be helpful. A log may be nothing more than a stenographer's notebook kept in the administrator's desk and used to note conversations that have potential for future proceedings such as grievances, discipline, or other labor-relations matters. The administrator should record the date and time of the conversation, topics discussed, and verbatim comments, where possible.

Confronting. An administrator must make his or her intention to terminate clear to the tenured teacher, as perceptual screens (hearing what one wishes to) often contaminate messages. The administrator should be straightforward in evaluations and conversations indicating that the teacher's performance is below the acceptable standard and that continued employment will not be recommended. Several administrators say that they have told teachers "As you know from our previous conversations, I find your performance unacceptable and I am going to recommend your dismissal, regardless of the time and cost that might be involved. Unless you agree to submit your resignation within the next week, I have no choice but to prefer charges [or make a recommendation to the superintendent or whatever procedure is appropriate]."

This approach is often serious enough to make the teacher realize that the administrator does indeed mean what he or she is sayhing and that an embarrassing situation may result if a resignation is not submitted.

Timing. Some administrators who look closely at a teacher's seniority status in the district may discover that the teacher in question has the least seniority and would consequently be the first to go if a reduction in staffing were made. One administrator noted the potential for eliminating an elementary teaching position. However, instead of cutting that position, the administrator reduced a resource teacher position by shifting some of that duty to a classroom teacher. As a result, a highly regarded elementary classroom teacher was retained and a reading teacher whose performance was less satisfactory resigned because the duties of the position were so reduced.

Isolation. A teacher whose greatest joy in life was in bragging to fellow staff about taking sick days illegally and in performing insubordinate actions against administrators without getting caught provided the school administration with a great deal of difficulty. Many staff members were tired of this teacher's behavior, but others reinforced him in the faculty room by laughing at his stories. Those who disapproved were too intimidated to challenge the teacher or the union president and others who reinforced his behavior. The administration responded by isolating the teacher both physically and psychologically. Instead of having a lunch period when many of his friends were also eating lunch, the teacher was given the same lunch time as a number of more serious teachers who neither supported nor approved of his actions.

The principal also observed that this teacher was habitually late for school. While documentation of tardiness was taking place, the principal would go into the faculty room on the days the teacher was tardy and ask one of the teacher's friends to cover his class until the tardy teacher appeared. Those who thought his behavior so humorous began to see less humor when they had to give up their own planning period and morning coffee.

Incompetence. Lack of competence can be a difficult charge to prove. However, an administrator who feels that this charge is the most appropriate and necessary to bring against a staff member may follow a number of steps:

Regular observation: The teacher in question should be observed and evaluated regularly. Observations should include specific suggestions for improvement and should also note clearly that improvements have not resulted since the last observation. Union officials may charge harrassment by the administrator. Because of this, evaluations must be constructive in phrasing and specific as to the shortcomings observed.

Objective analysis of results: A standard difficulty with incompetency charges is in trying to define competence and incompetence. A review of cases involving attempts to dismiss staff members for incompetence points out consistent disagreement on the part of hearing officers as to what exactly constitutes incompetent teaching. One good strategy for administrators is to collect *objective* data through the use of standardized test results. However, administrators should be wary of attempting a dismissal based solely on student data. Additionally, poor student test results coming from a single year are not likely to be acceptable justification to dismiss.

If administrators plan to use test results as part of a case, they should try to provide evidence that a causal relationship exists between the results and instruction that took place. In doing so, specific teaching behaviors should be identified, along with discrepancies between accepted behavior and what actually occurred in a teacher's classroom. Additionally, a trend of poor scores over several years should be provided to show that poor performance was consistent.

Objectivity is crucial, since the concept of incompetence is extremely subjective. Data from standardized tests are easier for administration to defend than teacher-made tests. Evidence that the same students had scored well in previous grade levels and in other content areas is also useful. Being able to point out that students were assigned randomly to the teacher being charged, as well as others in his or her department, also strengthens the case of administration.

The use of data alone usually makes a weak argument for dismissal. However, if carefully presented and coupled with other evidence, it can be useful in strengthening an administrator's case.

Survey results: Some administrators have found that a survey of former students has been useful in verifying that a problem exists. Surveys sent to students who graduated in recent years, asking how well-prepared they felt they were to handle school or work experiences after graduating, have been gathered a great deal of useful information. Questions did not ask opinions about individual staff members but did ask students, "How well prepared do you feel you were based on your education in each of the following content areas?" Valuable comments regarding the lack of preparation from specific courses were often provided.

Observation of colleagues: To show that efforts were made to help the targeted teacher change positively, that teacher may be directed to observe colleagues in the classroom, to see how they deal effectively with concerns that the problem teacher is unable to handle competently. Although this method may have occurred earlier, its continued use can have a stigmatizing effect that would convince the teacher to resign rather than having to face a charge of incompetence.

Outside consultants: Administrators have also used outside consultants to assist teachers whose positions are in jeopardy. Although such a strategy focuses on an opportunity for improvement, it may also have a stigmatizing effect.

The major role of the administrator who wishes to terminate the employment of an incompetent tenured teacher is to provide support and remedial assistance, while documenting the individual's lack of progress in meeting district standards.

Although termination proceedings are emotionally trying, the administrator must remember that the primary purpose of the school is children, and must keep that purpose in mind as he or she makes decisions about who will be educating those young people.

Confrontation. Many administrators, particularly those entering the profession, have been educated to believe that administrators must always support their staff. Such a belief is at best naive. Although the vast majority of the people staffing our schools are competent, able, and caring, a few individuals use poor judgement that endangers the physical, emotional, and educational well-being of children. The idea that an administrator should tolerate and support such actions is ridiculous.

One administrator's story shows how to handle a teacher who abused some of the children she was charged to educate. A number of complaints alleged physical abuse. The abuse was not so extreme that the children involved required hospital attention, but they complained of being slapped, pushed against walls, and other abusive behaviors. The administrator involved in the supervision of the teacher took a number of steps to build a case for dismissal.

Require psychiatric attention: The ability to require a psychiatric evaluation varies from state to state. Administrators should find out whether they have this right and how to go about exercising it—whether it can be done through the superintendent's office, through the board of education, or not at all.

Involve parents: Like most administrators, this one initially handled parent complaints by listening, speaking with the teacher (who explained that the circumstances were completely different from what students were reporting), and then reporting back to the parents, some of whom were extremely unhappy with the administrator's explanation and let him know that. After several instances, the administrator investigated more closely and learned that the allegations indeed merited greater consideration. As a result, he asked concerned parents to meet with the teacher and share their concerns with her directly; he made a point of being present but attempted to stay out of the conversation. In facing the angry parents, the teacher's attitude was different from what it had been when the administrator had to deal with the parents while the teacher was in a class or the faculty room. The teacher appeared ill at ease at having to discuss the issue directly with parents and was much more conciliatory than when she met with the principal alone. The administrator also asked parents to write down what happened for possible later use. The teacher was informed that this documentation existed, and warned that any further incidents could result in disciplinary action. One positive result was a significant reduction in the number of complaints from students and parents.

Involve the school nurse: Knowing that staff often have mixed feelings about an administrator who attempts to fire a teacher, the administrator realized that the school nurse was a major source for information in the school. By having the nurse also hear the students' versions of what had occurred, and to bear witness to any marks or bruises, the administrator was able to recruit a valuable ally.

Use of physical presence. An interesting strategy used by a female administrator involved the use of physical presence to emphasize the message she was trying to make. This administrator recalled that she often found that some men on the faculty tried to take an overbearing attitude with her, particularly in high-stress situations. She used a number of strategies to deal with such conflicts.

Dress: Whenever a showdown was necessary and she had to be the bearer of bad news, such as her decision to dismiss an employee, this administrator made a point of dressing in severe, businesslike suits.

Turf: This individual also held all meetings in her office at a set time rather in the teacher's classroom.

Office space: Although her office contained a coffee table with chairs around it, this woman made a point of always sitting behind her desk, to use it as a statement of distance.

Manner: Finally, the administrator used both body language and a strong verbal message. She admitted that she sometimes pointed a finger and began her comments with a phrase like, "Let me make this absolutely clear . . . ."

There is no formula that will guarantee that a tenured staff member will voluntarily resign, no matter what strategies are used. Tactics provided here are merely samples of methods successfully employed by experienced school administrators.

To suggest that administrators should not be aware of such approaches is naive. To suggest that problem employees do not exist is just as naive. One of the first jobs of administrators should be to confront individuals who have serious deficiencies and work with them in overcoming those problems. After an honest effort, the same administrators must be willing to take the necessary steps to terminate employees who cannot or will not meet the standards necessary to deliver high-quality education to the youngsters they have been charged to educate.

Final advice. A few common kinds of advice came from the administrators interviewed about the termination process:

Be sure: There should be no doubt that every reasonable effort was made to help the individual in question. Dismissal can have devastating personal and professional consequences, and such an initiative must be taken seriously.

Take care of yourself: Dismissal is often a trying process, both physically and mentally. The administrator should monitor his or her own health and well-being carefully.

Find a mentor: Almost everyone who had gone through this process had identified someone with whom they could discuss it, particularly the first time. The mentor was sometimes an administrator in the district, such as the personnel director or superintendent, or someone outside of the district who was also an administrator and could understand the stresses that accompany the process.

Self-monitor job behavior: The administrator must *never* lose control. This does not mean that he or she might not *appear* to lose control, although this should be rare or it will lose its effect. However, reactions that might come back to haunt the administrator (such as, "He told me I was a . . . , and that proves this is a personal vendetta") should be avoided.

Keep in touch with counsel: In most instances a labor-relations representative or school attorney will guide administrators through dismissal proceedings. These persons should be contacted as soon as the administrator senses that a case may develop; they must be kept informed throughout. Since the attorney or representative will probably be the one who acts on the district's behalf, their complete understanding and vested interest are critical.

In addition to the points listed, education law is an intricate and detailed business. Administrators should never begin to believe that they have the ability to handle highly sensitive and complex situations such as terminations without competent counsel. No other information, whether from a textbook or a university course, will substitute for able counsel.

Exit Interviews

One practice that can benefit a school district concerned with honest self-assessment is the exit interview. In many private businesses a central personnel manager who is not directly involved with an employee is responsible for meeting and interviewing employees within a few days of their separation. The exit interview may provide candid insights regarding the practices of the school and the handling of its employees. A similar procedure, utilizing a central office staff member, should be considered by school districts.

Letters of Recommendation

Professional personnel often ask supervisors for letters of recommendation that can be added to their university placement files. Letters are usually written on a form provided by the university. These forms typically provide a place to check "confidential," meaning that the employee will not see the letter, or "non-confidential," meaning that the individual does have a right to see and read the letter.

When an employee asks someone to write a recommendation, a qualified good faith immunity is attached. However, even with this immunity, a few words of advice are warranted. Whether marked "confidential" or not, writers should assume that the individual will eventually (perhaps sooner than later) see the letter. Often such letters have a way of falling into the hands of the person being discussed. Portions of the letter may be quoted by an interviewer: "It says in this one letter . . . ."

Cases from the private sector support the need for care in comments, in letters and orally. *Newsweek*[2] reported several cases in which private-sector employees successfully sued employers. In one case an insurance broker was told that he was being dismissed from his position because he was not making sales targets. The broker hired a detective to act as a prospective employer. An executive from the firm that fired the broker told the detective that the employee was "a Jekyll and Hyde person, a classic sociopath." The fired employee sued, and the case was appealed to the Supreme Court, which upheld an award of $605,000 for lost wages and other damages and $1.3 million as a penalty.

Recommendations by Phone

Administrators often receive phone calls asking for recommendations. Administrators who do not know the individual calling should ask the caller for name, phone number, and position, and then call back after checking the phone directory for verification. Many lawsuits concerning recommendations have resulted in administrators having to be careful about what they say and to whom they say it. "Honesty is the best policy" may be overshadowed by reasonable caution.

— SUMMARY —

This chapter provides an overview of the hiring and termination process, with a focus on teaching staff. Explanations of differences in the termination of probationary and tenured staff members are provided. In addition, other personnel procedures affecting employment status are also discussed—promotion, transfer, demotion, and reduction in rank.

A comprehensive review of employee discipline includes descriptions of just cause and progressive discipline; why discipline is sometimes required; why administrators often refrain from disciplining; how critical communications to staff members should be conducted; and a description of steps taken by administrators to gain the voluntary resignation of tenured staff members.

Every case is different, and school administrators are encouraged always to confer with their school attorney and/or labor relations representative when considering dismissal of a staff member.

— REFERENCES —

1. Hogan, John B., and Sarzynski, Edward J. *Hornbook of Topics and Forms Pertaining to Teachers.* Binghamton, NY: authors, 1986.
2. "The Revenge of the Fired." *Newsweek*, February 16, 1987.

CHAPTER

— 8 —

Compensation

Probably the area of greatest common interest to employees, whether new or experienced, is pay. This chapter discusses pay standards, reading a salary scale, employees not covered by a negotiated agreement, merit pay, and the compensation of coaches and advisors.

— FINANCING EDUCATION —

Although a desired candidate may find a particular position enticing, he or she may refuse it if the salary is too low. Salary levels are defined by regional standards; however, the concept of regionalism is often misleading. For instance, School District A contains a shopping center, a number of automobile dealerships, a private country club, a couple of large industries, and several small businesses; School District B, located next to District A, is 99 percent residential, containing no businesses other than a corner grocery store and a small family restaurant. In District A a $75,000 home may raise $500 per year in school taxes; a $75,000 home in District B may raise $1,000 per year in school taxes. Obviously, the great difference in tax base dictates, to a large extent, the amount of money local taxpayers will contribute to education.

In suburban areas with a concentration of highly educated residents, taxpayers may be willing to foot the bill for higher taxes if such support goes toward better education. In other areas, taxpayers may also value education, but may not be willing to provide the same amount of support because their ability to pay is more limited. Another factor that must also be kept in mind by school officials is that the majority of taxpayers in school districts are *not* parents. Consequently, officials about to put yearly budgets or school bonds up for a vote must identify the audience they are asking for support.

Such common differences in ability to pay give many school administrators, especially those in less-affluent districts, their share of headaches.

Depending on state law, some communities do not have a chance to vote on school budgets. In these cases a board of education may give less consideration to the attitude of the community in terms of compensating school personnel. This can provide a hostile environment, because school board members throughout the country are generally elected by the public. Most school board members wish to keep their positions and need public support. The term of office of a school board member varies considerably, but is usually from three to five years. One may think this provides security, but a school board member may wish to have more than one term of office. In fact, most school board members serve multiple terms in a school system. Therefore, the voice of the public can affect the thinking of individuals elected or appointed to a school board.

Attitudes of school board members also vary, and this variance can cause many difficulties within a school system. A board composed of several members may have some identified as fiscally conservative and others who are fiscally liberal. These individuals influence other members of the board of education. The number of people on boards also varies, but there are usually five, seven, or nine members. Having two people at extreme ends of the spectrum in attitudes toward financing can greatly influence the actions of other board members.

– DETERMINING COMPENSATION –

When compensation ranges for staff members are given to the local superintendent, he or she is responsible for carrying out the mandates of the board, regardless of whether the superintendent agrees or disagrees with the board. The tenure of the superintendent may also be in question, depending on his or her ability to respond with accurate information about compensation factors that affect the school system. The superintendent must keep the board fully informed of the impact caused by regional pay standards, which may make a difference in the district's ability to obtain qualified personnel. Although people may say that salaries do not make the total difference in deciding to move, often this area of concern takes a close second place, if not the first place, in making a decision to be employed by a given school district. Although a range of salaries and benefits plays an important role in obtaining personnel, the status of the whole organization is also important. Personnel assigned to hiring must be given latitude in terms of salary placement. They must also be reasonably consistent in terms of compensating personnel similarly for closely related experiences. Morale may be adversely affected by hiring standards that vary from individual to individual.

Supply and Demand

A frequent case of variation is one based on need. The factors of supply and demand could make a difference in the hiring process. If the supply of good applicants is high, compensation may be set at the same level as for employees in another known area of high supply. An extreme case relates to the demand created by a low supply, which may cause several regional school districts to vie for a well-qualified individual, who then can take the best offer. Salary is not the only consideration, but will strongly influence an individual in selecting a district. Either through contract or through practice, a superintendent may have the latitude to offer a salary with no reference to a person's experience or background. The morale issue arises when these variations occur, and employees discover that they do not make the same salary, although they may have similar experience and background.

Contractual Pay Standards

The contract agreement is established through the collective bargaining process. Concerns identified by employees and employers are reviewed according to the processes set forth in law and the procedures established in the local district. Through the superintendent and board of education, a school system must identify the maximum compensation that can be tolerated by the tax rate and by the attitudes of the groups involved in the negotiation process.

In some cases collective bargaining is done on an informal basis, even where the law may provide for a formal process. The contract or agreement that emerges will establish latitudes for hiring that will vary between schools within the same region. Although some states are broken down into large geographic regions, it is uncommon to find uniform standards for an entire region set by school boards within that area, because there may be variation in wealth, public attitude, status of the school system, and pressure from individual school district faculties.

A trend affecting decisions on who runs for the school board may be seen in an increase in elected board members who have a potential vested interest in the compensation process. These may include a staff member's spouse or a person who serves a personnel role in a neighboring district.

These individuals may express strong support for increased salaries for all employees in a district or at least for a specific employment area. The role of personnel administrators dealing with the employment process becomes extremely complicated when this factor exists.

The duration of contracts or agreements can also be affected by the board of education. Contracts range from one-year agreements to multiple-year agreements, with most having a two- or three-year range. In some cases, five-year contracts or agreements are settled. The question of duration of agreements is often affected by current or projected inflation rates. A period of high inflation sees salary agreement increases that are lower than the rate of inflation. As inflation falls, salary increases are set at rates higher than the inflation rate. This factor does not affect all employees in the same way. Personnel who have limited experience may look at this system favorably. Staff members at the other extreme, who wish to have their salary at the highest level before retirement, may find that during their final years, compensation is lower than inflation; this could affect employees' decisions to continue or leave employment in the district. Since more experienced employees receive greater compensation, the school board and superintendent may face a dilemma in terms of financial constraints affected by the continued employment of individuals who might normally have retired, especially when those individuals are in an area of high supply and would not be able to relocate readily.

Salary Comparisons

In many areas, either through school board associations or regional educational organizations, a comparison of teacher salaries is made. Comparison between the school districts in an area provides administrators with information that can be used by their boards in estimating the costs of offering competitive salaries.

One superintendent, new to his district, asked the board to make a commitment in their district policy to "compensate employees in a fair and commensurate manner." The board members briefly discussed his request and initiated a vote to pass the recommendation. Before they voted, the superintendent asked if they understood the obligation they were accepting. He explained that their teachers were the lowest-paid in the region. He informed them that he planned to bring the teachers' salaries up to the middle salary range in the region over the next three years and wanted the board's informed support. Following much further discussion, the board went along with the policy and the commitment.

Where Do We Want to Be?

A superintendent, director of personnel, or contract negotiator must determine how to get an agreement that will place the members of the bargaining unit in the comparative salary area that the board believes is fair. In other words, does the board believe the teachers in their district should be the best-paid in the area, would they prefer to see their teachers among the lowest-paid, or would they prefer salaries somewhere in the middle? This issue is also a worthwhile consideration for administrator candidates and prospective teachers who are considering positions in a school district. Some boards actually take pride in the fact that they have the lowest pay scale in their county. When candidates know this ahead of time, they may reconsider whether they want to be employed in such a district.

Reading a Salary Scale

"What you see is what you get" is not necessarily true in examining school district salary scales. For instance, a school system that wants to be in the average range directs its chief negotiator to offer benefits that would be comparable in that range. Points that must be considered include (1) the actual starting salary, (2) the number of steps on the salary scale, (3) the amount of dollars between each step, and (4) the distribution of district personnel on the scale (the number of people on each step). Each of these has an important effect on the actual cost of a negotiated contract to the district. Older and more established faculty will look for greater increases at the upper steps, and a younger faculty, particularly in poorly paying districts, will be more interested in the lower steps.

Who negotiates. Although not often discussed, *who* does the negotiating is often reflected in the salary schedule. Many veteran administrators and negotiators will note that the greatest increases are often at the middle or top end of the salary schedule when the negotiators representing the staff are in the upper steps of the scale.

One must also look at cumulative earnings over a number of years. If the total amount of money received is greater in terms of the cumulative amount received in one district than what would be paid in another, this might provide a selling point for a faculty member considering long-term employment in one location or the other.

Once a salary schedule is determined, an employee should receive the amount that is agreed to in a certain year or on a certain step. The fringe benefits should be similar for employees in a certain category. However, most school districts have different negotiating units for teachers, support, staff, and sometimes administrators. It is not always most economical to have separate fringe benefits negotiated for each unit, as a personnel administrator could be bogged down with a variety of formulas dealing with different groups. For instance, administrators might negotiate a half paid (50 percent) dental plan, teachers might negotiate a lesser amount (40 percent), and support staff might agree to yet another (33 percent). Administrators should carefully study the amount of time necessary to administer such a system, then determine whether they are better off trying to get consistency. The initial costs might not be as great as the hidden costs of administering this program. In negotiating, one must be cautious to consider real costs versus the figures listed in negotiated agreements.

A salary schedule would be similar to the following, with provisions made for differences in graduate, undergraduate, and inservice hours. In addition, other language might deal with compensation, such as allowances for years of service and degrees held.

B.A. degree or certified. The following is an example of a step schedule used for ten-month teachers holding only their bachelor's degrees. Each numbered step represents payment for one year of service.

1. 20,000
2. 21,250
3. 22,000
4. 22,750
5. 23,500
6. 24,250
7. 25,000
8. 25,750
9. 26,500
10. 27,250
11. 28,000
12. 29,750
13. 30,500
14. 31,250
15. 32,000
16. 32,000
17. 33,300
18. 33,300
19. 34,000

Additional Payments

In addition, payments are usually provided based on factors such as course work, length of time in the district (longevity), and additional days worked:

1.   **a.** Payment for Credit Hours approved will be in the following amounts, if teacher is certified or has a B.A.

        For graduate hours $44.00
        For undergraduate hours $30.30

    b. Payment to teachers holding Master's degrees will be $400.
    c. Longevity steps will be payable after a teacher has been on the prior step for two years. (Longevity applies to teachers who have advanced to the top of a salary schedule – in this case, step 19. Longevity is applied at certain agreed-upon years (for example, 20, 25, etc.) and should be separately stated in the contract.)

2. Teachers granted special cost-of-living or merit raises prior to July 1, 199__ will continue to receive the amounts so granted as long as they continue working in their current positions.

3. Prior experience will be credited at the discretion of the board.

4. For ten-month employees, one-tenth (1/10th) of salary will be paid for each additional month worked or one two-hundredth (1/200th) of salary will be paid for each additional day worked.

5. Terminal pay

    Any teacher who retires under the State Teachers' Retirement Plan, and who notifies the district superintendent of intent to so retire, will be granted terminal pay in the amount of eleven ($11) per day for the number of sick-leave days the teacher has accumulated up to the date of retirement. The application to retire must be made in writing to the district superintendent by May 1st of the school year prior to the year of retirement. The terminal pay amount will be paid in a lump sum in the teacher's final paycheck. The May 1st application date may be waived by the district superintendent.

8. Club advisors will be paid an additional $300 per annum.

9. Salary: Increases for unit salary for the next two school years will be 7 percent of the prior year's unit salary, to be applied to returning staff each year.

In this example, if a person with no previous teaching experience entered employment, that individual would be paid $20,000. The assumption is that such an individual would not have any graduate work or related experience, so compensation would be set at the $20,000 figure; that individual would also receive the fringe benefits guaranteed to all personnel in the bargaining unit. If a person had multiple years of service, the school board's representative could determine the appropriateness of that experience for salary credit, take into account the need to employ that person, and set the salary based on those considerations.

If the person had twelve years of experience, he or she might start at a salary of $30,500, in addition to being compensated for any graduate work. The assumption would be that the person had earned a Master's degree, and allowance would be made for the hours relating to that Master's degree. If the individual had thirty-two credit hours toward the degree, he or she would be paid $44 times 32 equaling $1,408, plus $400 for the degree itself, providing a total of $32,308.

However, some organizations show inconsistency in terms of how people are placed on steps and in the interpretation of graduate hours. In a high-demand certification area, an employer may, as in the example, provide complete recognition of experience. In the case of a low-demand certification area, an employer may calculate experience in a different fashion; a person may have twelve years of experience, but may be granted only one year of experience for each year of experience on the salary schedule. Therefore, a person with similar background as the earlier candidate, but in a low-demand area, would only be placed on Step 7, at a salary of $25,000, if the person also had a Master's degree and similar number of hours related to that degree. Assuming the second person had the same qualifications as in the previous example, this person would receive $44 an hour times 32 hours for a total of $1,408, and $400 for the Master's degree. The total salary of $26,808 for this individual would be significantly less than that offered the previous candidate. Since the allowance for experience was adjusted for each individual, a morale issue might well be created because of the difference of interpretation of experience credit based on the district's need.

In this case, no one has violated the contract if it includes a statement that says, "Prior experience will be credited at the discretion of the board." The board in this case accepts the recommendation of the superintendent, who is acting for the board and interpreting the contract, based on the needs of the district.

Interpretation of step placement may also be handled by the administrative staff. If the contract is silent on this matter, and if the administration has not been challenged on its method of interpretation, this procedure can be continued to establish placement of personnel for compensation purposes. In some situations a person may have no degree; this would be typical of individuals who teach in occupational programs and who possess a variety of backgrounds and skills relating to the area of occupational training. In these cases, salary schedules may be developed for no-degree, uncertified personnel. In situations such as this, the number of undergraduate hours should provide additional compensation for the individual. The application of outside experience to placement on the schedule may be interpreted by the employer.

Longevity. In the example provided, longevity is established at the top steps, 15 through 19. As one interprets the salary schedule and the language of the contract where it states that longevity steps will be payable after a teacher has been on the prior step for two years, steps 15 and 16 would be the same amount, 17 and 18 would be the same amount, and 19 would be the final step for an increase.

A teacher who is retiring and is on the top step would receive benefits for the final year according to salary, graduate or undergraduate hours, Master's degree, plus any incentive or terminal pay. In this example, no retirement incentive is offered other than terminal pay. Therefore, a person on step 19 would receive $34,000, plus 60 hours of graduate work times $44 per hour equaling $2,640, and a Master's degree for $400; the total annual salary would be $37,040. The rulings of various state or district retirement systems may limit the amount of salary credited for retirement purposes as different from the final salary agreed upon by the employer.

The interpretation of graduate and undergraduate hours may be constant, and the rewards for degrees and certification may be constant. However, the interpretation of percentage increases in the contractual agreement may vary considerably between school districts. In some cases, faculty may not receive compensation that is equal to increases in the cost of living. In a period of a high cost-of-living increases, individuals may be compensated at lower cost-of-living rates, and therefore receive less actual money in terms of keeping up with inflation. The reverse may be true if faculty members receive higher percentage increases than the cost of living, thus providing them with greater spending power. What the school board and administration have to determine is a level of equity between the times when individuals received less than the increase or more than the increase in comparison to the cost of living. A system that balances these two factors would be more equitable. However, it is important that the board of education understand the balancing factor between these differences.

Administrator Salaries

Teaching salaries have increased in the last few years, and administrative salaries have not kept up with these increases. The interest in moving from the classroom or service areas to administration has diminished, as teachers take into account the fact that administration works a longer year and longer hours and potentially has a higher level of stress.

State laws vary on the status of administrators in relation to security and compensation. In some states, administrators may not receive tenure or any type of job security that includes having discipline or dismissal judged by neutral parties. In others, some administrators may legally be provided with some security. Calculation of compensation is also dissimilar, in that in some states administrators are allowed to form bargaining units and negotiate contracts, and in others they are compensated strictly on an individual basis, at the discretion of the board. In yet other states, both models may hold true; administrators may have the right to organize and bargain, or may choose not to. In instances when administrators choose not to organize and bargain collectively, they usually are not paid according to any type of set schedule that recognizes graduate credit hours, degrees, certification, or years of service.

Where administrators do organize and bargain, a negotiated agreement may be a vehicle to identify differences that exist between union and non-union administrator organizations. Monetary awards are important to employees, but boards and administrators are often willing to improve benefit packages instead of improving salary schedules. Because administrative salaries are usually the highest in an area, they often get more public attention. By replacing financial remuneration with other types of benefits, such as fully paid insurance, additional insurance coverage, transportation allowances, or annuities, board members may find it possible to keep administrator salaries down and still keep administrators satisfied.

– EMPLOYEES NOT COVERED BY A NEGOTIATED AGREEMENT –

. In some districts, certain classes of employees, usually support personnel, are not covered by negotiated agreements containing wage scales. In such cases a policy statement from the board of education may suffice to establish wage scales. In establishing this policy, a board may wish to set supplemental guidelines that identify the expectations or standards for this class of employees in the school district.

Also, where employees are not covered by contractual arrangements, those individuals must be informed of their fringe benefits. Salary is important, but the fringe benefits an employee receives can make the difference between accepting or rejecting a position. Clarification should be made concerning such points as:

- Absence
- Attendance
- Definition of roles
- Equal opportunity employment
- Evaluation procedures
- Health insurance
- Holiday schedules
- Types of leaves of absence
- On-the-job injury

- Physical examination
- Retirement plan
- Sick leave banks
- Termination pay
- Jury duty
- Travel
- Vacation
- Wages
- Working hours

Since all jobs are important in the operation of a school system, it is difficult to place functions in a priority ranking. However, people must understand where they belong in the chain of command. The position can then be evaluated in terms of that status.

In a number of school districts, salaries are determined by agreements or methods that are not included in the collective bargaining agreement. These methods might affect different categories/classes of personnel. Individual salary determination may be based on the appropriateness of the present salary in relation to employee performance, on salary rates of other employees within the category, on the value of work performed, or on other structural factors.

Before salary changes are considered, the equity of the present salary structure should be reviewed. Employee performance should be measured based on the period covered in the evaluation plan. Performance appraisal provides the first step of individual salary determination. The second step is determined by the presence of, or rate of, performance improvement or decline. Individual performance level versus the performance level of other employees in the category must also be considered. This leads to consideration of salary relationships; ranking of employees in an organization can serve to point out any inequities that may exist. By using this approach, an administrator can plan individual salary decisions in accordance with the results employees have achieved. As the composition of a division or department changes, expertise becomes a consideration. Under this condition, it may be appropriate to increase or decrease the level of assignments.

Individual evaluations and evaluation charts (also known as scattergrams) that include all the employees in each pay category are essential. The results of comparisons, anticipated evaluations, current salary levels, and the salaries of other employees can be seen at a glance. By using this type of system, administrators can determine the cost of employees in comparison to each other, and the value of each employee's performance in assigned responsibilities. The paired comparisons and performance ratings can be considered with respect to the employee's current category and salary.

The evaluation chart helps to identify level and salary inequities within the organization.

One basic problem will always exist in any system in which salary determinations are based on personal judgment: those receiving salaries will always question the fairness of the system. A set pay scale makes it difficult, if not impossible, to reward financially the employees who are conscientious about coming to work regularly, arriving on time, and fulfilling their obligations in a meritorious manner. Unfortunately, the dollar amount given to one employee within a set salary scale is the same as the amount given to counterparts who regularly use up all of their sick days, are tardy, and consistently find excuses for errors or omissions in their work.

On the other hand, while a system without a scale provides the administration and board with the opportunity, more likely in small districts, to evaluate each employee individually, those who receive less money will almost always mutter that they are victims of politics, or that someone in a decision-making position is out to get them. This manner of decision making may be the fairest, but it undoubtedly places more pressure on the administrator responsible for recommending the compensation to be provided each employee.

— MERIT PAY —

The term "merit pay" is used in a variety of ways in educational literature. Because of the many different interpretations of merit pay, administrators must be fully aware of what is discussed in the literature and how it is understood by different groups within local school districts.

In some cases "merit" is considered to be more effective teaching. However, in many districts teaching is not the only consideration, and other factors are also taken into account. For instance, attendance; student achievement; volunteering to take more difficult teaching assignments; additional professional growth experiences or course work; and cooperation in reconciling local needs are weighted in some merit pay plans. The use of career ladders is also becoming popular in many school districts. Probably the best-known is the state-wide performance pay and career ladder program instituted with the support of former Tennessee Governor Lamar Alexander. Tennessee instituted the program in 1984, with an initial group of 106 master teachers identified to act as evaluators of other candidates. Factors required to become a master teacher included classroom visits; an interview with the teacher candidate; questionnaires completed by the principal, students, and fellow teachers; and a skills test.

If merit is used, goals and objectives become very important. Where goals and objectives are part of the plan, there must be agreement on organizational and individual goals by both the evaluator and the person being evaluated, so that merit can be considered in terms of how an individual performs in meeting the goals, objectives, and related activities. To determine merit, a variety of systems may be used. In some cases, formulas are used, with weightings given to each factor. In some districts a panel containing both administrators and teachers is involved in evaluating candidates. Unfortunately, there is no absolutely objective, fair method of determining who should qualify for merit increases. Invariably, those who receive merit increases regularly will see the system as just. Those who do not will be able to provide a number of justifications as to why they were shortchanged: they had a more difficult group of students, those conducting the evaluation did not like them, the principal had it in for them, or the system did not adequately evaluate what they accomplished.

Often the success or failure of a merit system depends on the level of compensation for merit. If the compensation level is too low, the value of the system may be questioned. Merit awards may also be controversial because of the dissension they cause among staff members.

To deal effectively with the merit pay process, employees must be clearly aware of the goals and objectives that are to be achieved by the organization in general, and the relationship of those goals to receiving merit pay. Some form of evaluation must be used to define whether an individual has met the standards for merit increases. The common difficulty is that personnel do not trust the evaluation process, both in terms of general feedback and in how well it determines the worth of employees. An example of a rating scale is shown in Table 8.1.

The interpretation of merit, as noted before, should be determined by goals and objectives recognized by the evaluator and the evaluated.

Merit pay may apply to all school employees, including teachers, administrators, clerical personnel, custodial personnel, and all those covered by bargaining organizations of each of those groups. In the case of clerical and custodial/maintenance personnel, piecework or safety incentives may have greater impact on merit than for other negotiating groups. Most merit pay criteria specify that employees must have consistently shown better-than-average performance in their role, as assessed through some evaluation instrument. There also may be a limit on employees' eligibility for merit increases. Statements that a percentage of employees will be eligible, or that any employee will be eligible only once within a given period, are not uncommon.

An employee can set such a standard that major merit increases are considered for a whole department. Increases may not be specifically related to income, but perhaps to reducing the work load in a department by

TABLE 8.1 Merit rating scale

Performance Category	Performance Points	Evaluation Criteria
Outstanding	16–20	In addition to performing all aspects of the job at the level expected, the individual has made noteworthy contributions, such as overcoming unusual obstacles, advancing the state of the art, or performing several functions with a special effort, to the benefit of the district.
Commendable	11–15	All aspects of the job have performed at or above the level expected, but not at a level to qualify for special recognition.
Satisfactory	6–10	All aspects of the job have been performed above the minimum acceptable level, although several functions could be improved.
Minimum	1–5	One or more aspects of performance are below the minimum scale. Level of performance will not be acceptable on a continuing basis.

adding employees or by employing new technologies that would not have been approved unless merit had been demonstrated by the whole department.

– NON-SALARY COMPENSATION –

A number of areas related to non-salary compensation are important to the worker. These include a variety of categories, but many involve leave potential, including but not limited to: family leave, leave following injury on the job, general leave of absence, child care leave, personal leave, religious leave, sick leave, sick leave bank, visiting days, holidays, military training leave, sabbatical leave, vacations, grievance procedures, life insurance, and health insurance.

Additional life and health insurance become more important as the costs of such insurance rise. An employee who receives certain life insurance benefits in one district may remain there if that benefit is not as good in another district.

The percentage paid for health insurance varies from full payment by the employer to a percentage shared by employer and employee. The rising costs of health benefits make payment for health insurance a key item for negotiation, especially when the cost of this benefit is shared by employer and employee. Elements of health insurance may include dental and vision plans that initially may be relatively inexpensive, but may increase beyond the board's expectation in future years. Other non-monetary agreements that have been considered by some organizations relate to geographical location, transportation allowances, parking locations, position growth, title of positions, ability to take staff development programs at no cost, and payment of dues for various organizations.

– COMPENSATION OF COACHES AND ADVISORS –

One area of compensation that is often a point of concern in school districts involves the remuneration of coaches and advisors for duties beyond their teaching assignments. Matters of controversy often result from questions such as: Do we have to pay Mr. Smith (a losing coach) the same as Mr. Jones (a winning coach)? Do we have to pay the women's basketball coach the same as the men's coach? Is it really fair that a first-year coach should make the same as one who has been coaching for twenty years? Why is our soccer coach paid $500 less than the soccer coach in a neighboring district? These questions, or some form of them, are asked in almost every school district sooner or later. An unsuccessful season, or an influential community or board member who is dissatisfied with the way his or her child was treated by a coach, are often the root of such questions.

Satisfactory responses to all such questions are virtually impossible. However, a rational approach to the compensation of coaches and advisors is the best means of minimizing conflicts.

One method of determining salaries is through the use of a compensation schedule involving a point system. Using coaches as an example, one system (example in Table 8.2) assigns points based on various categories.

TABLE 8.2 Point system for coaches

Number of Games (A)	Level of Position (B)	Squad Size (C)
16 = 10 pts.	Varsity Head = 10 pts.	36–40 = 10 pts.
14 = 9	Varsity Asst. = 8	31–35 = 9
12 = 8	Jr. Varsity = 7	26–30 = 8
10 = 7	Jr. High Head = 6	21–25 = 7
8 = 6	Jr. High Asst. = 5	16–20 = 6
6 = 5		10–15 = 5
		5– 9 = 4

Other categories might include: equipment management (responsibility for items issued), number of coaching weeks, compensatory hours (weekends and nights), hazards (injury potential), etc. As with the examples detailed in Table 8.2, each category has a number of levels, with points assigned to each. Once the point system has been established, a schedule is developed. The schedule would list each sport, juxtaposed with the categories determined for that sport, as in Table 8.3.

Once all points are assigned and totaled, a point conversion chart is developed and points are related to compensation, as in Table 8.4. The renumeration listed is in addition to regular salary.

Using this format, questions about compensation may be answered by showing that compensation is set equitably rather than by using subjective factors.

Although such an approach provides some objectivity, the process used to determine factors and assign points must be carefully determined. A committee approach might be used, involving coaches (both male and

TABLE 8.3 Categories of coaches

Sport	A	B	C	D	E	F	G	H	I	Total
Varsity Football	6	10	5							87
Asst. Football										
Head Jr. High Football			(Each category is rated and then points are totaled.)							
Asst. Jr. High Football										
Soccer										
Field Hockey										
Cross Country										

TABLE 8.4 Point conversion chart

Points	Conversion
85 +	$1440
81–84	1343
76–80	1279
71–75	1147
66–70	1009
61–65	921
56–60	840
51–55	756
46–50	620
41–45	560
–40	492

female), an administrator, and perhaps a board member, and/or a booster club parent. Such a committee should be limited in number, and some member should be familiar with areas such as negotiations and Title IX requirements. In addition, the committee should realize that their charge is *not* to determine actual compensation, but to provide the board of education and superintendent with a recommendation for a process that will ultimately determine compensation.

One final point: those structuring such schedules must consider Title IX requirements. Coaches of men's and women's teams should be remunerated consistently if duties are consistent; conditions of employment and access to facilities should also be equal. The system of points should be reviewed by the local human rights office or federal office of civil rights before it is instituted.

– OTHER SOURCES OF COMPARISON –

What districts do in other regions and in the local area may affect salary schedules and benefits. Information from elsewhere may travel quickly or slowly, but will surely have an impact on salary schedules in a given region. Information identifying statewide standards based on state regional projections of salary is often available through state organizations, and should be gathered from the most current publications.

If national data are desired, the *American School Board Journal* publishes information related to various administrative roles, and provides information on per-pupil expenditures, ratios, enrollments, handicapped and minority students, and testing data.

– SUMMARY –

Compensation established at the local school district level is not determined in isolation. Various data are identified in establishing proper levels of pay and in determining systems for compensation.

The level of compensation for employees is based on the importance or value given the employees, and is frequently controlled by legislation and collective bargaining agreements. Where collective bargaining is not in force, a board and superintendent have greater latitude in establishing compensation, but would probably not depart greatly from regional standards.

Merit pay, a controversial subject, can be most effectively administered if there is agreement by employees and employers on the definition of merit pay and the procedures to be used in the process.

Extra-duty compensation for coaching and advising is best determined through objective methods. The use of a point system developed by a committee of school personnel is one method of addressing this concern.

Resources for dealing with compensation can be found at local, regional, state, and national levels. This information should be utilized by superintendents and school boards to establish total compensation packages.

— 9 —

Bargaining and Administering the Negotiated Agreement

Contract administration is a cyclical process that commences once a labor agreement has been negotiated and continues until a subsequent agreement has been reached. In states where collective bargaining takes place, the activities involved in contract administration are similar. Nevertheless, some differences exist, due to statutory provisions unique to each state.

— HISTORY OF COLLECTIVE BARGAINING —

The first labor unions began near the end of the eighteenth century and were concerned with wages, hours, conditions of employment, and job security. Recognition for these early unions was difficult since British Common Law, on which much of our own judicial system is based, did not recognize unions, so unions were considered illegal.

In the 1920s a majority of the Boston police force went out on strike. The strike had profound effects in its resulting disarray. Massachusetts Governor Calvin Coolidge made a statement that public servants did not have the right to strike. Coolidge proceeded to support the police commissioner's refusal to rehire the strikers. This action laid the foundation for the public's refusal to support striking public employees.

Teacher unions were first organized in the 1800s. The National Education Association (NEA) emerged in 1857 and is the largest teacher union in the country, with approximately two million members. The second largest is the American Federation of Teachers (AFT), founded in 1916, which has approximately one-third the membership of the NEA.

In addition to teacher unions, school districts are home to various other organized union groups. Many districts have administrator associations that provide legal services for professional matters, including representation and negotiation services, and other areas related to job security and conditions of employment. In some cases, additional services include job assistance information, insurance programs, financial planning, and retirement counseling.

Teacher unions were not considered to be formidable labor organizations until the 1960s, when they were strengthened by the New York City teachers' strike. With the rise of unions came pressure to initiate collective bargaining. The process has existed in different forms for many years; recent attention has been given to collaborative forms of negotiations, aimed at enhancing working relationships between unions and school management by greater involvement of staff in decision-making issues.

– ORGANIZING FOR COLLECTIVE NEGOTIATIONS –

As noted, collective bargaining activities vary by state. In some states, teacher bargaining occurs at the discretion of the local board of education and in others it is defined by law. In some, bargaining in good faith is required, and in others the only mandate is for the school board to confer with representatives from employee units.

Before collective bargaining was widely used, school districts frequently had decentralized administrative structures that conferred significant discretion on school-level administrators in the budget process, recruitment and selection of personnel, the assignment of personnel within the school, and the allocation of resources. After the widespread use of bargaining became established, the negotiation process had a tendency to centralize authority and to remove this discretion from school-level administration.

Laws have created a duality of obligation by a public employer in the enforcement of public employee organization rights. First, a public employer is constrained by the statutory provisions of the laws, and accordingly, employers are not permitted to make unilateral changes in terms and conditions of employment without negotiating the changes, unless the public employee organization concerned has waived its right to negotiate. Second, public employers are constrained by the terms of the negotiated agreement itself. With respect to this second obligation, the negotiated agreement may provide its own enforcement mechanism through a grievance procedure and binding arbitration, or a negotiated agreement can be enforced by an action of law for breach of contract. Thus, the administration of negotiated agreements in many states is dependent both on statutory considerations and the contractual obligations of a public employer.

Mandatory and Nonmandatory Subjects

In preparation for bargaining, administrators and school board members should know exactly what items they can negotiate. These are broken down into three categories: mandatory or bargainable subjects that *must* be bargained; prohibited or nonbargainable subjects that *cannot* be bargained, and permitted subjects that *may* be bargained. States vary as to the process required for bargaining. In some, a meeting of management and labor to discuss items of concern is all that is required by statute. In such cases, the categories are not relevant. However, the majority of states do require a process for good-faith bargaining.

Courts have tended to avoid strict interpretations as to which subjects are bargainable. In doing so they have left such determinations to individual cases, weighing the power of boards of education to develop policies about teachers and terms and conditions of employment. This process has provided state employee-relations labor boards with great influence, since such boards are often regarded as neutral experts by the courts.

Common nonbargainable subjects include appointment and promotion of staff, tenure determinations, position eliminations, and budget decisions. Common bargainable subjects are those most closely aligned with terms and conditions of employment such as salary, benefits, and leave. Some states also provide a permitted category of subjects that do not have to be negotiated but *may* be. Class size is not a required subject in some states, but in others may be bargained with the agreement of management.

The Negotiating Team

One of the most profound effects of labor relations rights for staff members was the decision that gave employee organizations the right to bargain their contracts collectively. In preparing to negotiate, both the school board and the employee organization will have a negotiating team representing them at the bargaining table. Each team usually consists of a chief spokesperson, someone familiar with finances, a recorder, and a job specialist.

The chief spokesperson may be someone local: for management, an administrator assigned by the board; for the union, the local union president or another member who has filled this role before. Often boards and union officials decide to use outsiders, sometimes referred to as "hired guns," to represent them. For boards, representation may be by an attorney or a labor relations specialist. Union representatives are usually regional field representatives affiliated with the union's state or national organization. The choice to use outside specialists depends on a number of factors: what the other

other side chooses to do, the history of labor relations in the district, the level of trust that exists in the district, and whether many changes in contract language have been proposed.

The business specialist is usually the district's business official, and the union often has someone, usually a teacher (for negotiating teacher contracts) with a good knowledge of the salary schedule and the ability to process information through a computer. When the negotiations involve support staff members, financial review is generally done by the union's field representative.

The recorders, often an administrator from the district and a teacher or secretary from the employee association, take notes on what is discussed and record the intent of any language that may be added, deleted, or changed. These notes may be used later in arbitration hearings, should a grievance be filed regarding the interpretation of a particular provision.

The content specialists are often a school administrator for management and a teacher (for instructional staff) or a district-wide support staff employee who has some knowledge of working conditions.

These roles are not always filled as described here. A board of education may have an administrator-negotiator who has worked for them for many years. The board may have such complete trust in the individual and his or her knowledge of the system that this individual is allowed to represent them each year, and the board does not feel compelled to have a team of other people also sitting at the table. Consequently, one person may serve as chief negotiator, finance specialist, content specialist, and recorder. Although not the norm, this kind of arrangement is not unusual, especially in smaller districts.

– TWO-WAY NEGOTIATIONS –

Any discussion of the role of negotiators should note the peculiarity of the job of chief negotiator. Although most bargainers do not acknowledge it, those who wear the negotiator's hat really negotiate in two directions. Bargaining representatives must not only find a common ground with those sitting across the table, but must also try to persuade their own team members that a particular settlement offer is reasonable. Thus, the union negotiator who spends the majority of his or her career bargaining contracts is likely to have a good idea of how much the union is likely to gain during a particular negotiation. At times the staff members sitting at the table with the negotiator become greedy, believing they can and should get a lot more than it appears they are going to receive. At such times the negotiator has to convince his or her constituents that the offers being made are realistic and should be accepted. The same thing happens with the management negotiator, who must often educate board members and administrators regarding the reality of what they should plan to negotiate. A board member often uses his or her own work hours, conditions, and salary as a basis of comparison for what members of the staff should receive.

– SEQUENCE OF ACTIVITIES –

Collective bargaining that results in a negotiated agreement is only one element of administering the employer/employee relationship in a public school district. The sequence of activities to prepare for negotiations includes several events that recur throughout the fiscal year of a school district.

States have differing fiscal years. The activities included in the negotiation process do not necessarily occur in a particular order, and some of the activities do not occur except during the time when a negotiated agreement is to be renewed, but the general sequence of events may be as follows:

1. In the months preceding the expiration of the negotiated agreement, a public employer should review questions pertaining to unit composition. For instance: what employee job titles are included in the negotiating unit represented by an employee organization? Should department heads be included in a negotiating unit with classroom teachers in instances where department heads are responsible for evaluating classroom teachers and making recommendations for their retention or dismissal? Should directors who are system-wide program administrators be in a negotiating unit with other employees, or should they be eligible for coverage under the public-sector labor relations statute at all?

2. Once issues pertaining to representation status have been identified and initiated, a public employer normally reviews the contract agreement. The review process entails an analysis of disputes and grievances that may have been filed since the last agreement and an interpretation of individual provisions of the agreement. The input of administrative staff should be solicited so that problem areas in the relationship between the school district and its employees can be determined. Many school districts ask their administrative staff members to provide a written review of the contract prior to the formulation of proposals for the new agreement. This is a good means for identifying problems, but a better practice would be to require each administrator to maintain a file on contract problems. The files could be reviewed periodically so issues that need to be addressed may be stated as formal proposals for negotiations.

3. After a review of the current agreement, proposals are normally formulated by the school district's negotiator, whether that person is an attorney, private consultant, regional or intermediate-unit personnel relations specialist, or in-house administrative staff member.

The review should take into consideration the fact that preparing for negotiations should be a year-round process. Whenever a grievance occurs or management feels stymied in its effort to provide positive education, because of a contract restriction, notes should be made and filed. About a month prior to the initiation of contract negotiations, members of the administrative team should individually, then collectively, review the present contract, note problems experienced throughout the past year(s), and identify concerns unsuccessfully remediated through additions to the contract in past years.

Checklist. Some districts have found the use of a formal checklist useful in reviewing pertinent provisions and concerns.

CONTRACT REVIEW CHECKLIST

_____ 1. Recognition

_____ 2. Employment security

_____   a. Method of hiring personnel

_____   b. Dues checkoff

_____   c. Job security

_____   d. Other

_____ 3. Conditions of employment

_____   a. Loss of seniority

_____   b. Layoff and recall

_____   c. Maintenance of standards

_____   d. Subcontracting

_____   e. Other

_____ 4. No-strike pledge

_____ 5. Resolution

_____ 6. Grievance procedure

_____   a. Arbitration

_____   b. Just cause

_____ 7. Separation from employment

_____ 8. Equipment

_____ 9. Job duties and classification

_____ 10. Holidays

_____ 11. Leaves

_____   a. Sick leave

_____   b. Bereavement leave

_____   c. Personal leave

_____   d. Child care leave

_____   e. Military leave

_____   f. Jury duty

_____   g. Other

_____ 12. Insurance

_____   a. Health

_____   b. Life

_____   c. Dental

_____   d. Optical

_____   e. Orthodontal

_____   f. Prescription

_____   g. Other

_____ 13. Duration of contract

_____ 14. Salary

_____   a. Instructional (or administrative, or support)

_____   b. Extracurricular

_____   c. Athletics

_____ 15. Agency fee

_____ 16. Association rights

_____   a. Use of facilities

_____   b. Use of school mail

_____   c. Release time—union officers

_____   d. Other

The checklist in the accompanying box contains many of the common provisions discussed during the course of bargaining, but it by no means exhausts every possible topic for negotiations.

The superintendent or his or her designee should compile a master list that presents suggestions for modifying or deleting contract articles that management believes are misleadingly stated or inappropriate. These recommendations should then be reviewed by the administrative team in conjunction with the school attorney or labor relations representative. Following this review, the school board should be apprised of the negotiations plan. The agreed-upon recommendations become the proposals that the district will exchange with the union.

After a careful study of proposals, further questions may result that lead to the establishment of priorities. Cost factors are very important and must be looked at in terms of immediate costs, long-range costs, administrative costs, and alternative methods of implementing the contract. Proposals must also be workable with staff, students, and the system. Thus, it is important to have a list of priorities that will be acceptable to all and provide equity in the agreement.

To reach a negotiated contract, representatives from both sides of the bargaining table must ultimately agree and sign off on provisions. In addition, the labor organization must check back with its rank-and-file membership. Exactly what will become an issue is often a result of provisions that have been discussed in neighboring districts. The use of settlements from other districts as a lever is known as "whipsawing." Localities often pattern contracts on the successes of other negotiated agreements, but a local district must determine its own standards before the negotiation process. Some board members take pride in being the leaders in terms of pay to employees; other board members are proud to have their district at the bottom in relation to its neighbors. Still other board members will say they would like to have their employees at the top of the local pay scales, but cannot do so since their district does not have the resources of some of its neighbors.

Such factors become part of the directions communicated to the negotiating team. If both labor and management representatives understand each others' messages, negotiations will be easier.

Once various parties have had the opportunity to make recommendations, the proposals are normally reviewed by the superintendent of schools, to determine whether they are consistent with the needs of the school district. Thereafter, proposals are normally discussed with the board of education in executive sessions, during which preliminary parameters for negotiations are identified.

In most school districts, negotiations commence during the period from late January to early March. Some school districts have a simultaneous exchange of proposals by the employer and the employee organization. Other school districts maintain a practice whereby the employee organization submits its proposals first, followed by a second meeting, usually within approximately two weeks, where proposals are submitted on behalf of the school district. The latter process provides the employer with the opportunity to review the employee organization's proposals and react to them with its own counter-proposals or additional items of concern. While many employee organizations express the view that this process places the employer in an advantageous situation, it also has the benefit of reducing the number of items that the employer needs to submit. If the district is required to make a simultaneous exchange of proposals, the negotiations will need to raise issues about every topic with which the district has a potential problem.

Negotiations. The next step in the sequence of activities is the actual negotiations; the timing of this activity varies by district and often in each contract negotiation year. When public-sector collective bargaining statutes were first enacted, fifteen, twenty or even thirty sessions during contract negotiations were not uncommon. That phenomenon is less common today. Unless one of the parties is attempting to change the nature of the contract significantly, it is more likely that the parties will meet and negotiate an agreement or reach impasse in fewer than ten sessions, lasting no more than two to three hours each.

The reason for this is relatively simple. Most of the issues of concern to the parties will have already been reduced to a written agreement during previous contract negotiations, and the number of new areas of interest is limited.

Bargaining postures. Win-win and win-lose bargaining techniques are popular topics of discussion among negotiators. Win-win negotiations are also referred to as a "problem solving" approach, a process in which both parties acknowledge the need for mutual gain and loss, also referred to as "give and take." Proponents of win-win bargaining would describe the process as one of open communication, honest trading of information, and a businesslike atmosphere free of finger-pointing, shouting, or accusations. Those who use win-win bargaining have a sincere concern that their own constituents as well as their "opponents" will perceive themselves as having gained from the bargaining process.

On the other hand, the main concern of win-lose bargainers is to gain as much as possible for those they represent while giving as little as possible to the other side. Supporters of win-lose bargaining would argue that win-win is a contradiction, and cannot actually be realized. They see a gain by one party as almost always involving a loss of some sort by the other party. Practitioners of this method give little information to the other side, tend to stick to their own positions, avoid compromise, and use whatever means are necessary to win, including confrontation and intimidation.

Bargaining representatives.   If you were to ask any negotiators whether management or union representatives are win-lose bargainers, they might tell you, with a chuckle, "The other side is." Our observations would counter this. Win-win and win-lose postures vary from place to place, bargainer to bargainer, and sometimes by the particular bargainer, depending on the situation. The posture of a bargainer is often determined by those he or she represents. A bargaining representative will often hear complaints from his or her constituents because their team was not aggressive enough and the negotiating process went too smoothly over the last few contracts. In other words, constituents believe that their negotiators could have gotten more if they had not been so cooperative. Full-time bargainers make their living from those they represent, so they often find themselves "playing the game" for the sake of their own team members.

Impasse.   Another timeless facet of the process is impasse. As an alternative to legalizing strikes, most states provide for extensive third-party intervention in the form of mediation, fact finding, or interest arbitration. A request may be made by either party to a public employment organization for assistance. Impasse is rarely declared early in the process, for the parties have not yet completely explained their proposals to one another. Nor have they actually engaged in negotiation.

Once impasse has been declared, however, the public employment organization (such as a state public employment board or federal mediation service) will assist by assigning as a mediator either a staff member or a member from a panel that it maintains. The mediator will usually meet with both parties and attempt to persuade them to modify their positions so that an agreement can be reached.

In the event that the mediator is unsuccessful or in those instances where impasse is declared late in the fiscal year, the assisting organization will assign a fact finder. This individual is usually requested to attempt mediation first, then to engage in fact finding. At one time, fact finding was an adjudicated proceeding in which evidence was submitted, and the fact finder made conclusions and recommendations based upon the record produced at a hearing, together with written arguments contained in a brief or memorandum. More recently, fact finding has acquired many of the attributes of mediation, and the resulting recommendations of the fact finder are usually based not so much on the facts presented as on the views of the fact finder as to what will entice the parties into an agreement. Today, fact finding deals less with issues of equity and comparability and more with issues of acceptability and mutuality. After the fact finder has submitted his or her results to the parties, the results become public and the parties are then given a set number of days to reach an agreement.

If an agreement is not reached, the process includes further steps. Depending on the state, the steps may include various parties (union, superintendent, board of education) making recommendations for settlement. In addition, the state public employees organization may be asked to provide additional assistance to help the parties resolve their conflicts.

Conciliation. In some states, conciliation is sometimes known as post-fact-finding mediation. Some governing boards, such as county, village or city governments, may retain the right to convene a hearing that will take into consideration the positions of the chief executive and the employee organization as well as the needs of the public. Thereafter, the board may, if it is empowered to do so, impose terms and conditions of employment that are usually consistent with the provisions of the existing negotiated agreement.

In a number of states, including Pennsylvania, Wyoming, Rhode Island, Nebraska, New Jersey, New York, Massachusetts, Washington, Minnesota, and Maine, school districts involved in a negotiations impasse may submit the dispute to interests arbitration if both parties consent to do so. This procedure has rarely been used and is not controlled by the contract, but usually involves matters dealing with terms and conditions of employment. Other jurisdictions, such as Oregon and Iowa, have arbitration provisions for resolving school district negotiations impasses. In both states either party may request arbitritation.

Job action/strike. If the negotiations dispute continues for an extended period of time, job actions, or in some instances strikes, may occur. Both parties have an obligation, derived from their respective statutory duty, to negotiate in good faith and to continue the status quo with respect to mandatory subjects of negotiations. In many states, public employees may not withhold services that are normal and customarily performed. Similarly, an employer may not reduce wages or withdraw other benefits that it has been providing, regardless of whether those benefits were contained in an agreement or not. It is the generally accepted obligation of the employer to continue all of the terms of the prior agreement until a successor agreement is negotiated.

Work actions.   The official steps involving third-party intervention vary from state to state. However, when these steps fail to bring about an agreement, the union may conduct work actions, such as work slowdowns. Often staff members will meet before and after school to enter and exit as a group. Staff may also be visible at board meetings, using picketing as a way to make their feelings known to the community. Sadly, these actions may also result in unethical behaviors such as refusal to talk to administrators, anonymous threatening phone calls, vandalism, and picketing the homes of administrators and board members.

Teachers who cut back on the amount of student work required (i.e. no longer requiring a term paper for classes that in previous years involved a paper), or who take a week to hand back papers instead of the normal two or three days, may be involved in improper practices. Should this occur, the administration should determine its right to require staff members to treat their responsibilities consistently with what they have done in the past. A school board must employ an attorney conversant with education labor law in such instances. When actions might be considered, consultation with the board's attorney should take place before such actions are instituted, to make sure that they are legal.

Strikes.   Some states, including Hawaii, Maine, New Hampshire, Montana, Oregon, Pennsylvania, and Vermont, allow teachers to strike under specific statutory provisions. About half of the states do not allow strikes, and in some cases outline specific penalties that may occur if a strike takes place. In states where strikes are illegal, teachers may still strike, even if they are likely to be penalized by the courts for engaging in such activity. Regardless of the legality of a strike, disputes sometimes continue even after such a strong response takes place.

When strikes do occur, schools often attempt to continue to operate and serve the student population. This requires that the district have a strike plan that identifies who could be employed during this period. It is unlikely that all employees will participate in a strike. However, a district may have to provide additional personnel to allow instructional and other activities to continue with as little disruption as possible. The strike plan may also include pickup points for personnel who do not wish to cross picket lines by themselves. A communications person, preferably an individual not involved with the negotiation process and not a key employee in the organization, should be in contact with the media. This would allow questions to be answered on a general basis, as opposed to involving the chief school officer directly responsible for the negotiation process.

Strikes should be avoided at all reasonable costs, as the division they cause between administration and employees and among the employees themselves will remain with a district for many years, and is difficult to mend.

Settlements. In concluding the agreement, various factors should be taken into account. Both sides must agree to the written version of the agreement. Checking the fine points in the agreement is the role of both labor and management, so that no questions arise after an agreement is accepted. Finally, the presentation of the final agreement for signing must be conducted and approved by constituents. After all these activities have been completed, distribution of the agreement to all parties should take place in a timely manner.

— MAKING COLLECTIVE NEGOTIATIONS WORK —

If the negotiated contract is complete and both sides are satisfied with the points that have been settled and included, fewer problems of interpretation are likely to arise. Often this provides for an era of good feeling. It allows both sides to operate by the agreement at hand. If the language is clear and definitions are complete, little is left to the interpretation of either employer or employee. To allow for questions resulting from differences of interpretation, or if a violation of the contract is perceived, the grievance procedure included in the contract will define the steps that must be taken.

The length of the contract is often indicative of potential problems or disputes in a district. Often, having something in writing may indicate distrust by one side or the other on these points. On the other hand, a thin or brief contract can cover the legal requirements in the negotiation process, and few questions may arise because of positive attitudes and previous settlement of issues before reaching the formal grievance process.

There is no magic in a contract per se; it may offer direction for dealing with the conditions of employment, but differences in interpretation can always arise, regardless of the size of the document. In the end, a spirit of cooperation and a rational approach to differences will have more to do with shaping constructive resolutions than any negotiated document will.

— STATUTORY OBLIGATIONS —

Requirement of Good-Faith Negotiations

The obligation to negotiate collectively requires both parties to meet at reasonable times and confer in good faith about wages, hours, and other terms and conditions of employment for the negotiation of an agreement. This also applies to any question arising about the terms and the execution of the written contract incorporating any agreements. The obligation to negotiate does not, however, compel either party to agree to a proposal or require the making of concessions. Simply stated, the duty to negotiate in good faith requires that both parties be accessible to persuasion and that consideration be given to proposals and to the formulation of counter-proposals. The process does not require agreement to any of the other party's proposals or to making particular concessions. Nevertheless, the totality of one party's conduct will be considered, in the event that an improper labor practice charge alleging a failure to negotiate in good faith is filed.

Unilateral Change

The independent obligations of statute and contract require that both parties adhere to certain standards. Neither party can unilaterally repudiate the terms of a negotiated agreement unless that agreement provides for such an event.

Both during and after the expiration of a negotiated agreement, a public employer is constrained by statute. To demonstrate that the employer is negotiating in good faith, the employer may only act unilaterally in those areas where a term or condition of employment is not changed.

The public employer may also make unilateral changes in terms and conditions of employment in certain exceptional situations where: the employer has negotiated the term and condition of employment; negotiations have reached a state of deadlock; and the employer has a compelling need to make the change. An example might be the implementation of the school calendar when negotiations have not yet been completed and school is about to start. In such situations, the employer will be permitted to make the unilateral change, provided that the employer is willing to continue to negotiate about the subject matter in dispute.

The law in some states is more restrictive on public employer flexibility than in others. Iowa, for example, has a statutory management rights clause that reserves to management certain rights that may require negotiation in other states. Michigan and Wisconsin follow the decisions of the National Labor Relations Board and the United States Supreme Court regarding scope and duty of bargaining as they relate to unilateral employer changes.

– CONTRACT ADMINISTRATION –

The administration of a negotiated agreement, once it has been completed, involves several facets. On a day-to-day basis, line administrators are confronted with the need to resolve a variety of disputes. Administrators should determine whether the dispute involves the terms of a negotiated agreement, or whether it is simply a complaint being brought forward for resolution. If the latter, a number of mechanisms are effective in providing a resolution to the issues presented.

The resolution of informal complaints should be dealt with in a sensitive manner. A school administrator, in particular, needs to be careful in recognizing that the provisions of the negotiated agreement control the relationship between the employee organization or a union representing employees and the school district. However, many complaints are unrelated to that formal relationship and can be easily resolved by a brief conference and an adequate remedy to what may be important to an individual, but is a minor problem in the school district.

Conflicts should be resolved expeditiously at the lowest possible administrative level. It is essential that distinctions be made between the resolution of informal conflict and procedures for handling contract violations. When a teacher appears at an administrator's office accompanied by a union representative and perhaps a representative from the union's regional affiliate, such as the American Federation of Teachers or the National Education Association, something more that a minor problem is probably involved, at least in the teacher's perception.

In most instances, a school administrator should not be resolving contract grievances with field personnel from a regional union office. In circumstances where regional field personnel are present, an administrator should consult with the school district's central office to determine the proper procedures to follow, and should not participate in unplanned meetings or discussions.

If the complaint is an allegation that the employer has not fulfilled its obligations under the collective bargaining agreement, then the administrator must adhere to the terms of the agreement and follow the procedures contained in it for the enforcement of its provisions. Under normal circumstances, such complaints are called grievances, and grievance procedures usually require specific steps to be followed in presenting the grievance, to give the employee and his or her representative an opportunity for a hearing, and for providing a response. Each of the steps is important.

– DISPUTE RESOLUTION –

Complaint Policy

In a civil action in court, a complaint begins an action of law in which a plea is made to a court, to inform the defendant that a suit is being presented and why, and to demand relief.

Complaints in schools are less formal and often are not covered by a negotiated contract. An unwritten complaint policy may be conveyed from administration to staff in opening-day remarks and an open-door policy. On the other hand, some boards of education have complaint policies that may be quite formal or at least provide a minimum procedure aimed at complaint resolution. Complaints are often equated with faculty-room grumbling. However, the wise administrator recognizes that complaints should be placed in two categories: those that must be heard, discussed, and used as a basis for growth; and those that should be ignored.

Many progressive schools have oriented their boards of education and staff to deal with complaints through a joint labor-management team. A process such as this can be valuable. It prevents problems from festering over a period of time, and also illustrates that the administration is indeed concerned with bettering the school environment. It may also reduce a lot of the hostility that arises at the bargaining table and consequently may simplify the bargaining process.

Administrators, like athletic referees, must sometimes learn to "not hear" a concern. Not hearing is not the same as ignoring, since often the administrator is confronted by a staff member on an issue. However, the administrative role, often characterized as a lonely one, frequently requires the administrator to do no more than be a concerned listener. Staff members want the administrator, as the formal leader of a program, school, or school district, to hear and understand the dilemma they are facing. Action is not required and often would not be appropriate, especially if the conversation deals with a personal problem. Recent conversations with school administrators have pointed out that in recent years the administrative role has taken on greater responsibility for acting as a counselor to staff. Administrators are trained to react, so the role of listener is often an uncomfortable one, but also a necessary one that is largely ignored in administrator training programs.

Grievance Procedures

In a labor relations context, a grievance is usually an alleged violation of the contract under which an employee is working. Additionally, a grievance may involve employees' perceptions that their health or safety are threatened, working conditions and/or equipment are unreasonable, or supervision has been inconsistent or unfair. Although there is no absolute definition of a grievance, the areas indicated include some of the broad categories under which grievances are often initiated.

The grievance procedure is the formal process that the aggrieved party and his or her representative association (usually a union) must follow to settle a grievance. A grievance may be filed by an employee, but the employee organization (union) has a statutory right to administer the grievance procedure. The respective rights of the parties are established by the terms of the contract. In some instances a contract may limit the initiation of a grievance to an individual employee, and in other situations the union may have an independent right to file a grievance on behalf of an employee even without the employee's consent.

It is advantageous to both management and labor to have a well-written grievance policy or contract provision. The grievance procedure should give both parties a good idea of whether the alleged infraction is covered by the contract and therefore grievable. In cases where an issue is not covered by contract, management may argue that it is their right to determine how the issue will be handled, and labor will argue that an issue not covered is not under the province of management.

Strictly speaking, an arbitrator, under most circumstances, does not have the right to rewrite a contract. An arbitrator is not empowered to change the intent or language of a current contract provision, nor can he or she, under ordinary circumstances, add an item that is not covered.

A standard procedure for filing a grievance may include the following steps:

1. A written statement by the aggrieved party to outline the complaint and specify what provision of the contract has been violated. This statement should include as much detail as possible: what happened, when, where, who was involved (directly or indirectly), and any other relevant points. The contract should also note that a copy of the written statement will be provided to the superintendent of schools.

2. After a specified period of time, such as five days, a meeting should occur between the aggrieved party and school administrator to whom the aggrieved party reports (for instance, a teacher will meet with a school principal). Following the meeting, the administrator will have another specified period of time (five days is common) to consider and respond to the aggrieved party.

3. If resolution does not occur at this level, the aggrieved party has a right to appeal. This appeal is usually to the superintendent of schools. The superintendent follows the same procedure used by the line administrator—taking a period of time to investigate, considering the grievance, and then responding.

4. Assuming the superintendent refuses the grievance, the aggrieved

party may then take his or her concern to the school board. The board generally follows the same process outlined in Steps 2 and 3. Presentation of the grievance to the board usually occurs during an executive session of the school board, attended by the aggrieved party, his or her representative (union representative and/or attorney), and involved administrators. Other individuals may be invited to attend this meeting, depending on the circumstances and board's approval. Members of the public are not allowed to attend the executive session.

A well-organized board of education will have one person, usually the board president or possibly the board attorney, designated to respond to any questions by the aggrieved party and his or her representative. Some board members may have legitimate questions, and this is the appropriate time to ask them, but members should agree that the board spokesperson will provide responses. There might be an understanding that any questions will be submitted by other board of education members and administrators to the board representative, who will then direct them to the staff member. The board should not make any commitments in this meeting. Too often an emotional appeal may clutter objectivity, and although board members may want to agree to give in because they are sympathetic to a problem, they might find themselves creating an inappropriate precedent that they would not want to follow in future grievances.

Such meetings can become heated. Personalities may become involved, a poorly worded comment may be made, and tempers may flare. Such instances have been known to result in name calling, threats, and occasionally even physical violence.

The best method for preventing problems in the meeting with the board is the education of board members. If members understand their role and keep individual involvement to a minimum, meetings about grievances should go smoothly. Many superintendents will brief the board prior to the meeting, as a gentle reminder of their role.

5. Whether or not the aggrieved party has the right to go to a next step depends on the local contract. Some contracts specify the meeting with the board of education as the last step to which the aggrieved party may appeal. In this case the board's decision is final.

Many contracts provide the right to appeal to a third party. In such an instance, members of both parties (the board of education and union) must agree on an arbitrator. Usually the arbitrator is chosen from a list provided by the American Arbitration Association (AAA). This list will contain the names of a number of arbitrators, and the parties to the grievance must agree on at least one. Often, because of reputation or past experiences with an arbitrator, one party or the other will refuse a number of the individuals whose names are on the list. However, if an agreement cannot be made by both parties, the AAA will assign an arbitrator.

What does the arbitrator do? An arbitration hearing usually consists of two steps: first, determining whether the grievance is legitimate—whether an infraction of some provision of the contract has actually occurred. Next, the arbitrator or third party listens to arguments by both parties, and then has the job of determining right, wrong, and a remedy if one is appropriate.

Theoretically, the arbitrator should first listen to arguments on "arbitrability." If the grievance is not determined to be legitimate, the process stops. If the arbitrator determines that the grievance is covered by contract and the merits of the case should be heard, the arbitrator will then hear the case.

Arbitrators often travel great distances to get to hearings. Additionally, getting all parties together (aggrieved party, administrators, legal or management representation, witnesses, etc.) is so cumbersome that hearing officers will often listen to arguments for arbitrability and merit at the same meeting.

Arbitrators will take notes, accept evidence, and allow each party to submit written briefs following the hearing. Rules of evidence in grievance hearings tend to be much more flexible than those involved in court cases, and the formal rules of evidence do not apply. After consideration of testimony and the other related points of evidence, the arbitrator will give a written finding that outlines the judgment.

Usually, once the arbitrator's decision has been provided to both parties, the process ends. However, either party may refuse to accept the judgment and appeal to the courts to have the case heard. The right to appeal to the courts exists, but courts will usually uphold the judgments of third parties. Appeals are uncommon and arbitration statutes only provide for review in few circumstances.

The grievance process provides a series of steps that ensure, at least theoretically, the opportunity for employees to be treated fairly and in accordance with the negotiated contract. The process is often uncomfortable for school employees for obvious reasons: teachers and administrators are people-oriented and feel that confrontation is not a common or desirable state; school boards are often made up of community members who do not understand the rational nature of the grievance process and allow personal issues to affect their perceptions; and schools are relatively intimate places where a great deal of person-to-person contact between administrators and personnel takes place daily.

Types of arbitration.   Two types of arbitration exist: advisory and binding. Advisory arbitration is exactly what its name implies. Although an arbitrator will come up with a judgment to resolve a grievance, his or her remedies do not have to be accepted by the board of education if advisory arbitration has been stipulated by contract.

Binding arbitration implies that an arbitrator's finding will be accepted by both parties. Binding arbitration has its roots in private enterprise.

The effects of grievances.   People working in schools are much like people who live in small towns: Everyone knows everyone else, and when a problem exists, no secret is likely to be kept. A conflict between labor and management may spill over into other relationships and areas. Because the administrator had to deny one teacher on a particular issue, he or she may suddenly feel distanced by other staff members as well.

Unfortunately, while many teachers who have been involved in the labor relations process can be objective about accepting the outcomes of grievances, others take their involvement personally. Just being involved in a grievance causes them to feel disenfranchised by the school administration.

As a result, many administrators are intimidated by the grievance process. This feeling may be the result of perceptions by administrators. They may believe that staff members will no longer like them and consequently fear that they will become alienated and lonely. A concern with the effective schools movement and the belief that effective administrators are leaders in their buildings may cause administrators to believe that handling a grievance will cause them to lose the ability to lead. An administrator may feel that losing a grievance would have a negative effect on the administrator and/or the system.

These perceptions may actually contain both fact and fiction. Judgement of effectiveness should never be based on popularity. Administrators who do so are likely to spend more time concentrating on relationships than on moving their schools forward. Additionally, administration is a inherently lonely vocation, and administrators should realize that they are headed for problems any time they base their actions on emotional support from or personal friendships with staff.

A well-handled grievance is time-consuming. However, allowing an infraction to become part of everyday practice can become an even greater problem. For example, a superintendent who wanted to be seen as a nice person allowed two teachers to take a vacation day prior to the Christmas holiday, a clear violation of the contractual agreement. The following year one-third of the staff requested personal days just before the Christmas holiday.

Fear of losing a grievance is one of the poorest reasons for avoiding the process. As one veteran labor relations specialist put it, "So what? At least it clarifies once and for all where you stand, and if necessary you can always try to change it in the next negotiations." This approach, shared by many negotiations specialists from both labor and management, provides one means of cleaning up confusing language that may have become even more confusing because of practices that have been allowed to occur over a number of years.

Violations Turned Practices

Even if a practice that is a contract violation has been allowed to occur over a period of time, administrators may not be required to live with the violation forever.

Violations can be brought into compliance through a fairly simple process that emphasizes good communication. For instance, one new superintendent learned that teachers were leaving the building shortly after their students were excused each day; students left at 2:30 P.M. and teachers immediately thereafter. The superintendent read the contract and knew that teachers were supposed to be in school until at least 3:00 P.M. In questioning his administrators, he learned that this early departure had been going on for a number of years. He also knew that many parents complained that their children needed extra help, but that many teachers were not available after school.

The superintendent knew that his best approach would be through the minimax theory of economics. Minimax theory states that a loss (unhappiness on the part of some staff) is going to occur no matter how the problem is handled. Consequently, the good administrator should try to minimize the loss that will take place (try to explain why he or she is concerned, in the hope that staff will understand).

In this case the superintendent asked each principal to hold a faculty meeting on the same day, to explain why the administration was concerned, and to let teachers know that the superintendent would be sending a directive to each faculty member about the need to be in school until 3:00 P.M. The superintendent also provided a week and a half before the return to the 3:00 P.M. limit would take effect. This provided teachers with time to deal with baby-sitters or other necessary personal obligations.

Grievance Administration: A Method for Analyzing Grievances

Responsibile approaches to grievance administration require a systematic method of analysis. The majority of collective bargaining agreements in both the public and private sectors rely on grievance procedures culminating in binding arbitration as the basis for enforcing contractual obligations. In analyzing an allegation to determine whether a grievance exists, a three-tiered approach can be utilized. The three tiers can be described sequentially as: (1) personal and subject matter jurisdiction exist; (2) procedures of the grievance provisions are being followed; and (3) the allegation of a violation has merit. The following details one method is recommended as a means of reviewing pending grievances.

Jurisdiction.   The concept of jurisdiction can be equated with authority. Basically, there are two types of jurisdiction: personal and subject matter.

Personal jurisdiction.   Personal jurisdiction can be defined as the right of the persons in the grievance procedure to be involved in initiating, processing, and determining the issues. A determination has to be made concerning the rights of not only the persons or organizations to initiate and pursue a grievance, but also of the right and authority of the persons to whom a grievance is submitted to hear and decide the issues related to the grievance.

Subject jurisdiction.   Subject matter jurisdiction involves a determination that the grievance procedure permits the type of issue in dispute to be processed as a grievance. The basic and most important determinant is the definition of grievance. Other provisions of the grievance procedure and contract may also expand or limit the application of the grievance procedure. In public-sector labor relations, a commonly encountered definition of grievance is:

> **Grievance shall mean any claimed violation, misinterpretation, or inequitable application of the terms of the agreement.**

Unless the claim falls within the above definition, there is no authority or jurisdiction. Jurisdiction predicates in grievance administration are important. Grievances should first be reviewed to determine the existence or nonexistence of jurisdiction. If jurisdiction is lacking, the grievance should be denied on that basis before attempting any further analysis.

Compliance with procedures.   After reviewing a grievance to determine if jurisdiction exists, a decision should be made as to whether the procedural elements of the grievance process have been followed. The analysis must ascertain whether the proper persons filed the grievance at the correct step or stage, and that all the information required to process the grievance has been submitted. Strict adherence to all time limits is a requirement that should not be overlooked.

Many grievances have been dismissed simply because the person filing this complaint did not fully comply with the contract procedures. Arbitrators will often uphold the dismissal of even an otherwise meritorious grievance that is procedurally defective. However, the failure to assert a procedural defense at the first opportunity has frequently been held to constitute a waiver of the right to raise that defense later. Thus, if a grievance is initiated in an untimely manner and no objection is raised at the first possible stage for response, management will probably be unable to assert untimeliness as a successful defense in later arbitration.

Determination of the merits. After a grievance has been reviewed to determine if jurisdiction exists and the proper procedures have been followed, an attempt should be made to analyze the claim on the basis of the substance of the issue(s) involved. Both the jurisdictional and procedural defenses must be covered before the merits of a given dispute are weighed. This is so even if the grievance is to be resolved by admitting that the allegations are meritorious and the relief requested is provided.

In grievance administration, school administrators often cannot determine whether or not a contract violation exists. Even if an administrator believes a violation does exist, he or she may be unable to provide the relief requested. In these situations, an answer still must be made and appropriate defenses maintained.

Compromise or a final decision may have to await action by the superintendent of schools or the board of education. If a solution cannot be found, arbitration continues to be an alternative. Accordingly, attempting resolution of the dispute on the merits is inadvisable without considering the consequences of failing to reach a settlement. In any event, care must be taken to preserve all existing defenses during the processing of the dispute.

Grievances that are properly filed and processed and that have merit should be resolved at the earliest possible stage. However, the remedy must be consistent with the nature of the violation, and it is not uncommon to deny grievances and proceed to arbitration solely on the basis that the remedy sought is inappropriate. Sometimes, even if the person filing the grievance is right and the employer is wrong, the dispute will not be resolved because of the relief requested.

Grievance procedures have been designed to resolve disputes relating to the contractual obligations of an employer to an employee organization. Although settlement of disputes should be encouraged, employers and their representatives must be mindful of the limitations under which they operate.

A grievance procedure is a technical and contractual device that requires both parties to comply with its terms. The failure to adhere to the established requirements should result in a denial of the claim. Management must, without exception, meet the specified requirements of the grievance procedure and preserve all available defenses during the administration of the process.

In reviewing the merits of a grievance, a school administrator must not only be familiar with the actual provisions of the negotiated contract itself, but should also understand some elementary principles of contract interpretation. For example, in what context does the contract language appear? Is it part of an article or series of articles dealing with a particular subject? If so, the entire article needs to be read as a whole, and attention should not be focused on a single sentence or phrase.

The administrator should look at the past relationships between the parties, determine how the clause has been interpreted in the past and question what the actual practices in the school district have been with respect to this particular provision. Do other schools in the district follow a different practice, or does the contract provide specific provisions for elementary versus the junior or senior high school level in the school district? What were the origins of the particular language? Is it relatively new in the contract or is it something that has been in existence for many years? Was the clause or the provision placed in the agreement to resolve a specific problem, and is the grievance now facing the administrator related to that problem? Have there been prior grievances on the issue? Does an arbitration award or court decision exist that affects the dispute? Is it possible that the union is seeking, in effect, to negotiate an extension of the provision beyond what was intended?

Term of art. Many clauses in a contract have a special meaning and can be considered as "terms of art." For example, the term "just cause" is a term of art and is a long-standing concept that has evolved over the past thirty to forty years.[1] The term has both procedural and substantive aspects. Within school districts the terms "personal leave," "personal business leave," and "business leave" are terms of art that have special meanings. The specific inclusion of one of the three terms in a contract probably has a distinct bargaining history with respect to that term. In general, the three terms form a continuum in which personal leave is viewed less restrictive and business leave is more restrictive.

Frank Elkouri and Edna Asper Elkouri have published *How Arbitration Works.*[2] This book is widely regarded as one of the standard references for contract administration and includes chapters on grievances, standards for interpreting contract language, use of substantive law, custom and past practice, and several chapters concerning substantive areas of contract disputes.

– CONTRACT PROVISIONS –

Negotiating the contract is a major activity that receives a great deal of attention in a school district, since it affects the lives of virtually every staff member. However, the daily administration of the negotiated agreement is even more important. Negotiators must not simply give in at the bargaining table, thinking that they are bringing negotiations to a close in order to get back to the business of educating. This idea may sometimes be attractive, but the way that teachers and administrators do that educating on a daily basis can be radically changed if contract language has been allowed that alters the way the district has previously operated. For this reason, administrators and board members must fully understand what they agree to in a collective bargaining agreement.

An old saw in the world of labor relations specialists says that the thicker the contract, the more difficult it will be to administer. In the view of management advocates, information that is not contained in a contract comes under the control of management. Although these advocates toil to keep contract language to a minimum, there will still be the need, because of legal requirements or local determinations, to include certain language in a collective bargaining agreement (CBA).

It is advantageous to school administrators to confer with their negotiators long before actual bargaining takes place, for two reasons. First, discussion of current language provisions should take place, to identify provisions in the existing collective bargaining agreement (CBA) that have caused or might cause problems with school operation. Changes in this language should be considered, and administrative staff should be involved in recommending these alterations. In addition, new language that will better serve the district's needs may also be recommended by administrators.

In conducting a review of existing language, or providing consideration of new language, administrators should closely examine the ramifications of the provisions that are constructed. The number of different provisions is virtually endless, but common themes are often found in employee contracts. The sample provisions through the end of this chapter are from the New York State School Boards Association's publication, *Negotiations Proposals to Achieve/Avoid – 1989*. The sample provisions are quoted here with the generous permission of the New York State School Boards Association.

General introductory language. Many contracts begin with general prefatory language that is often lofty, aimed at impressing staff members and other readers with the high goals of the board of education. In reality, such language does little to encourage the efforts of the district, and it may provide for time-consuming, costly grievances.

Example—Introductory Language

The board and association firmly believe that the primary function of the board and its staff is to assure each boy and girl attending our schools the highest level of educational opportunities obtainable. The board and association believe that the objectives of the educational program are realized to the highest degree when mutual understanding, cooperation, and effective communications exist between the board and its staff.[3]

Although this preface is broad and seemingly harmless in nature, districts have been held responsible for behaviors that appear to contradict the spirit of the language. For example, the provision that states the commitment to provide the "highest level of educational opportunities obtainable." If a group of board of education members decide to spend several thousand dollars to attend a national convention instead of providing an additional teacher's aide for an unanticipated overenrollment in the third grade, would a grievable offense have been committed? In the eyes of staff, possibly. In the viewpoint of the board, perhaps not.

Recognition. A major issue common to all contracts is determining exactly who is represented by the document. Many school districts, when bargaining first came into effect, allowed extremely broad recognition clauses to be included.

Example—Recognition

The Board of Education of the Knudop Central School District hereby recognizes the Knudop Teachers Association as the exclusive negotiating agent for all teaching personnel.[4]

Such a provision lacks specificity and would make administration of the contract difficult for district administrators, who might often question who they were dealing with and under what protection those individuals were functioning. By language such as this, would substitute teachers be considered part of the bargaining unit? What about teacher aides who work directly with children in instructional activities, or teacher assistants who function primarily in clerical roles, but who have indirect instructional roles?

Counselors? Librarians? School nurses who provide once-a-year instruction in health classes? How about an administrator who team-teaches a class with a staff member?

These questions should provide an understanding of the need for specificity in identifying who is represented by a union. Not only does it benefit the administration to have clarity, but the members of the staff are equally benefitted by understanding who is representing them. Unions cannot arbitrarily choose to represent a group. Members must, at some point, decide to be represented. Thus, identification of representation is neither arbitrary nor left to chance. In the end, the union is generally made up of individuals who share common interests; in education these are usually job interests.

Agency shop. An organization that operates as an agency shop is one that requires all members of the bargaining unit to pay contract administration and collective bargaining costs in addition to fees and dues to the union. Individuals must pay certain fees, but they also have the right to refrain from joining the union. In such cases, dues for political action activities should not be collected from nonmembers of the union.

Unions are in favor of an agency fee, since it provides them with additional financing for their organizations. School districts usually resist allowing the agency fee to be collected, since it requires that staff members pay money to the union whether they want to or not. In organizations where concepts such as academic freedom and individuality are held in high esteem, the idea of an agency fee runs counter to the beliefs of many teachers, administrators and board members. In one case, *Abood v. Detroit Board of Education*,[5] the Supreme Court found that a Detroit teacher who had refused to pay the agency fee had to pay whether she chose to join the union or not. As a result, agency fees may be collected from any staff member employed in a bargaining unit that has such a provision.

Acceptance of an agency shop provision would require employees to pay a portion of their salaries to the union whether they chose to be union members or not.

Example—Agency Fee

All regular full-time employees, who are not members of the union, shall, commencing thirty (30) accumulated working days after employment and continuing during the term of this agreement while employed in the bargaining unit and so long as they remain nonmembers of the union, pay to the union each pay period, a service charge as a contribution towards the cost of administration of this agreement and the representation of such employees. The amount of such service charges shall be equivalent to the amount required to be paid as union initiation fees and dues by those employees who become members of the union. The board of education shall, following each day period, deduct such amounts from nonmembers' paychecks and transmit the amounts so deducted to the teachers' association.[6]

This example not only allows for an agency fee but also requires a fee payment equivalent to the dues charged by the union. Boards and their administrations should seriously consider the acceptability of such language before agreeing to incorporate it into a contract.

Facilities access. The locations where union activities take place may vary. In some districts, staff may be allowed time and space for brief organizational and/or subcommittee meetings in the school's cafeteria or in a classroom. In others, any official gathering of union representation must take place outside of the school district's grounds; this often has occurred as a result of precedent rather than by contractual agreement. Some districts require the union to hold its formal meetings off-site. As a result, some unions have requested language that would ensure them space for meetings.

Example—Facilities Access

Members of the association will have access to the school buildings at times other than their regularly assigned working hours under the following conditions: Each September, at his written request, the board will provide the association president with three (3) keys to one (1) exterior door of each main classroom building; on or before June 30, each year, the association president will return all keys to the district office.

Members of the association wishing to enter the buildings at times when they are normally closed may obtain keys from the association president or his delegated representatives. Access to buildings will be limited to faculty members only.[7]

Such language provides a number of potential difficulties and should be avoided. First, it allows access during any time except when regularly scheduled school activities are taking place. Although the provision was originally made in good faith, complications could easily arise. For instance, the school principal might allow a community group to use the school cafeteria for the same time the union had planned a meeting. A question could arise as to who has the right to the facility. In addition, many districts turn down heating and air conditioning when buildings are not in instructional use, so extensive union use of the buildings at certain times could be costly. Finally, security could be a significant problem when hundreds of staff members might have open access, particularly during work actions or strikes.

Personnel files. Unions may propose a restrictive provision about materials that are admissible in personnel files. Such provisions should be avoided by management, since they could inhibit the inclusion of pertinent information.

Example—Personnel Files

A. A teacher's official personnel file shall include the following materials only:
1. Application for employment.
2. Official statement of courses taken and degrees granted.
3. Teaching certificate.
4. Military discharge papers (if any) and pertinent correspondence.
5. Requests for salary reclassification.
6. Requests for leave.
7. Requests for transfer or promotion.
8. Recommendations from previous employers.
9. Principal's evaluations made subsequent to July 1, 19__.
10. All commendations.
11. Communications relating to service with professional organizations.
12. Reports of disciplinary action taken.

B. Each faculty member's file shall be available for inspection only to:
1. The superintendent.
2. The assistant superintendent.
3. The director of elementary or secondary instruction or pupil personnel services, depending on which one of these is appropriate to the particular faculty member.
4. The director of personnel.
5. The building principal.
6. The faculty member whose file it is.[8]

There are a number of problems with such language. First, staff members would have access to employment information such as letters of recommendation that might have been originally submitted as confidential. In addition to a question of the legality of such a practice, this access would result in a credibility problem for the district with other educators. Second, such language is limiting, particularly in situations in which employee discipline might be considered. For instance, although reports of disciplinary action have been listed as allowable, communications that the administrator considers minor might not be allowable. This could get extremely complicated when a disciplinary report from an administrator to a staff member is followed by a letter. The report may be considered allowable by contract language and the letter may not. Letters aimed at counseling an employee might not be allowed. Thus, potential exists for a number of grievances to clarify whether particular memos are authentic "disciplinary action." Restricting allowable materials would also work against the district if disciplinary action were to be taken against the employee, since the number and kind of communications could well affect the judgment of a hearing officer.

This provision also makes access to files less available. Board of education members would not be allowed to see information that might be pertinent to decisions related to tenure or promotion, and this could conflict with law. If a serious disciplinary action were to be taken against an employee, the district's attorney might not be allowed access to pertinent information. Finally, if a new administrative position were created or a present position retitled, the individuals filling those positions might not be able to review personnel files.

Evaluation.   One of the most sensitive areas of professional functioning is evaluation. Without question, evaluation has provided a number of dilemmas for administrators and supervisors throughout the history of education. The classic concern still stands: Can a teacher and an administrator have an honest discussion about weaknesses without concern that such honesty will produce damaging results for the teacher? Such damaging results might include negative or critical comments on an observation report, fewer opportunities for advancement, or being perceived by the administrator as less than able.

Unions have made an effort to protect their members from evaluative observations except within the strictest framework. These efforts have resulted in provisions such as the following:

Example—Evaluation

All monitoring or observation of the work performance of personnel will be conducted openly and with full knowledge of the person observed. The use of eavesdropping, public address or audio systems and similar surveillance devices shall be strictly prohibited. . . .

Complaints of a nature serious enough to jeopardize the employment of a teacher, made to the superintendent's office by anyone, will be promptly called to the attention of the teacher involved.[9]

Such statements could prevent administrators from being able to monitor effectively the classroom activities going on in their schools. The requirement of full knowledge could mean any number of things. It might be interpreted to mean that administrators must provide teachers with advance notice of any plan to come into the classroom. It could also mean that if an administrator was passing a classroom in which havoc was occurring and the teacher had completely lost control of the students, the administrator could not intercede and then note his or her actions in a followup evaluative report.

The second part of the provision is also restrictive and should not be allowed in a contract. As noted in the earlier discussion of progressive discipline, an incident that might be considered relatively minor and isolated would not usually call for a strong response by an administrator. A number of similar, recurring incidents might draw a stronger reaction. Thus, a single complaint might not, at the time it occurs, justify being called to the staff member's attention by the criteria in the phrase "serious enough to jeopardize the employment of a teacher." Further, although an immediate supervisor might have certain feelings about the gravity of an incident, a superintendent or school board might not be willing to act on a dismissal based solely on the immediate supervisor's recommendation.

Just cause. The concept of just cause is aimed at providing job protection to probationary employees before they receive tenure. Although just cause does not provide safeguards as comprehensive as those given to tenured staff, just cause may require an administrator to convince a hearing officer that the decision to terminate the employment of a staff member is justified.

In many cases a contract that contains just-cause language will provide protection that becomes effective in the second or third year of employment. If just-cause protection became effective during the second year, the administrator could only dismiss a teacher during the first year without having to be concerned about going before a hearing officer. As a result, if teachers' performance is marginal, some administrators consider it best to discharge them during or at the conclusion of their first year, to avoid worry about a possible hearing the district could conceivably lose. This creates an unfortunate situation for new teachers who have the talent and capacity to become good professional educators eventually, but who may need a little more time to mature and improve. The just-cause concept is probably most controversial regarding its effectiveness in protecting employees. In reality, unions may be doing some members a disservice by encouraging the inclusion of such language.

Example—Just Cause

No teacher will be disciplined, reprimanded, reduced in rank or compensation or deprived of any professional advantage or evaluated adversely, without just cause.

Any such action shall be subject to the grievance procedure set forth in this agreement.[10]

This is an example of broad language that could provide problems for both administrators and teachers. First, the provision does not specify whether it is aimed at probationary teachers, tenured teachers, or both. It might be interpreted as replacing the statutory dismissal procedure outlined by the state; substitution of locally bargained dismissal procedures in place of procedures outlined by state law or regulation is allowable in some states. The provision also gives protection from being deprived of professional advantages as well as from negative evaluations. As written, such broad protection could make daily supervision extremely difficult for administrators, even in terms of making constructive criticisms in classroom evaluations. Another disadvantage of such broad language is that it could restrict the amount of information placed in an employee's personnel file. Should the district one day decide to discharge the employee, a lack of documentation could make dismissal impossible. Finally, many hearing officers interpret just cause as requiring the application of progressive discipline procedures for any of the actions listed in the provision. This interpretation would greatly increase the amount of preparation an administrator would have to go through to prepare a termination.

Although just cause has been of high interest to unions for inclusion in contracts, such provisions may work against them with employees whose performance is questionable. Inclusion of such language has usually been resisted by school administrators and boards of education.

Appointments and assignments.   Many teacher associations are using the empowerment initiative as an argument to allow staff members to decide who will teach what courses. These arguments are resisted by most administrators and boards of education.

Example—Appointments and Assignments

All professional staff vacancies, teaching and supervisory, shall be filled with personnel certified or approved for the position for which they are selected by the Certification Division of the [state] Department of Education.

No teacher shall be assigned within or without his or her tenure area, except with his or her consent.[11]

Such language provides a number of potential problems for supervisory staff who are responsible for its administration. First, unnecessary language is best left out of contracts. Since certification is required in order to take a teaching position, a provision that reiterates this fact is unnecessary. Additionally, in instances in which a certified staff member cannot be located, the district may have to hire someone on a temporary basis. Such language could restrict the district's ability to make such decisions.

The second part of this provision is even more restrictive and could make it difficult to place staff members in positions that would most effectively serve students.

Class size. A limitation on class size is a standard union request at the negotiations table. Requested provisions may read as follows:

Example—Class Size

The board and association feel that there is something to be gained through more individualized education. We feel that further concentration on reading methods in the elementary grades can be advantageous and should be pursued.

The board and association therefore agree that in some areas size correction is advisable in obtaining these goals, and are willing to take a meaningful first step toward solution of the problem in elementary grades K–3 in order to conform more closely with the recommendations of the commissioner of education.

To begin to meet this problem the board and the association agree to the following approximate figures K: 20–22, first: 22, second and third: 25 maximum. Within the school district, classes will be divided equally where possible with transportation and family allowances considered. Within a school, classes will be divided equally. If at any time during the first few months of school problems arise which could negate the preceding recommendations, representatives of the board and association would meet to discuss possible solutions.[12]

Language such as this can lead to a multitude of problems, due to its potential for different interpretations. The first sentence actually says little regarding class size, but could be interpreted as a commitment by the board of education for future efforts toward individualized education. The second sentence is equally broad. Individual teachers could argue that a concentration on reading methods abridges academic freedom if specific initiatives are taken with the understanding that a shift in instructional emphasis will occur.

The second paragraph is extremely confusing. On the one hand it notes that "size correction is advisable," leaving the impression that the determination is optional. However, it continues by saying that the board and the association "are willing to take a meaningful first step toward solution of the problem. . . ." This sentence might be interpreted to mean that actions will occur to bring class sizes in line with the recommended figures.

The third paragraph provides the same contradictory type of language, noting in the first sentence to "agree to the following approximate figures." The absolute figures in the language are not approximate. The next sentence, referring to dividing classes equally, could also cause problems. Virtually *any* classes could be balanced equally, depending on the district's willingness to make such a mandate. A number of dilemmas could result, including separation of children from the same family by requiring them to attend different elementary schools, additional busing, and possible misplacement of students with special needs, to name a few. The next sentence provides for similar potential problems. If classes at a grade level were balanced and then a dispute arose between a teacher and student (or parent), it might be advisable to move that student to another teacher's classroom. Although usually undesirable, especially once a school year has started, such a transfer is sometimes the best action to take in the long run. However, it could also mean moving another child who is performing satisfactorily, in order to comply with the language in the contract about class size. Management might interpret this language as a suggestion, but the fact that it was included in the contract provides for an interpretation that it is enforceable. As a result, administrators are best advised to refrain from allowing any language about class size in a contract, unless this topic is a required subject for bargaining.

Maintenance of standards.   Maintenance of standards provisions are often presented to novice negotiators and are to be avoided at all costs. Such provisions, synonymous with past-practice provisions, essentially require that the school district refrain from changing the working conditions of any employee without returning to the bargaining table to negotiate the change.

Example—Maintenance of Standards

> The association and the district agree to meet and confer prior to the adoption of any change in past practices, not a part of this agreement, which might have a substantial effect on the educational program. Insofar as possible, no substantial alteration will be made in the working conditions of any employee covered by this agreement. Existing board policies, procedures and practices pertaining to wages, hours and other terms or conditions of employment will remain in full force and effect except where modified by the terms of this agreement.[13]

By agreeing to "meet and confer prior to the adoption of any change in past practices," the district has consented to bargain any change whether the association agrees to the merit of the change or not. Using class size again as an example, if the district had no more than 20 students in a third grade classroom, and an additional third grade student moved into the district, the language might be interpreted to mean that the addition of one student would indicate a change in working conditions. Further, exactly what constitutes a "substantial alteration" could be a question that results in a number of grievance hearings. Finally, the breadth of this language also threatens to affect board policies as well as procedures and practices.

— SUMMARY —

This chapter provides a brief overview of the history of collective bargaining and introduces the collective bargaining process, including how school districts prepare to organize, and subjects that are mandatory, nonmandatory, or permitted for bargaining. It describes the typical makeup of a negotiating team and the roles of each team member. Various steps in the process are described, along with approaches such as win-win and win-lose bargaining.

The stages that occur during an impasse, when it appears that neither side is willing to compromise further, are also described, as well as the types of work action that sometimes accompany impasse, such as slowdowns and strikes.

The chapter also introduces the process of contract administration and presents methods for analyzing grievances based on jurisdiction, compliance with procedures, and determination of the merits of grievances.

A number of sample contract provisions are also presented, with an explanation of the implications of each of these provisions for school boards and administrators.

— REFERENCES —

1. McPherson, Donald S. "The Evolving Concept of Just Cause: Carroll R. Daugherty and the Requirement of Disciplinary Due Process." *Labor Law Journal*, Vol. 38 (July 1987), pp. 387–403.
2. Elkouri, Frank, and Elkouri, Edna Asper. *How Arbitration Works*. Washington, DC: Bureau of National Affairs, 1985.
3. New York State School Boards Association. *Negotiations Proposals to Achieve/Avoid — 1989*. Albany, NY: 1989, p. 2-1. This and subsequent examples in this chapter are reprinted with permission of the New York State School Boards Association.
4. Ibid, p. 3-1.
5. *Abood v. Detroit Board of Education*, 431, U.S. 209 (1977).
6. New York State School Boards Association. *Negotiations Proposals to Achieve/Avoid — 1989*. Albany, NY: 1989, p. 4-1.

7. Ibid, p. 6-1.
8. Ibid, p. 11-1.
9. Ibid, p. 12-1.
10. Ibid, p. 13-1.
11. Ibid, p. 14-1.
12. Ibid, p. 16-1.
13. Ibid, p. 17-1.

— 10 —

Conditions of Employment

This chapter reviews various factors related to the conditions under which employees work on a daily basis. Areas to be addressed include absenteeism and freedoms such as the flag salute, loyalty oaths, academic freedom, and freedom of speech. It also addresses teacher appearance, sexual misconduct, unwed mothers, staff involvement in political activities, search and seizure, indemnity of staff, educational malpractice, corporal punishment, employee records, negligence, negligent hiring, age discrimination, and the rights of substitute teachers. The chapter concludes with a discussion of employee assistance programs as a way to help teachers coping with personal difficulties.

Absenteeism

Several studies have documented the fact that students learn best when taught by their own classroom teacher. According to an Educational Research Service report by Porwoll,[1] teachers averaged eight paid leave days per year. Of the eight, 5.7 were used for sickness and the remainder for personal and family leave. The report also noted correlations to other factors that seemed to affect the number of days used: absenteeism was greater in larger districts than smaller ones; city districts experienced more usage than rural ones; and districts that negotiated their contracts had higher rates.

The use of sick days has been an issue in districts, since the purposes for which they are used varies. In some areas teachers take sick days when their children are ill. Some districts allow the use of sick time to extend vacations and for personal leave time, such as to close the purchase of a house or attend a funeral.

School districts should make a point of clearly outlining the purpose and use of sick days in their contracts, and the supervision and monitoring of sick days should be consistent.

— FREEDOMS —

Flag Salute

Teachers enjoy the same freedoms as other citizens, yet also have certain professional responsibilities that may run counter to their personal beliefs. For instance, teachers may choose not to take part in ceremonial activities such as the flag salute or pledge in their personal time, yet may have such responsibilities as a result of school policy to conduct the ceremony.

Only when compelling state interests intercede, as in activities involving the health and/or safety of students and staff, is a school district likely to be successful in requiring a staff member to adhere to a directive that runs against beliefs of a strong religious or political nature. For example, requirements for vaccinations have been upheld by courts.

Loyalty Oaths

In some instances teachers are required to sign loyalty oaths by the state in which they work. The Supreme Court has supported oaths that ask candidates for teaching positions to refrain from unlawful actions that would be a threat to the state. At the same time, oaths that require the signer to refute membership or association with subversive organizations have not been upheld, because their wording is vague and someone could innocently join a group without knowing that it had dangerous goals.[2] In summary, the use of a loyalty oath by schools is permissible if proper wording is used.

Academic Freedom

The concept of academic freedom, by its nature, implies an abstract that is difficult to define. As a result, the subject has received much attention in cases that have occurred in postsecondary institutions. However, some cases have emerged, particularly in secondary schools, in which the courts have attempted to balance the rights of teachers with the need of schools to maintain neutrality in the information that is presented to students.

The contradictory findings that have resulted provide no specific guidelines as to what constitutes academic freedom. In some situations, local school boards have been given the responsibility of determining values and levels of community acceptance; in others the courts have interceded by reinstating teachers who refused to obey a district directive banning a book.[3]

Speech

The right to free speech is protected by the First Amendment to the Constitution. However, the courts have also found that educators, because of their sensitive position in society in general and in their communities in particular, are held accountable for their behavior both on and off the job. As a result, the courts have sought to find a balance between the constitutionally guaranteed right of free speech and a school district's right to limit personal comments. Free-speech cases are usually the result of a school board's argument that what has been said is insubordinate. The Supreme Court ruled that the right to free speech is not an absolute, but that there must be a "compelling state interest" to overrule a teacher's right to make statements that are of interest to the public. In *Pickering v. Board of Education,* a teacher criticized a school board's fiscal management; the court ruled that Pickering's right of free speech was the same as that of any other member of the school community to criticize the official policies and actions of a board of education.[4] However, the Court also noted that an important basis for its decision was the fact that the teacher's criticism was not aimed at anyone with whom the teacher was in contact "in the course of his daily work," nor did it have any potential disrupting effect on discipline by immediate supervisors or maintenance of harmony among co-workers. These concerns will have an effect on a judgment. In *Connick v. Myers,*[5] another United States Supreme Court case, an assistant district attorney who was unhappy about a job transfer distributed a questionnaire asking fellow employees for their views regarding the office transfer policy, morale, and whether a grievance committee would be favored. In a five-to-four decision, the court found that her speech was unprotected, and noted the need to weigh each case on its individual merits.

Ratliff v. Wellington Exempted Village Schools Board of Education involved a middle school principal who criticized his board of education at a public hearing and was fired eighteen months later. The United States Court of Appeals for this circuit found for the principal and determined that his termination was a result of his public comments. As a result he was awarded approximately $175,000 for mental anguish, violation of his First Amendment rights, and back pay. The court found his comments to be constitutionally protected and that they were a key reason for his firing.[6]

Free expression also goes beyond comments made at meetings and in the classroom. Cases involving the use of allegedly inappropriate media to teach have resulted in the dismissal of teachers. In *Krizek v. Cicero-Sickney*,[7] an English teacher's use of an R-rated movie led to the nonrenewal of her contract. The court found that the use of the film was poor judgment and that the film was unrelated to the curriculum.

In a related case, *Fowler v. Board of Education*,[8] a fourteen-year teacher allowed students to watch an R-rated "Pink Floyd" movie that contained nudity, on the last day of classes. Although she had a student in the class cover the screen during parts of the movie she felt were inappropriate, she was terminated for conduct unbecoming a teacher. Fowler appealed her dismissal, using First Amendment protection as a defense. The court did not agree.

Appearance

A number of cases related to teacher dress have occurred and have provided mixed results. Although a board of education's right to require changes in the dress or grooming of a staff member whose appearance would inhibit the educational program would not be disputed, neither the amount of constitutional protection provided teachers nor the proof needed to sustain or overturn regulations have been clearly defined. As a result, the courts have not provided consistent results that can be used to determine what dress and appearance would be acceptable and what would not.

In some cases, districts have been allowed to terminate teachers for the refusal to trim or remove hair, beards, and sideburns. In other cases, schools have been required to prove the necessity for a grooming restriction before they were allowed to regulate or discipline a teacher for hairstyle.

One case involving grooming in the field of education that received a great deal of attention was *East Hartford Education Association v. Board of Education*.[9] In this case an English teacher, Brimley, refused to wear a tie and was reprimanded and directed to wear one. After internal appeals failed, a lawsuit ensued. The court of appeals pointed out the right of local communities to make determinations regarding daily operations, as long as those decisions do not counter basic constitutional rights. It admitted that although some determinations "may appear foolish or unwise," the court nonetheless may not overturn those decisions. In this case, the defense argued that Brimley's refusal was a form of "symbolic speech" and thus was protected by the First Amendment. The court found that the symbolism of Brimley's refusal was vague and lacked focus. Additionally, the Court noted that Brimley failed to show that the board's code was irrational to the point of being arbitrary. As a result, the board's right to establish and maintain the code was upheld. Although a board's right to provide a dress code has been upheld in other cases, a college instructor's dismissal for refusing to shave off his beard was held unconstitutional in *Hander v. San Jacinto Junior College*.[10]

– NEXUS –

In reviewing cases involving unusual behavior by staff members, it is useful to understand the concept of "nexus," which is often referred to when reviewing cases involving allegedly improper actions. A nexus is the establishment of a link between private behavior and fitness to teach. The California Supreme Court defined "nexus" as:

a. Likelihood that the conduct might adversely affect students or fellow teachers.
b. Proximity or remoteness in time of the conduct.
c. Age of the students.
d. Likelihood of recurrence.
e. Aggravating or extenuating circumstances surrounding the misconduct.

Consideration of a nexus, or connection between actions and ability to instruct, is likely to be a primary consideration in making judgments.

Dismissal for Alleged Sexual Misconduct

School districts, like other employers, encounter instances of sexual misconduct by their employees. Sexual relationships between employees and students form the basis for disciplinary action in most school districts. Aberrant sexual behavior that is not employment-related is a more controversial area, for it is unclear whether a person who is homosexual is automatically subject to discharge because of his or her sexual orientation. One of the leading cases is the decision of the New York Court of Appeals in *Matter of Gary Goldin v. Board of Education of Central School District #1*, Towns of Brookhaven and Smithtown.[11] *Goldin* involved a case in which the school district preferred charges against a guidance counselor for having sexual relations with an eighteen-year-old female student during the summer following her graduation. Goldin raised the defense that the disciplinary charge violated his constitutional right to privacy. The court rejected the proposition and concluded that "what might otherwise be considered private conduct beyond the scope of licit concern of school officials ceases to be such in at least either of two circumstances: if the conduct directly affects the performance of the professional responsibilities of the teacher, or if, without contribution on the part of school officials, the conduct has become the subject of such public notoriety as significantly and reasonably to impair the capability of the particular teacher to discharge the responsibilities of his position." In reaching its decision, the court relied upon the California decision in *Morristown v. State Board of Education*[12] and on *Beilan v. Board of Education*.[13]

In instances where a relationship has developed between a homosexual school district employee and a student, the matter is usually treated as one of sexual misconduct and discipline may follow. Homosexual conduct by teachers has often led to termination. At one time, allegations of homosexuality could result in discharge of a school district employee. More recently, however, homosexual status itself has been found not to form a basis for discipline or discharge unless the conduct meets tests such as those set forth in *Goldin*.

As with other cases involving highly personal, sensitive behavior, no existing standard would clearly be grounds to remove someone from the education profession. In *Sarac v. State Board of Education,* Sarac was arrested for fondling the genitals of another man on a public beach. He pled guilty to disorderly conduct and was charged with immoral conduct by the state board of education. He admitted he was homosexual and what had occurred. A nexus was found in that in "view of the appellant's statutory duty as a teacher and his necessarily close association with children, there is an obvious rational connection between the homosexual conduct on the beach and evident unfitness."[14]

However, in another California case, *Morrison v. State Board of Education,* the defendant admitted he had engaged in a physical relationship with another man a year earlier. He claimed the incident was isolated and that he had not felt homosexual urges in twelve years. The board revoked his credentials, but the California Supreme Court reversed the decision with three judges dissenting, saying the board had not proven unfitness to teach. In their finding, the court listed factors relevant to proving unfitness:

a. The likelihood that the conduct that occurred had already harmed students or teachers.

b. The degree to which such adversity might be anticipated in the future.

c. The likelihood of recurrence of the conduct.
d. The extent to which the action may have chilling effects on discipline.[15]

In summary, although the courts have been inconsistent, a general conclusion seems to suggest that teaching effectiveness is most affected, and a nexus established, when a relatively high degree of public attention has been proven.

Sexual harassment. Sexual harassment usually involves behavior by someone in a position of authority who attempts to use his or her position to receive sexual favors from a person of less authority. Title VII defines this concept in terms of supervisors and supervisees in employment situations, and also provides a basis for cases involving teachers and students in educational settings. Title VII states:

> Unwelcome sexual advances, requests for sexual favors, or other verbal or physical conduct of a sexual nature constitute sexual harassment when 1) submission to such conduct is made either implicitly or explicitly a term or condition of an individual's employment, 2) submission to or rejection of such conduct by an individual is used as the basis for employment decisions affecting such individual, or 3) such conduct has the purpose or effect of creating an intimidating, hostile, or offensive working environment.

The landmark case, *Meritor Savings Bank v. Vinson,*[16] established that the responsibility of an employer is broad and that although an employer is not automatically liable for the misconduct of an employee, neither is it automatically free of liability even if it has not been notified by an employee about an incident of alleged discrimination on the part of a supervisor.

Several cases of teacher misconduct toward students are found in education. Administrators should be familiar with the rights of staff members in their respective states, since some variations exist. In *Fadler v. Illinois State Board of Education,*[17] a tenured teacher was dismissed after being charged with fondling two female students. A hearing officer ruled that the teacher had in fact fondled the students, that his behavior was irremediable, and dismissal was appropriate. An appeal was made to a trial court, which upheld the actions against the teacher. On appeal, the teacher argued that his behavior was not irremediable since no harm to the student or district had been proven, and therefore a written warning was required before he was terminated. The court disagreed and found that sufficient evidence of harm to the students and school was provided to justify the board of education's dismissal. The harm involved damage to the trust put in teachers and the school system itself. As a result, a written warning would not have served an adequate purpose in repairing the damage that had occurred.

Overall conclusions cannot be drawn regarding such cases, and specifics of situations and pertinent laws and regulations must be considered. In *Brandt v. Board of Cooperative Educational Services,*[18] a substitute teacher was asked by administrators to resign after allegations that he had been involved in sexual misconduct with students. The teacher refused and requested a name-clearing hearing; the hearing was not provided, and he was dismissed. The teacher brought suit, asking to be returned to his position, along with back pay and removal of any material regarding his termination from his personnel file.

The court supported the teacher's termination, but found that he had a right to an in-court name-clearing hearing. The teacher brought suit again in federal court, claiming violation of his Fourteenth Amendment right to liberty, and requested a name-clearing hearing, damages, and attorney's fees. Liberty interest would involve an individual's ability to gain future employment. The court's finding noted that when an employee's liberty interest is involved in his or her dismissal, the employee is entitled to due process of notice and the opportunity to a hearing. In this case, the fact that such charges were included in his personnel file would damage his ability to secure future employment, since they could possibly be shared with a prospective employer. As a result, the teacher did not need to prove that the allegations against him were false in order to justify his right to be heard. On remand the employer demonstrated that it had not published any information from the employee's personnel file affecting his liberty interest and that publication would not occur. As a result, in this particular case, there was no requirement for a hearing.

The findings in sexual harassment and misconduct cases have varied and include any number of results: firing, suspension, reinstatement, name-clearing hearings, and quiet resignations with conditions agreed upon by the employee and district. Since the courts have not agreed on a consistent manner for handling such cases, and since laws and regulations vary from state to state, such consistency may never occur. Local school administrators should be aware of all laws and regulations affecting them. A local policy that outlines exactly how charges against employees will be handled should be established and closely followed.

Unwed Mothers

Several cases have occurred in which school boards have attempted to terminate the services of female teachers who are not married and become pregnant. Courts have usually upheld the teachers, with defenses based on Title VII of the Civil Rights Act of 1964, Title IX of the Education Amendment Act of 1972, and privacy rights. However, boards have had success in such cases when they have been able to establish a nexus between the teachers' condition and ability to teach.

— POLITICAL ACTIVITIES —

The political activities of a school district employee are usually protected under the First Amendment to the Constitution. Attempts by school board members or other employees to discipline or discharge a person on the basis of political affiliation have frequently resulted in litigation being successfully initiated against the school district.[19]

However, although teachers maintain their right to personal political beliefs, those beliefs cannot be brought into the school without qualification. A teacher does not have the right to expound political beliefs when the topic is not relevant to the school curriculum, nor can a teacher share beliefs without providing a balanced viewpoint so as to show neutrality.

Passive, symbolic speech has been upheld by the courts in *James v. Board of Education*,[20] when a teacher wore an armband to express opposition to the Vietnam War; the court did not accept that the armband condoned partisan political activities or interfered with the educational process.

— SEARCH AND SEIZURE —

Public employees, including school district employees, are protected against unreasonable search and seizure by the provisions of the Fourth Amendment to the Constitution. The standard to be applied before an employer may search an employee is one of reasonable suspicion as opposed to probable cause. The decision of the United States Supreme Court in *O'Connor v. Ortega*[21] indicated that where an employee has an expectation of privacy with respect to his files or work location, the employer is not free to make random searches. The employer must have a reasonable basis to suspect that the employee has engaged in a violation of rules and regulations or in other misconduct. If an employer has determined that the employee has violated a rule, the standard for the search is less than what would be required for a law enforcement agency to conduct a search.

— INDEMNIFICATION —

State and federal laws distinguish between types of immunity that may limit liability. Legal protection of school district employees is provided in some states; this in essence frees individuals from suits based on incidents that arise during the conduct of educational duties because the school district accepts any liability. Exactly how much liability will be placed on an individual will differ based on legal protections provided and on court decisions. In instances where statutory protection is extended to employees, their legal defense and payments for any resulting judgments may be covered.

— EDUCATIONAL MALPRACTICE —

With the exception of the state of Montana, educational malpractice is not recognized in the United States at the present time. Even in those instances where an employee acts in violation of existing standards, a cause of action is not created that would hold the employee liable in a civil action for damages. In this sense, malpractice must be distinguished from negligence and the failure of a school district employee to supervise students properly, with a resulting personal injury. Educational malpractice cases tend to arise from allegations of failure to learn or failure to diagnose learning problems and provide remedial assistance.

— CORPORAL PUNISHMENT —

School employees must be extremely careful about almost any type of physical contact with students. Charges of assault and abuse are common against teachers and administrators in school districts. Some states, such as Massachusetts, New Jersey, and New York, have gone so far as to prohibit, either by regulation or by statute, the use of corporal punishment. California requires parental permission, and others allow the use of corporal punishment, although even in these states a school staff member can still be held liable for injury.

In Texas, a state statute allows corporal punishment to maintain order and discipline in the schools. Thus, in *Cunningham v. Beavers*,[22] the court found that while the right to use corporal punishment was provided, students who believe they received disproportionate punishment have the right to redress through state common law.

– EMPLOYEE RECORDS –

A school district should maintain one set of official records on employees. Private records may be considered an unfair labor practice as in one case in Oregon, when the dismissal of two teachers was based on personal notes kept by the principal. Since these notes formed the basis for the ultimate dismissal of the staff members and they had no knowledge of or access to the notes, the state's employee relations board found that the failure to disclose the existence of the notes was a violation of the collective bargaining agreement.[23]

– NEGLIGENCE –

Suits against school employees for negligence have become more common in recent years, and as a result personnel should be educated regarding their rights as well as their responsibilities. Employees are expected to act with "reasonable care" in carrying out their duties. This was outlined by the California Supreme Court in *Lehmuth*:[24]

> It was not necessary to prove that the very injury which occurred must have been foreseeable by the school authorities in order to establish that their failure to provide the necessary safeguards constituted negligence. Their negligence is established if a reasonably prudent person would foresee that injury of the same general type would be likely to happen in the absence of such safeguards.

In *Logan v. City of New York*,[25] a twelve-year-old girl was asked by her teacher to fetch papers that had been left in another classroom. While she was responding to the teacher's request, the girl was raped by another student. The mother of the girl sued the school district for negligent supervision. The court found that the school district had taken precautions to protect students and that to prove the security was inadequate would require a historical review of violent instances that had occurred in the school.

This reasoning was reinforced in *Best v. Houtz*,[26] when an eighth grade student broke his elbow after he slipped in a puddle during a physical education class. In a suit against the board of education and two physical education teachers, the court found that the teachers had provided reasonable supervision and that neither of them had knowledge of the problem that had caused the puddle to form.

Negligent Hiring

Because of the vague nature of this concept, negligent hiring has become a popular ground for suits against school districts by parents and students. In *Scott v. Blanchet High School*,[27] a male teacher who was alleged to have had a personal, romantic relationship with a female student was relieved from his duties at a parochial high school. The father of the student brought suit against the school, charging negligent hiring, negligent supervision, and negligent supervision of a student. The negligent hiring charge was dismissed by the court because no evidence was available to prove that the district had not exercised reasonable care in hiring the teacher.

As outlined in the chapters dealing with recruitment and selection, adherence to a well-defined policy is probably the best defense against negligent hiring claims. The hiring of some individuals will always be regretted later by school boards and administrators, but care in conducting the hiring process will help reduce the likelihood of bad selections, and will also provide a stronger defense if a negligent hiring claim is filed against a district.

— AGE DISCRIMINATION —

Some school districts have instituted mandatory retirement for bus drivers, using age as the justification for their action, but the courts have found that age is a legitimate reason only if it can be proven to be a bona fide occupational qualification for an employee to function. In the case of school districts, a district must prove that the qualification is reasonable.

— SUBSTITUTE TEACHERS —

The status of substitute teachers varies by state, their rights are generally defined by state employee relations boards. The Iowa Public Employment Relations Board ruled that substitute teachers were public employees and consequently were entitled to the benefits outlined in the Public Employment Relations Act. In New York, substitute teachers have the right to organize and establish a bargaining unit including only substitutes, or to request admission to the bargaining unit of the teachers' association in the area where they are employed. In such instances the courts will generally defer to state employee relations boards, as in the Iowa case.

— EMPLOYEE ASSISTANCE PROGRAMS —

Staff members in schools may have the option of an employee assistance program (EAP) as one way to receive help in overcoming personal and professional difficulties. Recent contract requests by teachers' associations have often included the incorporation of such programs for staff members. The problems occurring in the lives of school personnel are no different from those of the larger population: adjustment problems with jobs; marital difficulties, including divorce; drug and alcohol misuse; coping with aging parents; and the stresses of parenting their own children.

Support of and interest in employee assistance programs are a response to these concerns and have been positively received by many employers. The same arguments may be made for supporting employees through personal difficulties as were made for retaining rather than firing employees: recruiting and training new employees is costly and time-consuming, a sincere commitment to staff members sends an important message to all members of the organization, and the skills and expertise of present staff should be utilized and nurtured whenever reasonably possible.

Personal difficulties often get in the way of effectiveness on the job. When this happens, an EAP can provide an easily accessible source of support.

Defining an EAP. While various models exist, an EAP is usually a counseling program and/or resource center that an employee may use at his or her own discretion. Involvement may result from an administrator's suggestion, but the decision to participate is left to the employee. In addition to counseling services, other assistance through an EAP may include social service, and health, financial and legal support.

Procedures. Confidentiality is stressed for individuals who choose to participate in EAP programs. For obvious reasons, people are often embarrassed to have others learn that they are having personal problems. As a result, administrators may or may not be aware of the fact that an employee has sought help.

Financing of programs. As a result of being incorporated into contracts, the cost of an EAP is usually covered through an insurance program, or a district may finance participation through a per-person flat fee.

Refusal to participate. Some districts have agreed to refrain from taking disciplinary action, at least for a prescribed period of time, against employees who have been evaluated as ineffective, if those individuals will agree to seek help. If employees are unwilling to participate, or if their performance does not improve, even with the support of the EAP, normal disciplinary procedures may be initiated.

– SUMMARY –

School administrators and boards of education have become increasingly vulnerable to lawsuits by employees. The potential for actions based on a variety of causes requires school officials to be well-educated regarding appropriate practices. This chapter reviews factors that may result in actions to, or by, school boards, including absenteeism and various civil freedoms enjoyed by staff members. It also introduces the concept of nexus (the link between private behavior and fitness to teach), cases of questionable sexual behavior, sexual harassment, search and seizure, indemnification, malpractice, and corporal punishment. Suggestions on employee recordkeeping are made, and cases involving school district negligence in care and hiring are provided. The chapter concludes with comments on age discrimination, the status of substitute teachers, and employee assistance programs.

– REFERENCES –

1. Porwoll, Paul J. ERS Report, "Teacher Absenteeism, Experience and the Practices of School Systems." Educational Research Services, Arlington, VA, pp. V–VI.
2. *Elfbrandt v. Russell*, 384 U.S. 11 (1966); *Wieman v. Updegraff*, 344 U.S. 1983 (1952).
3. *Parker v. Board of Education*, 237 F. Supp. 222 (D. Md.), *affd.*, 348 F.2d 464 (4th Cir. 1966).
4. Supreme Court of the United States, 1968. 391 U.S. 563, 88 S. Ct. 1731.
5. *Connick v. Myers*, 461 U.S. 138 (1983).
6. *Ratliff v. Wellington Exempted Village Schools Board of Education*, 820 F.2d 792 (6th Cir. 1987).
7. *Krizek v. Cicero-Stickney*, 713 F. Supp. 13 (1989).
8. *Fowler v. Board of Education, Lincoln County, Kentucky*, 819 F.2d 657 (6th Cir. 1987).
9. *East Hartford Education Association v. Board of Education*, 562 F.2d 838 (1st Cir. 1977).
10. *Hander v. San Jacinto Junior College*, 519 F.2d 273.
11. *Matter of Gary Goldin v. Board of Education of Central School District #1, Towns of Brookhaven and Smithtown*, 35 N.Y.2d 534, 364 N.Y.S.2d 440 (1974).
12. *Morristown v. State Board of Education*, 1 Cal. 3d 214, 461 P.2d 375 (1969).
13. *Beilan v. Board of Education*, 357 U.S. 399 (1958).
14. *Sarac v. State Board of Education*, 249 Cal. App. 2d 58, 57 Cal. Rpt. 69 (1967).

15. *Morrison v. State Board of Education,* 1 Cal. 3d 214, 461 P.2d 375, 82 Cal. Rptr. 175 (1969).
16. *Meritor Savings Bank v. Vinson,* 477 U.S. 57 (1986).
17. *Fadler v. Illinois State Board of Education,* 506, N.E.2d 640 (1987).
18. *Brandt v. Board of Cooperative Educational Services,* 820 F.2d 41 (2nd Cir. 1987).
19. *Harlow v. Fitzgerald,* 475 U.S. 800 (1982).
20. *James v. Board of Education,* 481 F.2d 566, 573, 576 (2nd Cir. 1972).
21. *O'Connor v. Ortega,* 480 U.S. 709 (1987).
22. *Cunningham v. Beavers,* 858 F.2d 269 (5th Cir. 1988).
23. *Oregon School Employees Association v. Lake County School District,* 93 Or. App. 481, 763 P.2d 160 (1988).
24. *Lehmuth v. Long Beach Unified School District,* 148 A.D.2d 167, 53 Cal. 2d 544 (1960).
25. *Logan v. City of New York,* 543 N.Y.S.2d 661 (1st Dept. 1989).
26. *Best v. Houtz,* 541 So. 2d 8 (1989).
27. *Scott v. Blanchett High School,* 50 Wash.App. 3, 747 P.2d 1124 (1987).

CHAPTER
– 11 –
Employee Data

The success of an organization depends on the effectiveness of its employees. This effectiveness in turn relates directly to the adequacy of the organization's personnel system. An adequate personnel system is anchored in accurate, useful information that the employer can utilize in making organizational decisions. The key ingredient in this is the kind of information and data that are accumulated. Employers differ and the data each seeks may vary. However, an organization's personnel system should respond to a number of critical questions:

What information do we need?
How do we get this information?
How will we use needed information?
How should information be processed?
What information should be retained?
How should information be stored?
How should information be secured and protected?
How should information be disseminated?
What legal factors should be a part of an information system?

The personnel system must systematically collect and maintain important organizational information such as personnel folders, records, reports, lists, and histories. For example, a district's employment needs could not be satisfied unless the information system identified the number of jobs to be filled, the kinds of employees needed, the skills and strengths necessary for the organization's continued health, and projected organizational requirements. Current employee information and its relationship to the long-range needs of the district is the essential ingredient in the conduct of an effective employee recruitment and selection program. To determine employment needs and ensure a stable and productive working environment for employees, a district should develop and maintain an employee information system that deals with at least three major areas:

Collecting data
Using data
Processing data

– COLLECTING DATA –

A school district should continually examine its data collection process. The information system that is developed should reflect:

Characteristics of current staff
Needs of current staff
Future staffing needs
Steps necessary to satisfy staffing needs that are identified

The method may differ from district to district, but consideration should be given to collecting the following kinds of information:

Employee background data: Education, special competencies and skills, outstanding achievements, previous jobs and positions, promotions, reasons for job changes, and job preferences.

Personal data: Social security number, retirement system number, birth date, addresses and phone numbers (regular and emergency), health information.

Employee evaluation data: Record and assessment of continuation and advancement, placement possibilities, need for assistance and training, and potential to satisfy additional needs of the district, such as teaching in different tenure areas, and advising or coaching abilities.

Employee position data: Salaries, fringe benefits, salary and fringe benefit history, attendance records, employment data, and promotion dates.

District needs data: Organizational chart, number of certified positions and their location, current vacancy list, current retirement list, current leave list, current resignation list, current preferred eligibility list, and projected position needs list.

Means of Collecting Data

There are many ways to collect data, but generally they can be categorized under two headings—oral and written.

Oral. There has never been a clear definition of what should be included in the oral collection of data. It is an endless process that involves the telephone, or casual or accidental conversations over the fence, at the market, or at the club; the process may be direct or indirect. Talk never stops, and whether it is directed or not, the oral collection of data invariably takes place, whether welcome or not, and occurs in a number of forums. The greatest weakness of the oral form is its lack of reliability. Administrators are caught in a double bind. On the one hand, most educated people acknowledge the potential for inaccuracy that occurs with information gained through conversation. On the other, often the adage, "where there is smoke there is fire," turns out to be at least partly true. Most administrators do not like to be the last to find out that an employee is involved in a situation that in some way affects the school. As a result, most administrators cautiously and quietly use their professional and personal networks to ascertain whatever information they can, then determine whether they should actively explore a matter.

The area of legal rights of employees is burgeoning with test cases. Administrators who decide to confront an employee about a matter that may involve questionable behavior should, before acting, be sure of the employee's rights as well as their own right to question the staff member. Even if an earlier decision was made to terminate the staff member for reasons other than the one in question, an administrator could still be accused of making the termination decision in violation of the staff member's rights. Thus, situations must be handled with forethought and planning. This planning should occur in conjunction with some type of legal counsel. Administrators should be aware of comments made about a member of the staff, be ready to weigh those comments judiciously, know what to investigate further, and be prepared to defend any actions, if necessary.

Written. Forms for collecting data on personnel are specific in content and include checklists, applications, standard letters, resumes, specified histories, evaluations, and other related materials. Accounts are more general in content. Examples include personnel studies, payroll lists, certification status lists, and seniority lists. The important consideration is that once data needs have been clearly identified, the format for collection and the person responsible for collection must be clearly defined.

The questions that need to be addressed are: Will data be collected by one person and then disseminated, as in a centralized system? Or will data be collected by a school principal or unit supervisor, then transferred to a central point, as in a decentralized system? Or will both systems be used?

Unless data are accurate and complete, they will be of little use to the organization. A vacancy list is of little value if it is not kept current. An inaccurate callback list for employees who have been laid off due to reductions in force is detrimental and can have negative results if one name is omitted. A budget cannot be developed and controlled if the payroll roster is not up to date; promotions may not be made if evaluation records are lacking. Keeping information accurate and complete is relatively easy with the use of new technologies, but may be expensive. Numerous systems can help in accomplishing this task, but costs are often a prime consideration when acquisition decisions are made.

Updating data. Also of key concern is the establishment of a screening system to review all data collected. Required data must be separated from unneeded, outdated, duplicated, or inaccurate data. Screening should be conducted on a regular basis, at least annually. Each form and account should also be corrected and updated annually, and one person, usually the personnel administrator, should be held accountable for this process, if the data system is to be of use to the employer. The collection of data is the first step in an information system and is critical to subsequent activities.

Using Data

Although Chapters 3 and 4 detail the recruitment and selection processes, brief references are made here to these matters, since they affect the employee data process.

Employee and institutional information should be used in securing, retaining, excessing, training, and projecting the workforce needed to satisfy the mission, goals, and objectives of the organization. This is the primary reason for having an accurate and thorough employee information system. Discussion here will be limited to critical workforce issues that affect the employee and the organization.

Recruitment. To identify the best individuals for positions, a number of candidates must be attracted for consideration for each available position. This can only be done when the information system reveals the number of positions open, competencies and skills necessary for each, salary and fringe benefits to be offered, responsibilities to be assigned, and education and experience required. Recruitment brochures, applications, letters, and various methods of advertising have to be developed, routed, mailed, and, when returned, collected and stored in a retrievable manner.

Selection. Once a sufficient pool of candidates has been established, completed forms and accounts are given to individuals in the organization who are responsible for the selection decision. Employee traits, background, and experience are evaluated by those involved in selection. Candidates whose traits and experience are compatible with position requirements are invited for interviews. Interview questions are also a key part of the data system. Questions should be structured to elicit responses that will further match the competencies of those interviewed with the position requirements. When references are called, responses should be documented.

Following collection, all employee data should be recorded and evaluated, so that a final assessment can be made and the position offered to the person selected as the best candidate.

All data accumulated during the recruitment and selection process process become the first part of the employee's permanent record. This record will be added to and updated as the employee accumulates a history with the school district.

Post-Selection

Information collected about unsuccessful candidates should be stored for a period of time, in the event of future vacancies and to accommodate applicable laws and regulations. Some states require that such information be stored for a specific number of months or years.

Once the employee is hired, the district initiates a prescribed orientation program (see Chapter 5). Each employee receives information about the community, the system, the school, and the position. Although the orientation program is standard in format, certain aspects, based on the needs of new employees, are emphasized. These needs are identified by reviewing the data collected about each new staff member. Data help to determine the kinds of orientation activities that should be emphasized for different employees. As the orientation process unfolds, additional data about employees may surface that will be appropriate for retaining in the individual's personnel folder.

— EVALUATION —

One of the district's most important personnel functions is to provide an effective evaluation system. This system should contain useful data for personnel decisions. It should give positive reinforcement to individuals who do their jobs well. It also identifies those who need assistance, training, and monitoring. Additionally, it initiates decisions about promotions, demotions, transfers, retentions, and dismissals. Finally, it initiates the recruitment and selection program by revealing the skills of the current workforce and the competencies needed in new employees.

Whatever system is used, recorded data should reveal the answers to the following considerations:

If the employee's performance meets the expectations of the district;
If the employee's performance merits consideration for promotion;
If the employee's performance indicates a need for assistance;
If the employee's performance indicates the desirability of separation;
If the employee's performance indicates special talents and skills for other jobs.

— TRAINING —

The evaluation segment of the personnel function leads directly into the training component. Training should serve the needs of the individual as well as the district. Training serves the individual when it improves performance and creates career advancement opportunities. Training also serves the district when employees improve and upgrade their performance.

Staff development efforts directly related to the ability to instruct students are usually of great interest to teachers. This type of education may be available through the district or through a local college or university.

In some cases, particularly when school districts find themselves witnessing dramatic fluctuations in student enrollments, it may be possible to maintain staff members by planning ahead. For instance, if secondary enrollments are dropping, a review of employee records may identify secondary staff members who are certified, or close to meeting certification requirements, to teach at the elementary level. Although some time and additional course work may be needed to fulfill certification requirements, by promoting this the district may be able to transfer internally and prevent the layoff of present employees.

– EMPLOYEE DATA AND COLLECTIVE BARGAINING –

The test of accuracy is critical when applied to collective bargaining. The negotiation process deals with many issues, but two are paramount: money and power. Money concerns include salary, fringe benefits, and extra salary for extra duty. Power includes virtually everything else, but in a real sense implies control over those who enter and leave the system. Power translates into protecting current staff members from infringement on their rights and promoting their ability to hold and conduct themselves in a job. Accurate and timely data are essential if a district is to plan and participate in the collective bargaining process.

Information on salaries, fringe benefits, certification, performance, vacancies, arbitrations, negotiations history, and any other relevant data dealing with personnel matters has to be readily available and accurate, to enable the employer to construct proposals and react to counterproposals. This need accelerates when a third-party arbitrator, mediator, or fact finder enters the bargaining process to effect a resolution.

– CAVEATS –

It is essential to identify who will have access to a district's information system and how that accessibility will occur. Only those who have responsibility for personnel decisions or those in confidential positions who provide support should have access to the information system, and then only to data essential for their personnel decision-making responsibilities. Thus, prime consideration needs to be given to the following questions when developing and implementing the system:

Who is authorized to receive data?
Who is authorized to access data?
Who is authorized to release accumulated data?
To whom can accumulated data be released?
How are data to be released?
How will data be duplicated?
Who is responsible for controlling, coordinating, operating, and making decisions about who uses and has access to the district's information system?

— PROCESSING DATA —

The collection and use of data rely totally on how information is processed and its storage and retrieval. The amount of data, the assortment of data, and the demands for data use and transfer will determine whether a district should consider use of an electronic or manual system.

Manual recordkeeping. Since all electronic systems require manual input, a small district might find that such systems require additional work without providing greater efficiency or faster information retrieval. In a small district with a relatively stable staff, data on areas such as tenure, seniority, and certification can be handled efficiently through manual recordkeeping. In many cases, selected records can be maintained on microcomputers. This type of system generally provides software that allows the district to compute and sort data; project costs, enrollments, taxes, and other related information; and then write reports based on the stored data. As the volume of data increases, small districts might look toward a regionally based mainframe computer to maintain and record personnel data. In some cases, with the increasing power of office computers, districts may be able to do a good part of their recordkeeping with an in-house system.

Electronic recordkeeping. Larger districts with vast amounts of data would benefit from electronic systems that store, update, and instantly retrieve all of their employee data. In some computerized systems, the updating of records in one file can automatically change the information in other files. This provides the capability to change the address of an employee in the personnel file and at the same time make the change of address in the payroll, retirement, health insurance, and business files. This type of system also provides immediate access to current data on questions such as tenure, seniority, certification, position control, retirement, and budget balances.

In addition, some systems allow authorized users to generate reports or lists from a wide variety of individual files. Other examples range from simple file management programs that store lists, to full-fledged database management systems that allow linking of different data files and include their own programming languages to meet individual needs.

— FREEDOM OF INFORMATION —

Periodically, school districts are faced with requests from community members asking for information about a particular employee. Fulfilling such requests may or may not be legal, depending on the nature of the information requested and the laws governing records protection in that state. The federal government and individual states work under freedom of information laws. Federal laws essentially govern the maintenance of records by federal or federally funded agencies. State laws usually differ from federal ones, and the requirements vary from one state to the next. A personnel office is especially sensitive to freedom of information requests, and administrators must understand their responsibilities in handling these requests. State agencies are generally glad to provide descriptive information and answer questions.

In the best interest of a school district, *one* individual should be responsible for handling all information requests. This process provides a number of advantages. First, a district would be unlikely to need a number of people trained in this area; one expert in a district is sufficient. Second, having one person handle all requests will ensure greater consistency in the way inquiries are handled.

— SUMMARY —

A formidable amount of data is generated in the operation of a school district. Organization and access to information are critical. Additionally, accountability for maintaining information and for making that information available to the public is the legal responsibility of every school district.

The personnel function, and ultimately much of the health of a school district, is based on the employee information system. The adequacy of the system is related to the accuracy and thoroughness of the data collected, processed, and then applied.

— 12 —

Administering Support Staff

"We're treated like second class citizens."
"No one communicates with us."
"We realize we aren't teachers, but we'd at least like to be treated with respect."

These are actual comments made by support staff members in a survey. Ask any administrator, "Who has the greatest influence on your ability to do your job successfully?" The vast majority of veteran administrators will say, "My secretary."

Unfortunately, support staff are often the forgotten people in the education business. The irony to this lies in the fact that the majority of support staff members in most school districts are residents, often long-term, and are far more involved in the fabric of the community than most of the teaching and administrative staff.

A review of most school district contracts will show a great difference in the salaries and benefits of support staff members in relation to those of educators and administrators. The fact that professional staff (administrators and those working under the teachers' contract) usually make significantly more money than support staff members is due to educational background and job responsibilities. However, it is sad to observe that other benefits given to support staff are often less than those of the professionals. A number of factors contribute to this. For instance, support staff members are generally less educated and often feel intimidated in the labor relations arena when negotiations take place. Support staff are usually grouped into smaller units within a district and are often fragmented; whereas teachers meet and confer in the faculty room on a daily basis, support staff members do not have planning periods that provide the chance to congregate. In many districts, a number of support staff bargaining units exist, for bus drivers, maintenance workers, food service personnel, etc. Such a breakdown provides for greater common interests within groups, but it substantially reduces the ability of the total support staff to unite and pressure management by lobbying. Finally, although teachers in schools usually are the first to give credit to the importance of support staff members, teachers will usually not go out of their way to assist support staff in any substantial manner.

– NATURE OF SUPPORT STAFF POSITIONS –

Support staff operate under various titles. "Noncertificated" and "noninstructional" have both been used in the past to label members of this group. The positions support staff are asked to fill are the most diverse in a school district. Teachers may be categorized by level (elementary, middle level, high school) or subject (science, math, physical education, etc.), but they all conduct themselves in behaviors that are similar—instruction of children. Likewise, although the responsibilities of administrators and supervisors may be different, their general duties still place them under the heading of "bosses," with similar overall goals to achieve within the district.

The diversity of the support staff's responsibilities sets them apart from other members of a district's staff. The variation in duties from the boiler room to the cafeteria, or the office to the playgrounds, results in a number of different job interests. However, some generalities should also be applied in the way jobs are constructed, so that employees have a better understanding of what is expected of them and how their success will be evaluated.

– SUPERVISION –

The matter of who supervises a support staff member usually depends on the size of the district and the location of the position. In many districts, responsibility for the supervision of support staff goes to the assistant superintendent for business or business administrator. This may vary, and in districts large enough to have a personnel director, this individual may have supervisory responsibility for support staff.

In smaller districts, the superintendent or a business manager will often take direct responsibility for support staff. Responsibility is sometimes split, depending on the district and the interests and abilities of the superintendent and his or her business manager. In others, support staff supervision may be decentralized so that each school administrator has responsibility for respective support staff members.

Supervision of support staff members is often difficult to outline clearly in terms of "line-staff" relationships. For instance, building maintenance personnel may be in the "line" of a maintenance supervisor, but on a snowy, wet day on which potentially dangerous conditions exist in a hallway, a principal may ask the building janitor to give immediate attention to the wet floor. Obviously, it would be time-consuming and inefficient for a building administrator to have to locate the head of maintenance, who could be anywhere in the district, to ask him or her to have the janitor mop the floor.

In many districts, the support staff working in individual buildings report directly to the building administrator when needed for unexpected duties, and report to the head of maintenance for normal daily schedules and responsibilities, special projects, and summer and vacation duties. This may cause problems in some districts, especially if a new administrator enters and has a different idea of how support staff members should function. The best way to keep such problems from occurring is to have line-staff responsibilities clearly outlined on the district's organizational chart, accompanied by job descriptions in the school board's policy handbook. Although always open to review and revision, such information should at least answer concerns a new administrator might have regarding the district's organization.

– RATING POSITIONS –

As with the hiring of professional staff, the first step to take place in hiring support staff is determining whether the need for a position exists, for either a new position or one that has been vacated. A review of district needs in relation to the job should take place. If the position is needed, a review to determine whether changes in the job responsibility of an existing position might be warranted should also be considered.

Once review has been completed and the determination made to fill the position, the employees who are candidates should have a clear understanding of the position and how its responsibilities and remuneration have been determined. In addition, the district should decide whether any change or reclassification must be approved by the appropriate civil service office, if the position falls under their authority.

Once responsibilities have been determined, a position description should be developed. This description should include an explanation of work responsibilities; the minimum education, knowledge, skills, and abilities required; any special requirements for the job; relationship to other positions; and benefits and remuneration that can be expected.

Work responsibilities. This includes a list of the job functions an employee will be responsible for during the course of his or her duties, and should provide an approximate breakdown of the percentage of time in each major function. The list may not include every duty (and this fact should be noted), but it should at least enumerate major functions in order of importance. These functions should be clearly outlined in recognizable language; educationese should be avoided.

Education, knowledge, skills, and abilities. If minimum educational requirements exist, these should be listed. How additional requirements, such as knowledge, have been fulfilled may be more flexible. For instance, former job or training experiences may be acceptable. In terms of skills, the ability to perform certain job-related tasks may be required and should be listed.

Special requirements. Any special licensing or certification required should also be listed. For instance, a position that requires driving a school bus may mean that a particular age must have been reached and a license is needed, depending on the stage.

Relationships to other positions. Individuals should know who they will be reporting to and that person's authority. Likewise, they should know whether any staff members will be reporting to them. Finally, if they will be working closely with other persons, that information should also be provided.

Benefits and remuneration. An applicant might find a position very attractive, but cannot consider it because of financial reasons. Consequently, pay should be listed so prospective candidates will know before filing an application whether the salary and benefits will be acceptable. Making this information clear from the first may reduce unnecessary paperwork and time in screening and interviewing.

Job rating. One practice often used in rating support staff positions involves the use of a point system based on various job-related factors. Major categories are established that are common to most support staff positions. Examples of categories include: ability, responsibility, safety, demands, and work conditions. Once the categories have been established, appropriate job-related factors are identified and assigned points on a scale. Once points have been assigned to each factor, they are added and each position is provided with a maximum total. This total is used to determine how positions should be ranked and remunerated.

JOB RATING

This job rating is based on the following criteria:

Category: *Ability*

Educational Background

Level 1:   Requires demonstrated ability to read and write simple directions and non-technical information. No diploma or degree requirement (1–5 points).

Level 2:   Requires a high school diploma. Must be able to do literal and basic interpretation. Requires demonstrated experience with reading manuals and instrumentation (6–10 points).

Level 3:   Requires a high school diploma. Must be able to pass state test for certification to operate appropriate equipment (11–15 points).

Level 4:   Requires two years of college or demonstrated ability. Involves the ability to interpret technical information from engineering manuals, blueprints, and architectural drawings (16–20 points).

Level 5:   Requires a degree in engineering. Must be able to read and interpret engineering manuals, blueprints, and architectural drawings; identify and repair problems; complete reports to governmental agencies; and handle compliance requirements for governmental agencies (21–25 points).

Factors	*Points Assigned*
1. Educational background	_____
2. Experiential background	_____
3. Demonstrated expertise	_____

The example in the box on page 261 would be used to rate educational background requirement. A separate rating would be developed for the other factors.

— RECOGNIZING SUPPORT STAFF —

Inherent differences exist in comparing the responsibilities of support staff jobs to the positions of other school staff. The empowerment movement by teachers stresses the importance of feeling some control over one's work life. The same concerns are echoed by support staff members, who may feel that they are at the bottom rung of a school district's decision-making hierarchy. A number of factors contribute to this. Support employees have much less autonomy, both in making decisions and in structuring their daily schedules. Additionally, the types of tasks they are asked to do vary greatly. At one moment a support staff member may be responsible for the safety of a number of children in a bus on a treacherous road, and a short time later the same person may be directed to clean up the result of a child's becoming ill in the school's entrance.

These differences often contribute to feeling inferior. The feeling of being second-class citizens is reinforced not only by the discrepancy in salary and benefits that often exists, but also as a result of being left out of many of the daily operations and opportunities available to teachers, administrators, and board members in schools. For instance, significant amounts are usually budgeted to provide professional and management groups with the chance to attend conferences and workshops, or to receive on-site staff development, but often such opportunities do not exist for support staff members. Try to think of the last time an inservice day for staff members included programs for support staff members as well as teaching staff.

Another example deals with working conditions. As discussed in Chapter 13 (Empowering Teaching Staff), labor-management committees have become popular for resolving the concerns of teaching staff members. Unfortunately, support staff representation on such committees or parallel committees for support staff are not common.

Wise administrators realize the importance of support staff and the amount of power they have to make a school function effectively. The influence of support staff is more subtle than that of teaching staff, but it can also be more powerful in the long run. Teaching staff may become publicly vociferous during a difficult contract negotiation and, along with their union, are often sophisticated in how to use the press to stir up public support. However, this strategy may not always work, since some teaching staff may not be community members, and since the demands of teaching staff have a direct effect on the amount of money local taxpayers must provide, so teachers may not always receive a great deal of community sympathy. On the other hand, support staff members are usually well established in the community, and dissatisfaction with the way they have been treated by an administrator is more likely to be shared over a cup of coffee in the local diner or at the supermarket. Such comments can and do spread quickly and have the potential to affect reputations significantly.

Roles. The importance of support staff cannot be overstated. Consider their roles alone. The importance of first impressions is acknowledged. The office secretary is the first individual a parent or outsider to the district will meet. Even prospective job candidates have been known to mention how impressed they were by the way they were treated by the school secretary. However, when an individual walks into an office and is ignored while standing at a counter, or is required to wait while the secretary is engaged in a conversation with a co-worker about a personal matter, the impression of the entire office is affected. As a result, the secretary who offers to take a coat, offers a cup of coffee and a comfortable seat, and tells the visitor, "Dr. Smith is on the telephone and should be with you shortly," creates a powerful impression.

Maintenance and transportation staff are equally important to the operation of a school district. Many districts, especially those with relatively small school populations, have only one or two employees with jobs that require critically important knowledge and skills. (Critical is used here to define a function that could mean the difference between whether school might be opened or closed.) For instance, a small school may have only one person on staff who is knowledgeable about the workings of boilers. On the cold January day when the main boiler breaks down and the backup does not want to start, a school may have to cancel attendance if the boiler expert is out of the district. The operation of the district bus garage could be a similar concern; if the one maintenance mechanic is ill or away from work, a district may find itself in a crisis. Safety is always a critical issue in school districts. Think for a moment of the responsibility placed on a school bus driver, who may be charged with the safety of sixty or more students at a time on any given day.

These examples are common ones that can be generalized to almost every support staff area in every school district. The impact is felt directly on the instructional program. If students are not in school, they are not learning. If they are in school and the library aide is out for the day due to illness, the instructional program suffers because the library cannot be opened when the librarian is off for lunch.

Needs. A literature search about the role and support of staff members results in little information. Although they play a crucial part in schools, little attention has been paid to the needs of these employees. The importance of keeping up with one's area is taken for granted in other professions—teaching, law, medicine, etc., but little attention is paid to the needs of support staff.

Providing inservice training for support staff personnel would result in a number of benefits. First, it would give them an opportunity to improve at what they do. Just as administrators and teachers try to sharpen their skills so they can better serve children, support staff need to gain information and abilities that will allow them to perform better the duties they have been assigned. Second, as noted, this group often suffers from the feeling that the perquisites provided to teachers, administrators, and board members are unfair, since support staff work equally hard, and also happen to be members of the public who pay the taxes to support those privileges. Finally, inservice training for support staff would provide administrators the opportunity to send them a positive message. A periodic pat on the back may be appreciated, but actions do speak louder than words. The financial investment in programs for support employees may be more than the cost of substitutes to cover their job areas while a program takes place or additional dollars for after-school participation. The payback will be more than just the appreciation that someone cares enough to listen and provide them an opportunity. Better skills and higher morale are likely to result in staff members who are willing to go the extra step when asked.

With regard to constructing staff development programs for adult learners, Hendrickson[1] presented several factors that should be considered. Some of these included:

a. Consideration of the relationship between a pleasant social atmosphere and a satisfying educational experience.

Providing inservice with style is essential. The ever-present feeling of being looked down upon must be replaced with a classy environment. The same amenities afforded professionals should be provided to support staff. If an administrator's goal is to make staff members feel important, they must be treated as significant persons.

b. Involvement in the staff development experience.

Educators are sensitive to the need for involvement by learners of all ages, and involvement is especially important in addressing adult learners. Students and teachers are used to sitting in classrooms for lengthy periods of time; most support staff members are used to active, busy schedules.

Asking them to learn by listening rather than doing may result in little attention to the goals of a staff development effort.

c. Utilizing employees as a prime teaching resource.

The best teachers are the people who roll up their sleeves and actually do the job each day. The amount of talent, skills and knowledge that exist among the staff members of a school district is usually very impressive. Using these valuable resources provides a number of benefits. First, it recognizes individuals and gives them a chance to receive some attention from administrators and colleagues. Second, the intimidation factor that may result from use of an outsider is prevented. People are likely to feel comfortable with a fellow employee and may be more willing to ask questions and engage in discussion. Finally, the best inservice programs provide follow-up and do not let an initiative end at the close of the session. An expert on staff can provide that follow-up for an extended period of time, whereas an outside consultant is not as accessible.

d. The importance of concrete, immediate goals.

Staff development efforts for professionals are often initiated with a theoretical background that lays out the rationale for particular approaches. This is a logical first step, but programming for support staff should emphasize practical, useful ideas and methods that can be used to help them do their jobs more effectively.

e. Recognition of the potential for physical and mental fatigue.

Participants in staff development efforts, particularly those not used to spending time in classroom environments, may find workshops to be difficult experiences. Taking in large amounts of information at one time may result in a feeling of overload. "Chunking," or taking in smaller amounts of information in separate sessions may be a better way of approaching the inservice needs of support staff.

Another consideration should be given to planning sessions strategically. For instance, use of inservice days may be preferable to asking staff members to stay after work, which would lengthen what may have already been a long day.

Programming

In addition to training programs that will allow employees the opportunity to learn and upgrade job-related skills, Castallo and Papalia[2] noted general areas that all support staff would be likely to find useful.

Stress management. Due to the stressful nature of the positions held by many support staff, stress management is often of interest, since it will help employees deal with concerns related to their positions and have the potential for greater happiness, satisfaction, and physical health in their personal lives. Programs that provide the means to identify stress and methods for dealing with stressors are usually high-interest topics. Involving staff in discussions with colleagues not only results in personal benefits, but makes them aware that they are not the only ones suffering from stress-related concerns. The screens that many individuals use to block discussion of such matters are more likely to disappear when stress reduction is the focal point in a workshop environment and other people are also opening up and sharing their feelings.

Communications. Communication skills are another topic of common concern. The diversity of skills among support staff makes this an interesting topic, since some of the district's best communicators are its school secretaries, who practice communication activities over the telephone, in written form, and in face-to-face meetings each day. At the other extreme, many support staff members are almost never asked to engage in written communication, their use of the telephone may be minimal, and their amount of face-to-face communication is often limited. At the same time, all of these individuals are critical to a district's successful operation and a commonly heard complaint is that they are not communicated with effectively. As a result, programs that focus on communication with and between members of the support staff are almost always timely and fruitful.

Time management. Another general topic of interest to most staff members involves better management of time. Helping staff identify how they use their time, what activities they engage in that waste their time, and teaching them how to plan by prioritizing their work responsibilities are likely to be of interest.

Although these are general topics, each subgroup from the support staff will have job-specific concerns that can be addressed. A review of interests raised with administration may provide a good starting point for developing appropriate programming. Formal needs assessments can also be developed in conjunction with staff, as a means of identifying areas of interest. More knowledge on safety issues such as toxic substances; types of word processing programs available to secretarial staff; and discipline programs for bus drivers—such programs will provide all staff members with the opportunity to get better at what they do. The opportunity will be most appreciated if it is presented in a manner that is interesting, meaningful, and treats participants with dignity.

– SUMMARY –

Support staff members in a school district are often overlooked and their importance understated. Because the work locations of these employees are throughout a district, and their self-esteem is often less than that of professionals, they frequently feel that they receive less respect than other employees. A motivated support staff will have a great effect on a school district in terms of climate and areas such as physical appearance and efficiency.

One of the most obvious differences between support staff and professionals is the wide variety of duties associated with support positions. Because of the diverse nature of support jobs, many districts find that a rating process that outlines employment-related categories, such as ability, responsibility, safety, demands, and work conditions, provides a fair and objective means of setting hiring and salary determinations.

Many personnel administrators have recognized the importance of a motivated support staff. Ongoing staff development has been accepted as a primary means of acknowledging the significance of the roles these employees perform, and of providing them with the opportunity to learn and expand their abilities.

– REFERENCES –

1. Hendrickson, Andrew. "Adult Learning and the Adult Learner." *Adult Leadership*, Vol. 14, No. 8 (Feb. 1966), pp. 255, 256, 286, 287.
2. Castallo, Richard, and Papalia, Anthony. "'Hey, What About Us?': Professional Development for Non-Professional Staff." *Impact on Instructional Improvement*, Vol. 21, No. 1 (Spring 1987).

— 13 —

Empowering Teaching Staff

A review of labor history in schools shows that the advent of collective bargaining in the 1960s and 1970s in many states, accompanied by an increased membership in unions, resulted in the adoption of what was the most common format for labor relations at that time, the industrial model. This approach was also known as distributive or win-lose bargaining. The basic principle behind such bargaining was that a finite amount of authority or power existed. Inherent in this model was the fact that when decisions had to be made, boards of education had the authority to give or keep, depending on what they decided. On the other side, unions had the advantage of numbers.

Students and communities often found themselves feeling like pawns in a power struggle between giants. Failure to support their school board would send several messages. First, that the board members did not have their support. Second, that more costly operation of the schools was acceptable, since many of the issues had direct or indirect financial impact. Third, that lesser services to children might be acceptable, if the negotiations resulted in the elimination of programs, larger class sizes, or fewer dollars for teaching materials.

Involved teachers were often neighbors or friends with whom taxpayers had long-term relationships. The arguments of the employees often sounded reasonable, and many community members felt sympathy for these professionals who, they were told, were laboring for substandard wages under difficult working conditions.

Following precedents in the private sector, teachers in various states subsequently became involved in work actions and often strikes. In most cases these early strikes were times of bonding for staff. They received the sympathy and support of fellow teachers throughout their state and sometimes, with proper union publicity, throughout the nation. That strikes occurred was not always coincidental. More than one school superintendent can tell of hearing that his or her district had been targeted for a strike "within the next few years." During such situations, spokespersons for both sides, often people who did not work in the district on a full-time basis, including regional representatives for the unions and legal representatives for the school boards, would make public statements that were contradictory and confusing. Exactly who wanted what, for what reasons, and how far apart they actually were, was often difficult to determine.

Unfortunately, work actions and strikes often took place at the end of the school year, coinciding with final examination periods for students. Using children as bargaining chips became acceptable in some districts. This became a tactic aimed at getting students and parents to pressure school board members to bring closure to unpleasant situations and get on with educating.

Sooner of later matters became settled. The outsiders from the union's regional office and the district's attorney would advise those who had to live and work in the district that they should not take what occurred personally, that it was just a process to work through, and they should shake hands and work together for the good of the children. Theoretically this was sound; realistically it was impossible.

– AS IT IS –

These young teachers and administrators of the 1960s and 1970s are now the veteran teachers of the 1990s. According to Evans,[1] as we look at the entire teaching community, we recognize that the majority of staff members are in the middle to later part of their careers. The average age of these staff members is nearly fifty, and three-quarters of them have been teaching ten years or more, with half of them teaching fifteen years or more. The majority have only taught in one or two schools during their careers.

Obviously, how these veteran teachers perceive their careers and the work they do varies from one individual to the next. Ability to move into leadership positions has been limited to moving out of the classroom and into administration. For many, this has not been a desirable option. In some cases, individuals do not perceive themselves as having the kind of skills or personality needed to be effective as an administrator. Many state that they enjoy the contact that they have with children and feel that leaving the classroom would substantially change that contact. Some have personal reasons, such as spouses who also work, so geographical relocation is impossible. In recent years, better wages for teachers have resulted in many veteran staff members making more money in the classroom than they would in entry or mid-level administrative posts. Whatever the reason, a large percentage of graying teachers are now remaining in classrooms. For those who have not been active in formal professional associations or other growth programs, little stimulation is available. As a result, boredom, disenchantment, and poor performance are common. Many fail to enjoy the work they have been doing for years, and burnout has become all too familiar in faculty rooms.

Several efforts have been made in individual schools to combat this concern, but a widespread remedy is lacking. By exercising the scientific management mentality, some decision makers believed that increased pay and improved working conditions would ameliorate this problem. Follow-up studies found that such was not the case.

— THE FUTURE —

Recent efforts have taken a different approach and have suggested giving staff members more control of their professional activities. Through various strategies with differing titles, such as school improvement, school-based management, and teacher empowerment, initiatives are being taken to change the way schools make decisions and operate. Whether this will be the answer is still to be determined.

Students of administration often lament programs that are theory-based and, in their view, lack practicality. These same students are usually at the point of being ready to start new careers in administration, and are looking for hands-on answers to the daily challenges they think they will be facing. Defenders of theory-laden programs point out that this approach provides a foundation that allows practitioners to look at their organizations from a broad perspective, also called seeing the whole picture. When options are viewed from their respective extremes, the best answer probably lies somewhere in the middle.

One complaint that has wide support concerns the difficulty students of administration often have in understanding *how* theory can be applied to the job. The recent glut of linkages between theory and practice for teachers has provided a number of ideas and strategies for instructional improvement. A similar link between management strategies and practices is more difficult to find, and students of administration often experience confusion in trying to understand how study findings and theories relate to on-the-job application.

The concept of staff empowerment in schools might be viewed from three levels: the individual, individuals in relation to their stage of life, and organizational factors.

— MOTIVATING THE INDIVIDUAL —

As the teaching staff of our schools become older, many school people have become interested in methods for increasing teachers' motivation. Administrators, particularly at school levels, have undertaken various initiatives in an effort to revitalize staff members. Traditionally, efforts have included various ideas:

Changing the grade or content level an individual teaches;
Reorganizing staff into teams, requiring them to work together in planning and instruction;
Exchanging teachers with other grade levels and/or other schools;
Encouraging major changes in curriculum;
Initiating committee formats for various school efforts;
Developing teacher centers;
Changing physical environments (classrooms);
Sending staff members to conferences and bringing inspiring speakers into the school to share ideas;
Encouraging classroom research, followed by publication in professional journals;
Designing workshops and faculty meeting presentations for teacher-to-teacher sharing.

These efforts are commendable, but too often they are limited in scope. Job dissatisfaction has been a focus of educational research, and findings have been enlightening. According to Blase and Greenfield,[2] teachers reported concerns with supervisors who failed to listen to them, were critical and directive, and showed little willingness to support them. A major concern was with being put into classes of students identified as having lower ability levels. This type of teaching, year after year, provides little stimulation or growth. As a result, teachers often feel both physically and emotionally drained.

In attempting to determine what ideas might motivate staff members, little consideration is given to the natural changes that occur in the lives of people in general and educators in particular, and how schools might better accommodate biological and psychological needs.

Maslow's Theory of Motivation

Any discussion of motivation theory would be incomplete if it failed to recognize the contributions of A. H. Maslow. Maslow conceived of motivation as a hierarchy of levels, and suggested that truly happy, productive individuals must achieve each of these levels, more or less in order, to achieve maximum effectiveness in their lives.[3]

Maslow's original work was theoretical, and provided the basis for other motivation theorists who have expanded on his original principles to look at human behavior in the work place.

Maslow describes five levels of needs individuals must have in order to be fully productive, satisfied beings:

Physiological needs: These are the most basic drives, encompassing needs such as hunger, sleep, or thirst. If these lowest-level needs are not met, other needs of a higher order may not develop.

Safety needs: Since needs are seen as hierarchical, once physiological needs are met, individuals strive to meet safety needs, including physical safety, predictability, order, and routine, and show the ability to anticipate and plan ahead.

Love needs: The third step in the hierarchy involves love needs. These include belonging, satisfactory associations in work and social groups, affection, and love.

Esteem needs: With a few pathological exceptions, esteem needs include two types. The first involves the desire for self-respect: strength, achievement, adequacy, and confidence; the second, the respect of others: recognition, attention, and appreciation.

Self-actualization: The highest level on Maslow's hierarchy is self-actualization. If a person has achieved the lower four levels of needs, he or she may become restless. To ameliorate this, the individual must be involved in challenging, personally satisfying activities. To be self-actualized, a person must be able to create, express, and function at maximum capacity.

Using Maslow's theory, administrators might approach the motivation of employees through a series of efforts to eliminate or satisfy the kinds of concerns suggested in the various levels. Adequate salaries would provide shelter, food, and the potential for a personal environment and opportunities to satisfy other needs for gratification.

In the workplace itself, administrators should exhibit consistent, behavior. Doing so on a daily basis will make employees feel secure in knowing their own range of authority for decision-making, how they can expect to be treated, and what types of behaviors are valued.

This recommendation should be given strong consideration, since new administrators often struggle with determining what kind of style they should use as they assume leadership positions. Maslow's ideas indicate that being oneself rather than trying to play a role is the best advice any administrator can take.

Schools, as well as other organizations, are made up of informal systems. Acknowledging the existence of those systems by giving them consideration when making decisions, showing concern for the well-being of their members, and supporting after-hours activities that enhance such well-being are important behaviors for successful administrators. The administrator should not be seen as the social director, but involvement through presence and selective participation can enhance status.

All persons need to feel that they have value. This esteem most often results from accomplishments made through their work. As public institutions, schools are unable to provide trips to exotic islands or monetary bonuses to employees. As a result, administrators become the primary source of recognition for employees who have performed above and beyond the call of duty. Letters, recognition in faculty meetings or in the community, and just a pat on the back often have a great deal of meaning to employees.

Administrators can provide some support for the efforts of individuals to meet the first four needs, but self-actualization is more personal than the others. Essentially, the individual must be happy and satisfied with his or her work and believe it is truly his or her calling in life. Any real support provided by an administrator can be through noting appreciation for the person's work, not just through letters and memos but through meaningful conversations. Any outstanding contributions, whether in a lesson taught, a game coached, or a musical directed, provide an opportunity for such support.

Motivation-Hygiene Theory

Herzberg's[4] studies of motivation suggested a two-factor theory. Herzberg and his colleagues proposed that gaining one set of factors led to job satisfaction and the lack of certain factors led to job dissatisfaction. The opposite of job satisfaction is not job dissatisfaction. Herzberg labels the first set "motivation factors" and the second "hygiene factors."

Motivation factors that must be satisfied in order to provide satisfaction and hygienic factors that lead to job dissatisfaction are outlined in Figure 13.1.

FEATURES TO INCLUDE IN LETTERS
OF COMMENDATION

1. *Be timely.* Send the letter shortly after the employee has done something you believe is praiseworthy.
2. *Be specific.* Let the person know what you are praising and why you appreciate it.
3. *Make it personal.* Use "you," "I," "we."
4. *Share it.* Send one copy for the superintendent's attention and another to the employee's personnel file. Make sure you put a "cc" on the bottom so the employee knows where copies are being sent.
5. *Emphasize points.* In writing the letter, capitalize and underline a word or two in order to emphasize. For instance: "Your commitment is EXTRAORDINARY . . ."
6. *Personalize.* Put a single line through the typed spelling of the employee's name at the beginning of the letter and handwrite the name above the typed copy. At the conclusion of the letter, handwrite a few words of additional praise or thanks.
7. *Use the power of the pen.* An exclamation point or two at the end of a phrase or sentence helps strengthen a point you are trying to make. An additional aside can be made in parentheses.
8. *Utilize the opportunity.* Capitalize on the event by handing the letter to the employee yourself and by providing both a verbal and physical pat on the back at the same time.
9. *Add a bit of artwork.* An administrator's comfort with this varies from person to person. Some administrators find a smile face or some related illustration adds to the point they are trying to get across. For some administrators, the many options now provided by word processors also allow for added illustration.

Job loading. According to Herzberg,[4] "job loading" is used as a means to affect job satisfaction. Unfortunately, although managerial intentions may be aimed at improving a worker's feelings about his or her job, they may actually exacerbate existing dissatisfaction by increasing the factors that cause dissatisfaction. This phenomenon has been labeled by Herzberg as horizontal job loading. Schools engage in this process in a number of ways. For instance, an administrator might suggest to a teacher whose students are performing poorly in reading that students should read eight pages a day instead of four. To use a sports analogy, if a golfer is having difficulty with

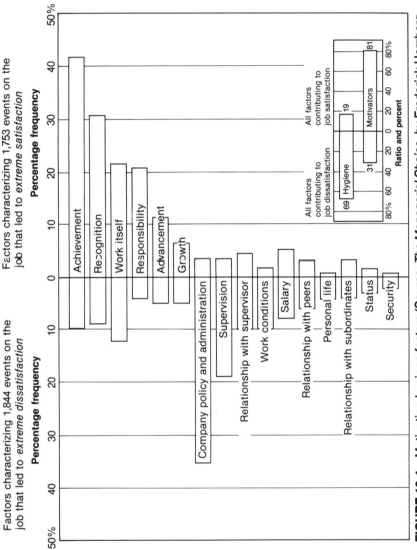

FIGURE 13.1 Motivation-hygiene factors (Source: *The Managerial Choice*, by Frederick Herzberg (Homewood, IL: Dow Jones-Irwin, 1976). Reprinted with permission of the author.)

the swing, the answer for correcting it is probably not to go out and hit dozens of practice balls, which will only serve to reinforce the fault that exists. Instead, a lesson that diagnoses the fault and provides suggestions for its remedy is more likely to ameliorate the problem.

Another example is the elementary teacher who claims dissatisfaction with teaching science, and as a result is told that he or she no longer has to teach the subject. Thus, the teacher never has the opportunity to grow, and the problems that originally caused the difficulty remain.

Vertical job loading, on the other hand, is aimed at job enrichment and involves efforts intended to improve job satisfaction. Herzberg suggests several principles associated with vertical job loading.

PRINCIPLES OF VERTICAL JOB LOADING

Principle	*Motivators Involved*
A. Removing some controls while retaining accountability	Responsibility and personal achievement
B. Increasing the accountability of individuals for own work	Responsibility and recognition
C. Giving a person a complete natural unit of work (module, division, area, and so on)	Responsibility, achievement, and recognition
D. Granting additional authority to an employee in his activity; job freedom	Responsibility, achievement, and recognition
E. Making periodic reports directly available to the worker himself rather than to the supervisor	Internal recognition
F. Introducing new and more difficult tasks not previously handled	Growth and learning
G. Assigning individuals specific or specialized tasks, enabling them to become experts	Responsibility, growth and advancement

---

— THE INDIVIDUAL AND LIFE STAGES —

Various theories of motivation exist, but few take into account the natural changes that occur in people's lives. An administrator can address motivation through the theories proposed by Maslow, Herzberg, and others, but consideration should also be given to theories of adult development.

Levinson[6] described the lives of the men he studied, noting that life is a cycle from birth to death, containing a number of stages or seasons, each with its own distinct character. According to Levinson, these stages include common biological, psychological, and social changes. Sheehy[7] also viewed life as cyclical, and described the various psychological changes that affect the lives of both men and women. Sheehy also noted various stages, but she also described the stages differently. Thus, when a man's career may have been through a number of years of development and be approaching its peak, his female age counterpart may be at an initial or intermediate stage. How schools consider, or do not consider, these life stages is worth discussion.

Life Cycles and the Organization of Schools

Schools do little to meet the changing biological, psychological, social, and professional needs of their teachers. In part, this is due to a lack of focus on these changes until recent years and to the fact that schools are ill-equipped to handle such changes. Salary schedules are established according to years of service and amount of education; giving extra time and working harder will probably not be financially rewarded. Enthusiastic younger teachers who are in their peak years physically often apply for after-school jobs such as coaching and advising. Payment for these positions is generally substandard, and work conditions can often become undesirable if parents complain about the lack of playing time their children receive or become critical of the way a teacher directs the pep band or yearbook club.

Young professionals strive to gain a foothold as senior executives in their firms, but this opportunity is not available to teachers in most schools— once a teacher, always a teacher. The twenty-two-year-old first-year staff member has the same title as the sixty-year-old with almost forty years of experience: teacher. Opportunity to gain recognition or advancement are precluded by a structure that lacks any kind of career ladder, although concern for this problem has recently resulted in a small number of schools implementing career ladder programs.

Perhaps one of the most difficult and frustrating problems for teachers is the perception held by those outside of their profession. An office supply salesman has little trouble taking a new position as a salesman of luxury boats because his success in one sales position is an indication of potential for success in another sales position. Teachers are not afforded this consideration. Usually, excellent teachers, particularly those who have spent a number of years in the classroom, find it extremely difficult to convince private-sector employers that they have a high potential for success in anything other than entry-level positions. As a result, teachers are likely to see the classroom as a cell from which they have little hope of escape. This perception becomes more acute in mid-career, when individuals become security-conscious while still comparing their salaries and style of living to friends who have significantly higher incomes. In their twenties and either still single or newly married, teachers find the option of trying something new is not as threatening as when approaching 40, with years invested in a retirement system; children and a spouse to support; and the gnawing concern about having no other skills than teaching with which they could earn a living. The constant, predictable organization of schools does little to reduce this phenomenon and if anything, continues to reinforce it each September when the school doors opens and yet another year begins.

Organizational Factors

A number of strategies for addressing staff motivation have been provided, but history shows that even the best efforts have resulted in little change. A number of reasons exist for this lack of success. For one, the hierarchical structure of school districts requires that those adults at the bottom of the decision-making hierarchy (teachers) take cues from superordinates— administrators. This organizational plan has become imbedded and is accepted in many cases by teaching staff, who find it easier to function in the privacy of their classrooms, with the only visit from an "outsider" being the required annual observation by the school principal. For those attracted to a life of little disruption or challenge, such a pattern works well. Another reason why change is so difficult results from the present teacher tenure laws in most states. Once teachers are given tenure, their dismissal is an extremely difficult exercise in terms of time, financial costs, and emotional stress. As a result, tenured teachers become very insulated, with little motivation to change and improve. Such a system provides security, but can also encourage mediocrity. The tenure system also sends the message to teachers that their practices must be effective, since the administration and board of education have granted them tenure.

Probably the greatest problem with the use of the various theoretical models is in the way their implementation has been interpreted. Since the models address the needs of individuals, the reaction of administrators has been to determine ways to encourage staff members on an individual basis. However, if a district is large enough to support a full-time school personnel administrator, he or she will probably not have the time to get to know the needs of every member of the district's staff, much less respond to all of their needs. Similarly, a principal with responsibility for hundreds of students and dozens of staff members will not have the time to meet the motivation needs of every individual in his or her school.

The reform reports of the early and mid-1980s pointed out that the present education system is failing to meet the needs of students. Overloaded supervisor-staff ratios make it impossible to identify and meet the needs of each staff member. One response to the reports has been to suggest reorganization of the governance structures of the schools. Motivation theory has resulted in efforts aimed at individuals, but schools have recently witnessed the emergence of empowerment as a means of increasing motivation by changing school governance patterns. This concept may hold some promise and benefit, but one of its most difficult features is a lack of definition. No universal understanding has yet been established, so when empowerment is mentioned in conversation or in text, people have no common understanding of its meaning. As a result, a number of different activities take place in schools under the same general title of empowerment.

This confusion as to definition has caused many school superintendents to be skeptical about the adoption of empowerment initiatives. A survey of superintendents that asked them to define "empowerment" resulted in the following responses:

I don't understand the term.

Shared decision-making in professional areas of expertise; for instance, curriculum development, textbook selection, some personnel recruitment, but *not* in management areas.

Accountability for areas in which they (staff) make decisions.

A formal vehicle for decision-making in the school that is incorporated into the union structure.

Giving away the store; teachers getting control over terms and conditions of employment.

It is a very effective way of gaining statewide changes in contracts without calling it negotiations.

The lack of definition may be the root of some confusion, but may also be empowerment's greatest advantage. Empowerment has resulted in a variety of efforts under a variety of subtitles such as open-door policy, peer supervision, school-based management, shared decision-making, career ladders, and others.

In considering whether to move toward this concept, schools and school districts must determine their readiness to adopt empowerment efforts. For instance, one teachers' union president who was invited to address a meeting of personnel directors gave an example of empowerment that she believed to be legitimate and important for her school district. According to her, the district was to study a proposal to give union leadership the contractual right to review and sign off on any new construction or capital project modifications. Her logic was reasonable: the people who have to spend a good part of their lives in classrooms should have a say in the way those classrooms are constructed. Those present agreed with her rationale, but they also pointed out that, in their experience, the union leadership might refuse to sign off on such an agreement during a period of intense labor strife, such as a breakdown of negotiations. The union president said that she did not believe such a thing could happen in her district.

Undoubtedly, the observations and beliefs of the union president were honest, and her district had developed a healthy climate that allowed them to sort out their differences over labor and management issues. The personnel administrators, on the other hand, had been exposed to different approaches and motivations that made them wary of including such language in the negotiated agreement. One administrator in the meeting had brought along copies of contracts he had recently acquired, which had been proposed by various teachers' union groups. The administrators present could appreciate the need for more collegial relationships, but they felt the focus of the unions had remained distributive in nature and that the only aim of many unions was to continue to gain power rather than promote collegiality. Recommendations in some of the provisions would have required boards of education and administrators to give decision-making authority to unions in areas such as evaluating and recommending all appointments—instructional, support staff, and administrative, and included making tenure recommendations for administrators. In addition, the unions wished to have the authority to determine the hours of the school day, work schedules of all staff, approval of planning activities, and determining physical plant needs and requirements, staff schedules, and assignments.

The arguments of the union president were undoubtedly sincere and worth considering in the most rational of organizations, but school districts tend not to function as highly rational, logical structures. As a result, most administrators are cautious about recommending language that could impede a district's mission as a result of labor disputes. The personnel administrators involved in this meeting had enough experience to believe that such "torpedoing" of efforts could occur in some districts, and as a result were not strongly receptive to endorsing such contractual additions.

Contractual options.   In addition to identifying what if any empowerment efforts a district will consider, a primary responsibility of school administrators is to determine how these efforts will be incorporated into the system. Essentially, three options exist. One is to include empowerment activities as part of the negotiated contract. A second is to incorporate ideas into the contract on a trial basis, allowing either side to back out after a predetermined time has passed, and the third is to implement ideas on a noncontractual basis.

Union leadership has emphasized to its members the importance of including empowerment language in contracts. Boards and administrators will vary, depending on philosophy, past experiences, and goals. There is no correct answer for all parties. The readiness of a district in terms of its labor-management atmosphere needs to be considered. Consideration should not be based only on the present climate of the district, but also on the district's history and potential for long-term stability. Districts that see themselves as having long-term positive relationships between management and labor will undoubtedly feel more secure about engaging in contractual empowerment agreements that will bind both parties. Districts that have had stormy relationships are best advised to refrain from any contractual agreements; temporary agreements should be used, if any are desired. In any case, administrators should never enter into a bargaining agreement that allows for empowerment activities if they believe that doing so will provide a show of good faith and remedy existing problems. To do so is like concluding that two people who are dating, but do not always get along well, will find that all of their conflicts will disappear if they sign a contract and get married. Not only are such provisions likely to have little positive effect, but they are more likely to accentuate existing problems.

— EMPOWERMENT INITIATIVES —

The lack of definition for the concept of teacher empowerment has resulted in a number of initiatives taken in various forms.

Sample Empowerment Activities

- School improvement programs
- Student placement
- Curriculum selection/development
- Selection of teachers
- Selection of administrators
- Administrator evaluation
- Mentoring
- School calendar
- Scheduling
- Staff assignments
- Textbook selection
- Student discipline
- Student promotion
- Teacher discipline
- Teacher evaluation
- Teacher recognition
- Capital project efforts
- Allocation of space
- Classroom activities
- School policies

* Budgeting
* Purchasing

* District policies

Mechanisms for empowerment activities committees. The option of including empowerment initiatives in contracts exists, but the means for implementing such efforts are not usually included in contracts. Districts use a number of methods for involving staff. Probably the most popular is involvement through committees.

Sample Empowerment Committees

* Sick leave bank
* Sabbatical leave
* Evaluation
* Professional development
* Insurance
* School board advisory
* Principals advisory
* Grade level teams

* Personnel
* School improvement
* Curriculum
* Textbook
* Coaching
* Superintendent advisory
* School advisory
* Content teams

— INITIATING EMPOWERMENT —

Obviously, the types and means of empowerment activities are broad. Personnel in most school districts, on looking at these lists, would probably note that they are already engaged in such activities and have been doing so long before the idea of empowerment became fashionable. For those districts interested in pursuing empowerment initiatives, this observation provides good justification for the board and administrative staff to engage in some assessment activities before determining what they want to do and the methods they will propose to the union. "Propose" is used because empowerment implies joint involvement with staff members, and the board and administration will no longer direct. The initial discussions should no longer include union representation, whose presence could restrict points that members of the board or administration might want to make about past events in the district, potential threats to operations that might result from the adoption of particular empowerment activities, or concerns with individual union personalities who might try to redirect the intentions of empowerment efforts.

These discussions should include the district's school attorney, who will keep the board members and administrators aware of legal implications of any decisions being considered. In addition, the attorney will educate the board as to legislated responsibilities that cannot be shared.

The use of outside expertise in conducting such discussions can be useful for a number of reasons. A consultant will have no vested interest in a particular issue. A correctly chosen consultant should also be in a position to give board members and administrators an orientation to empowerment, what it means, the types of initiatives taking place, their implications for district operation, and how they have worked in other school districts. Finally, an outsider is almost always better able to broach sensitive issues and make statements regarding the implementation of the process than is someone already working in the district.

Such discussion might come in a meeting of administrative staff and board of education members in a retreat setting. After breaking the total group into subgroups of five or six with a mix of board members and central office and school administrators, the following questions might be posed to provide starting points for discussion:

1. Define empowerment. Is empowerment synonymous with shared decision making?
2. Give examples of empowerment.
3. What elements must be in place in order to institute empowerment in a school district?
4. In the group's shared perception, what is the district's state of readiness to become involved in empowerment activities?

Once each group has answered these questions, an overhead projector, a blackboard, or newsprint should be used to make a master list of the responses. Each response should bring about some discussion and clarity, so that those in attendance can leave the meeting with both a common vocabulary and a common understanding of what is meant in the school district when a board member or administrator uses the term "empowerment." Once this meeting has occurred, the board of education, personnel director, and superintendent should meet and have further discussion to identify the expectations of the board. If movement toward empowerment is to continue, the superintendent and personnel director should have a clear idea of the guidelines they are to follow. The superintendent and personnel director should also be prepared to outline for the board, either at this meeting or in the near future, the process they plan to follow to pursue discussions with staff representatives. Once these discussions begin, the board should be kept aware of the status of the efforts.

The lists of empowerment activities and committees contain most of the common efforts being considered or implemented in school districts, and the following examples provide more detailed descriptions of popular empowerment initiatives.

School-Based Management

The use of a school-based management program calls for a change in the way schools are presently organized. It provides for decision-making by a group or council at the school level that is authorized to make critical decisions that in the past have been the province of the school administrator with the support of the central office. The advantage to school administrators includes the fact that responsibility for decisions is shared rather than falling solely on individual administrators. As a result, ownership in decisions belongs to all involved, enhancing credibility with various school constituencies, and the opportunity to utilize the expertise and knowledge of several persons becomes available.

Disadvantages must be considered as well. A great deal of efficiency is lost when decisions must be held in abeyance until the school's council can meet. Decisions that could previously be made in the privacy of an office or faculty meeting are now the responsibility of the school's council. Power, in terms of the ability to make final decisions, is now shared. Perhaps most important, building administrators who have often spent their entire careers working under one type of management approach are called upon to learn a new set of skills.

The purpose of a council is to provide guidance and direction in a number of daily decisions. After first forming a council, schools should begin with decisions that are relatively simple and that can provide the council with the opportunity to be successful. For instance, a council might be involved in personnel areas such as hiring. The council might be provided the opportunity to become knowledgeable about job openings by reading job descriptions and questioning professionals. Council members might then be asked to help construct questions that will be asked during interviews, take part in interviews, and participate in making recommendations. Other areas in which council members might become involved include determining school goals, reviewing student discipline procedures, assessing program requirements, and building a budget.

Probably the greatest concern to be addressed is the actual authority of a council. To be truly effective, a council must be aware of the extent of its power. Will their recommendations be adopted? Are they replacing the principal in the line-staff relationship? In some cases it may be the council's role to recommend and the superintendent's and board's role to adopt suggestions officially. Is the principal an equal member of the group, or must he or she approve decisions before they are sent on? Or is there a sliding scale in which some decisions are the administrator's and others are not? These are all legitimate questions that must be answered at the beginning of a council, to be sure that all members have a clear understanding of the scope of their authority.

Councils will vary, based on local situations, but a few observations are worth sharing. The role of the principal in a school-based management program is critical. If a program is initiated by a principal who is directed to do so, and that principal is recalcitrant, the program is doomed. To be successful, a principal's role in decision-making begins to look somewhat similar to that of a superintendent. He or she is asked to coordinate council activities; help develop agendas and disseminate minutes; provide information, resources, personnel records, and historical records; and fulfill other related requests for information council members need to make intelligent decisions. As a professional, the principal also takes responsibility for educating council members about the types of questions they should be asking and information they should be requesting. This education should be given serious consideration, and members should regularly be provided with inservice sessions on topics such as procedures for decision-making, education law, interviewing procedures, etc. In many school-based management programs, the principal retains the power of final approval or disapproval. If this power is used too often, council members are likely to perceive their role as marginal, become disenchanted with decisions that are made, and decide that they would prefer to resign their membership.

The council must also be aware of its authority in relation to the superintendent and school board. Certain authority is provided the council, but the superintendent and board of education have legislated authority that cannot be transferred to any other body. Examples of this authority include approval for hiring or terminating staff members and adopting policies.

The membership of school councils varies in different districts. In some, the council may be made up of the building administration, a group of teachers, and possibly support staff representatives; in others, the council may consist of a cross-section of school community members who are representative of various groups that have vested interests. As such, teachers, parents, members of the school's support staff, community representatives (business and/or political), students, and the school principal are included on the council. The actual number of members will vary, but schools that adopt such a structure might consider a membership such as four to six parents, the same number of teachers, and two students. The actual number of representatives from other groups must be based on the school's size and geographic location. One other point is worth noting here.

Obviously the initiation of such a program is a highly significant move. Any school seriously considering such an effort should thoroughly research its purpose, make sure its board of education and central office are comprehensively educated, and spend time visiting other schools that are operating under such a system. An effort of this type is not to be implemented on a trial basis, with the idea that if it does not work well, it can be dropped at will. Doing so could seriously damage the reputation and credibility of the board and administration that originally encouraged community members to participate, and then terminated the effort.

Another point administrators should consider relates to union support for councils. Although there seems to be general support for empowerment activities, this support is usually given with the understanding that shared governance means teachers will have more say in decision-making. Unions may be less interested in this concept if the council also includes parents and students.

Specific authority, procedures for decision-making, relationships between the council and superintendent and board of education, makeup of council membership, and roles should be fully outlined in board policy. All members of the school community should have a clear understanding of the council's role and scope of authority.

The operation of a school functioning under school-based management is different from traditional settings. The purpose of moving toward such an effort is to provide the best educational program for all children. To do this, school-based management advocates subscribe to the belief that decisions about what is best for children are best made by those working closest to them. As a result, critical decisions and problem-solving are dealt with by councils rather than through a district office or traditional hierarchy.

Whether council members are provided with stipends for their participation also varies. In some districts, a fund is provided for use by the council, who may opt to use their funds to provide stipends for members. Another council may decide to use its funds to support what it believes is a needed position in a school, such as a curriculum specialist. How funds will be expended to best respond to the needs that have been identified in the school is left to the council.

Role of the school board. Individual schools are given responsibility for determining how best to meet their own needs, but the board of education continues to play an important role by providing standards and expectations. In addition, the board's mission statement should provide a model for the mission statements of each of the district's schools; the individual schools' mission statements should not be expected to replicate that of the board, but their statements should be reflective of the district's overall mission.

In addition to leadership in providing direction, the board of education must continue to exercise its legislated responsibilities. The board continues to maintain fiscal, personnel, and related legal functions for district-level operations and for appropriate school-level activities. However, the board may also give up certain areas of authority by contractual agreement.

Waivers.   One practice that has been adopted by districts engaging in empowerment initiatives is the use of waivers to allow an individual school to waive a contractual obligation for a specific period of time, usually a year, in order to try an approach or alter a practice that they would not otherwise be allowed to do. Generally a district council made up of administrators and teachers reviews requests for waivers, which must then be approved by the union local.

Administrators' concerns.   Few educators would argue the legitimacy of the concerns that now exist with American education. However, some administrators have objected to empowerment practices. Empowerment programs refer to teacher involvement in decision-making and in some cases to extra or added remuneration for their efforts. Additionally, empowerment often refers to teachers taking responsibility for programs.

Personnel involved in school-based management programs agree that such efforts require more work for members of school staff, including administrators. However, although teachers are generally provided extra remuneration for their efforts, administrators are usually expected to take on their additional responsibilities without receiving extra compensation. In addition, few have incorporated accountability measures for staff members in a way that would parallel the responsibility taken by administrators. For instance, if goals and expectations are not adequately met, teachers continue to have the protection of their contract and of legislated measures such as tenure laws. In states where administrators are not given tenure, poor results can be a threat to job security. Additionally, even in states that do provide tenure, administrative raises and benefits are commonly determined on an individual basis by school boards. Thus, an administrator who is perceived by the school board as a poor producer may find himself or herself in disfavor when annual raises for assignments are determined. Again, concern with performance may be reflected in a board's decision, but the power of an administrator to alter or affect that decision without the advocacy of a large collective bargaining unit is limited.

Peer Evaluation

One recent effort toward empowerment in some school districts has been the adoption of peer supervision involving teaching staff. A number of justifications exist for such a process. First, it is not reasonable to expect school administrators to be expert in every content area. Also, master teachers in most schools are the people who spend the majority of each day instructing children and who will have a better understanding of the personal and instructional needs of the children being taught. Third, the idea of a collegial relationship between administrators and staff members might be perceived as a contradiction, since administrators must evaluate staff and make decisions regarding their tenure and possible promotion, and also provide them with comments about positive teaching behaviors and with critical comments where appropriate. Because of this relationship, staff are often hesitant to admit weaknesses or ask for help if they fear that such honesty might make them appear to be weak or lacking.

As a result of concerns such as these, peer supervision programs seem to be gaining more acceptance in schools. As with almost all empowerment activities, how the programs are implemented varies from district to district. One model that has received a great deal of attention comes from the city of Rochester, New York where a program initiated by contract includes a number of empowerment initiatives, including peer supervision. The Rochester effort involves peer assistance for staff members who receive from their supervisors evaluation ratings that are less than satisfactory and who volunteer for assistance.

The program outlines a number of procedural steps for identification and referral, and also allows a teacher who is eligible for assistance to refuse. Efforts are made to provide assistance from teachers who are in the same certification areas and have an understanding of the content-specific and classroom management needs of the identified teacher. In most cases, a period of two full semesters is allowed, and regular status reports are provided, to include information such as the concerns addressed by the teacher and peer supervisor, strategies being used to improve instruction, who will be involved in providing assistance, and updates on progress.

Labor–Management Committees

A number of school districts have explored, and in some cases implemented, the use of labor-management committees (LMCs) at both district and school levels. Most districts initiate such committees as a means of improving communication and providing staff members with an opportunity to be involved in decision-making. District-wide committees usually consist of administrators and teachers. In some cases, school board members are also represented on the committees. As with most committee structures, local conditions dictate many of the parameters for the formation and membership of the committee. However, the following are considerations that might be discussed prior to forming such a committee.

Determining committee purpose. Perhaps of most importance is the identification why such a committee has been formed and what needs it intends to address. This is an important question, since the answer should provide guidance about the concerns that the committee will discuss. A committee's role might be to enhance communication in the school district; it might intend to improve the educational efforts of the district; or it might aim to improve labor-management issues in the district. The distinction is crucial. Exactly what efforts the LMC adopts must be made clear to its membership as well as its constituents.

Determining committee makeup. Representation of various constituencies should be considered in determining the number of people who will be on a labor-management committee. Teacher representation will usually include individuals from the elementary, middle school, and high school levels. Special areas are often represented as well. Administrative representation usually includes staff members from each of the levels represented in the district and members from supervisory and pupil personnel staffs.

Some districts also include a board of education member on their committees. From an administrative viewpoint, this practice may hold certain advantages. It can provide confirmation of information that administrators share with the board, but that might otherwise be received with skepticism from individual board members. Additionally, as a member of the committee, the board representative is more likely to act as an advocate for recommendations that result from committee efforts.

Appointment. Membership to the LMC may be by appointment or election. Union representation may be through the president or governing committee of the union; administrative appointments may be through the superintendent. In some cases, representatives are elected by constituents.

Rotation of membership. Membership of a committee should change annually. Unless representation changes, individuals may become entrenched and continue to advocate concerns of personal importance. At the same time, stability is also important. Consequently, a structure that calls for a change of one or two members from each constituent group each year is preferable. By this means, new representation and ideas have the opportunity to arise, and continuity is provided for issues of ongoing importance.

Roles of superintendent, board of education president, and union president. The presidents of the school board and association and the school district superintendent should be excluded from the LMC. This allows members to discuss issues of concern openly, without deferring to one of the district's leaders. Additionally, it provides a buffer for leaders by allowing LMC members to discuss issues and come up with possible solutions without committing their respective leadership. Finally, if leaders were present, most discussion would end up being between these individuals, and other committee members might feel their comments to be of less importance.

Consultants. A district may use consultant assistance in structuring the LMC. A specialist from outside the district can be useful, since he or she can make comments and recommendations that insiders cannot. Should a representative from labor suggest a different method of determining agenda items, management members might question the motivation for this recommendation. An outsider whose primary interest is in the successful functioning of the LMC is more likely to be above suspicion and can evaluate suggestions and make comments objectively.

Guests. Members of the LMC should be encouraged to be creative in examining concerns and identifying potential solutions. A method of enhancing such efforts is through the use of external sources. Once potential concerns have been identified, the LMC should attempt to identify people whose knowledge or abilities will help facilitate problem-solving. These individuals should be utilized on an ad hoc basis and involved with specific concerns for a limited time.

Governance. The concept of formalizing empowerment is foreign to most school districts. Many administrators will attest to the fact that staff have had the opportunity to be involved in decision-making over the years, but that involvement has often varied, depending on the personalities who have made up a district's administration and school board. Since most empowerment activities have been avoided in contracts, continuity has been difficult to guarantee. The 1990s threaten to change the status quo, as unions press for the incorporation of empowerment in local contracts.

Determining scope of authority.   History and local labor contracts may have an impact on the amount of decision-making authority staff members have in a district. For instance, many districts have a provision for a group of teachers, often union representatives, to meet with the superintendent on a monthly basis to discuss concerns. This group might deal with specific issues about working conditions or day-to-day matters. In such a case, a labor-management committee might be unnecessary or might deal with matters not covered by the present group.

Chair.   Two of the most important jobs on the LMC involve chairing the group and recording minutes of meetings. Chairing the LMC should be shared by labor and management representatives on a monthly rotation, with one member from labor and one from management alternating during the year. In other words, Teacher Jones might chair the first, third, fifth meetings, and so on. Principal Smith would then chair the second, fourth, sixth meetings, etc. As with responsibility for chairing meetings, taking minutes that will be provided to staff should also be rotated.

Relationship to other committees.   Members of the LMC must be careful to reflect *often* on the purpose of their committee. It is easy to slide into discussion of issues that have traditionally been in the province of another committee or individual, or are legislated matters falling under the authority of the superintendent or board of education. To avoid this, representatives from all sides must regularly communicate with the leadership of their constituencies to discuss issues under consideration.

Structure of meetings.   Determining when meetings will be held, and for how long, is often difficult, since various schools in a district may have different ending times (elementary schools usually dismiss before secondary ones); board members often have jobs that require their attendance, some distance from their homes, and administrators have after-school duties. It may be difficult to find a good time for all members of the LMC to meet. As a result, some LMC meetings are held shortly after students are dismissed from school; others find it easier to meet in the evening. This scheduling may determine membership, and should be decided as early as possible. Another issue that needs agreement is the actual length of time that the LMC will meet. One-and-a-half to two-hour meetings are the most popular. Restricting the time is advantageous, since this forces participants to attend to concerns.

Agenda planning.   The use of an agenda, in addition to determining what will or will not be placed on it, is a critical concern. An agenda for each meeting must be made. Meetings should not be held without all members being fully aware of what will be discussed and having the opportunity to prepare for the meetings. Agendas should be developed by members of the LMC at their preceding meetings. In other words, suggestions for future meeting topics should be determined before the end of earlier meetings.

The types of issues that might be discussed will vary according to local needs, interests, and agreement by all sides. Some committees may determine that certain items are out of bounds, and should be handled at the negotiating table or by another, more appropriate committee. Matters that are discussed by committees have included the following:

- Scheduling
- Smoking policies
- Busing
- Copy machine use
- Communications
- School climate
- Professional duties
- Faculty concerns
- Release time for staff

- Public relations
- Telephone access
- Proper attire
- Student discipline
- Secretarial/aide assistance
- Role of department chairs
- Inservice programs
- Addition of advisors and coaches to the contract

To be effective, the LMC must also have the flexibility to discuss emerging issues that might arise unexpectedly. The ability to do this should be understood by all committee constituencies and their representatives. Likewise, the decision *not* to discuss an unexpected concern must also be provided. All staff members represented should have the chance to suggest matters they would like to see on the agenda. This opportunity is critical if staff are going to feel involved and if they are going to be asked to buy into any changes that might occur in the district as a result of the LMC's efforts. However, the ability to veto a topic should also exist for members of both parties. Should either side determine that an issue is better handled through another group, or that they are not well enough prepared to handle a particular topic, they should have the option of refusing to discuss the matter. This refusal might be permanent or the matter tabled until a later date.

Approval and dissemination of information. Approval of minutes from LMC meetings should require action by the whole membership. This action should take place either at the next meeting or through an agreement that the minutes will be provided, accepted, and acknowledged through an initialed note by each member. Minutes absolutely should not be disseminated without approval. Once approved, minutes should be available to all staff members.

Decision-making. One important factor that the LMC must determine is how it will go about making its decisions. Consensus decision-making is the best method, when possible. By requiring all members of the group to agree, any decisions that are made will have greater support. Conversely, if a few members do not advocate an idea, and even work against it, adoption by the full staff will be much more difficult to gain. Requiring full agreement also has the additional effect of enhancing the relationships among group members. By struggling through a concern together from inception to closure, LMC members are more likely to develop a sense of identity and joint mission.

Maintenance of records. Although different in spirit, the principle behind good recordkeeping for the LMC is the same as the need for good recordkeeping in negotiations. As time goes on, membership changes, concerns vary, and the exact intention of a decision often becomes distorted. Staff members in a school district may find themselves, a number of years after a decision was made, with different interpretations of that decision. By having accurate records from LMC meetings, future misunderstandings can be minimized. Records should include agendas, minutes, and notes. Agendas should be brief and topical. Minutes should provide some explanation of the agenda items. Notes might include specific examples, comments, or clarification of discussion that would not ordinarily be contained in minutes. Both notes and minutes should be jointly agreed upon before being filed. All information, once accepted, should be kept in a central file accessible to members of all groups.

Determining annual objectives. Once a committee has determined its purpose, it should next decide on its general objectives. This is usually done on an annual basis and helps to provide the LMC with direction for the year. New issues will certainly arise during the course of the year and will need clarification or even in-depth study, but annual objectives force the LMC to give attention to one or two major concerns that they should be able to look at as important organizational contributions. The objectives should be closely monitored and discussed at each LMC meeting. As noted in Chapter 2 (Planning), goals should be attainable and contain specific criteria to measure their success: criteria to be met, methods for evaluation, correlated activities, and identification of who will be involved in various activities.

Career Ladders

As noted in the discussion of theories of motivation, education provides little opportunity for the recognition and advancement of talented classroom teachers. The reward systems of schools have been limited, either by tradition or by legislative restrictions. As a result, the outstanding teacher who has wanted to make a career change but still remain in education has been limited to moving into administration, or in some cases returning to school for a doctorate, in order to move into higher education.

Many districts have initiated career ladder and career lattice systems that allow teachers to gain further recognition and rewards for their performance. The Charlotte-Mecklenburg schools in North Carolina have adopted a four-step ladder system. The first step is the probationary period; the second follows the probationary period and asks teachers to maintain their regular classroom responsibilities, in addition to assisting new teachers and conducting curriculum evaluation. Teachers at the third level may become involved in volunteering to teach in a school that has been identified as being in need of help, in research activities, and in other organizational assistance, as needed. Teachers who complete five years at this level are eligible for the highest level, which requires involvement in teacher training, research, and curriculum development activities and reduces classroom duties. Each step beyond the probationary period provides a stipend.

Career lattice programs are similar in principle to career ladders and provide opportunities for staff in non-classroom roles such as audio-visual coordinator, counselor, and librarian.

Additional pay for additional responsibilities appears to be a standard in districts that have adopted such programs. One district provides a stipend at each step above the probationary. Another provides involved teachers an additional 10 percent of their salary, plus another 10 percent for accepting other professional assignments; an additional month of work may also be required.

— SUMMARY —

A review of the history of labor unions in education shows that they originally operated in a manner similar to private industrial unions. Negotiations were the focus of most union activities, and concerns with pay and working conditions often resulted in work actions and strikes.

Recently, the work force in the teaching profession has taken a greater interest in initiatives such as school improvement, school-based management, and teacher empowerment programs, which will give them more involvement in decisions affecting their schools. As a result, many administrators and students of educational administration are called upon to view the operations of schools differently than they have in the past. Means of making teachers and support staff members more effective have included efforts at motivating individuals by responding to their personal needs and interests, by better understanding the common life stages individuals go through and how they relate to schools as organizations, and by implementing specific programs to provide teachers with a sense of empowerment.

Empowerment efforts have been conducted in various ways. In some cases they have taken place informally, based on the agreement and interest of local boards, administration, and teachers. In others, formal language has been bargained into negotiated agreements. Perspectives vary on whether it is better to operate such efforts formally or informally, but any initiative calls upon staff members to reexamine and redefine their roles and means for making decisions.

— REFERENCES —

1. Evans, Robert. "The Faculty in Midcareer." *Educational Leadership*, Vol. 46, No. 8 (May 1989), pp. 10–15.
2. Blase, Joseph J., and Greenfield, William. "Motivating Teachers: Understanding the Factors That Shape Performance." *National Association of Secondary School Principals Bulletin*, Vol. 65, No. 448 (November 1981), pp. 1–10.
3. Maslow, Abraham H. *Motivation and Personality*. New York: Harper & Row, 1970, pp. 35–47.
4. Herzberg, Frederick. "One More Time: How Do You Motivate Employees? Part I." *The Managerial Choice*. Homewood, IL: 1976, pp. 53–60.
5. Herzberg, Frederick. "One More Time: How Do You Motivate Employees? part II." *The Managerial Choice*. Homewood, IL: 1976, pp. 128–136.
6. Levinson, Daniel J. *The Seasons of a Man's Life*. New York: Knopf, 1978.
7. Sheehy, Gail. *Passages: Predictable Crises of Adult Life*. New York: Dutton, 1976.

CHAPTER

— 14 —

Policy and Procedure

There is a fine distinction between policy development and the procedures that are established to follow through with a policy resulting from board of education action. That fine line is often difficult to draw. Boards frequently move beyond policy development into areas that have been set aside for administration—those of procedure, regulation, and practice.

Policies are the broad guidelines by which the district is governed. The development and acceptance of policies are the result of action; policies may emanate from various sources. Often the administration may offer recommendations to the board of education about the need for policies that are necessary to operate the school system more effectively. In doing so, the superintendent or a member of his or her staff will identify a policy that is necessary for board approval. It should be fully understood that this is only a recommendation and not an official action by school administration. States usually provide a framework of law for the operation of boards of education. As a result, the handbook of policies developed by a board of education is used to carry out the guidelines of law established by the legislative body. The board, in its development of policies, stands as the legislative body in the discussion of school districts. Its resolutions have the force of law. The superintendent is the executive officer of the board and reports to it on the status of policies in operation and proposed changes. These changes should be reviewed on at least an annual basis. Board policies provide the administrative staff with positive direction in developing regulations and procedures that will be translated into practice. The result of these will be another handbook, for employees, to deal with these topics.

The philosophy determined by the board guides the staff in the administration of responsibilities assigned under the law. The organization undertakes or arranges only those educational programs or services that the board has established. This is usually provided in a general statement of

297

educational philosophy. Generally, policy is broken down into the following categories: community relations, administration, business and noninstructional (or support) operations, personnel, students, instruction, and by-laws of the board of education.

Since the line between policy and regulations/procedures is so fine, a breakdown of the various areas of policies should be considered.

— COMMUNITY RELATIONS —

Under community relations, items such as communications with the public, printed materials referring to types of publications and their review, and copyright and freedom of information data would be included, as well as employee involvement. A simple statement regarding communications with the public might be:

> The board of education will encourage the use of all appropriate means to keep the community accurately informed about the educational inservice programs within the school district and to seek information about the community's attitudes and aspirations for the programs.

This may constitute a policy statement on the subject. That general statement may relate to other policies drawn from the topic. For example, in referring to printed materials, the policy might say something like:

> The board of education will encourage wide distribution of all printed materials including, but not limited to, newsletters, news releases, budget statements, and brochures. The board encourages the development of materials and publications that:
> 1. Are of direct use in the educational process.
> 2. Inform the public, personnel, and the teaching profession concerning the policies, activities and accomplishments of the district.
> 3. Aid and promote the improvement of instruction. Such publications and materials should be of high professional quality and appropriately reviewed before publication. Standardization of format should be used when possible. All publications will be dated at the time they are issued.

Simple statements such as these provide the district with guidelines that can be followed in more specific detail. The board may indicate that publications developed under their jurisdiction shall be:

1. *Publications officially presenting the policies, opinions, and statements of the board:* Publications in this category must be approved by the board prior to their publication.
2. *Publications of various divisions or departments:* Publications in this category should be reviewed by the superintendent or his or her designee, to ensure their conformity with the policies of the board.
3. *Publications jointly developed under contract between the board and other boards or approved agencies.* Publications in this category should state the names of all the cooperating agencies and the individuals representing each in their development, and the names of the principal authors. They will be approved by the superintendent or his or her designee, for appropriateness and quality of content.
4. *Reports of projects, studies, or surveys conducted under grants or contracts with the state or federal agencies or private foundations:* Publications in this category will include full information concerning the source and purpose of the grant or contract and the names of the principal author or authors and advisory committee members. They should include a statement such as the following:

> The work presented or reported herein was performed pursuant to a contract with the board of education. The opinions expressed herein do not necessarily reflect the position or policy of the board, and no official endorsement by the board should be inferred.

These general policy statements form the basis for the district to provide a variety of information in printed form about district efforts. A copyright policy may also be suggested, since the district may produce a variety of materials that represent individual effort and that should not be copied for general purposes in other areas of the educational community. Such policy may deal with copyright statements such as: "The use of the copyright law for selected materials produced through the district will be implemented for specific classes of items when recommended to the board by the superintendent." All unpublished materials should have copyright identification protection under common law literary property.

In addition, financial commitments in developing materials are important and should be recovered when possible from users outside the district. With this in mind, administrators should coordinate their recommendations through the superintendent about items that should be considered for copyrighting. The superintendent would then recommend this process to the board and provide the rationale related to each request.

Since the board also may want the public to be aware that the district abides by freedom of information laws, it may include a policy statement on this subject, stating that the district is in compliance with applicable laws and regulations that are mandated by state and federal governments. Further, the board has the responsibility to comply with the provisions of such laws and to make those records available for public inspection, as set forth in statutes. A simple statement of this nature clarifies the position of the board, and the public then can determine whether the board is meeting its policy or not.

In dealing with employees, both the board and employees of the district must be fully informed about policies and programs that come from the district. A simple affirmation that the board recognizes the need to keep all employees as fully informed as possible about policies and programs should be stated. Conversely, employees should be aware that they are to keep the board fully informed of all unusual activities dealing with programs that reach groups or individuals in the district. This information should be supplied to the board through the office of the superintendent. A statement should also be included about visits to programs supported by the district. This relates to any members of the public involved in the school district.

Board of education meetings should be used to encourage community members to appear and bring before the board any matters aimed at the improvement of the district. The board agenda should normally provide an opportunity for any individual or group to be heard on subjects pertaining to the policy or administration of the district. In this area, more definition should be included to identify who should be contacted and how topics will be scheduled for discussion at the open-hearing session of the board.

A policy statement may also be included to deal with the use of buildings and facilities in the district. As a corporate body, the board has the legal responsibility to conform to state education laws concerning the use of public school buildings. Buildings should be available for community use within the limits of the law, to the extent that such usage does not conflict with the instructional program.

— ADMINISTRATION —

In the areas of administration, board policy may include statements related to central administrative and supervisory personnel and to management of the district; the latter could include terms of employment or appointment, employee compensation, vacation time, leaves of absence, health insurance both in current employment and post-retirement, conference attendance, work-related travel, and statements relating to civil rights compliance and smoking.

– BUSINESS AND NONINSTRUCTIONAL OPERATIONS –

Items included in this area include budget, income expenditures, accounts, and noninstructional operations. More specific statements relating to the preparation of budget documents, the development and implementation of procedures for annual budget construction, and the responsibility for budget activities should be developed. Statements should include authorization of programs to be established by the district and also the transfer of responsibility within budget categories. Frequently, state laws or regulations establish limits as to which budgets can be transferred by personnel having the authority to do so within the district. Regarding the administration of the budget or spending plan, it should be clearly stated that the superintendent is responsible to the board for the administration of the budget. The superintendent has the responsibility to acquaint district employees with the final provisions of the program budget, and to guide them in planning to operate efficiently and economically within these provisions.

Under the superintendent's direction, a designee may be identified to maintain the records of accounting control required by state or local laws or regulations. The board may settle on the procedures deemed necessary and should keep the individual areas of budgets under the person of authority. A summary report by program or major functions should be provided to the board in a timely manner. The board, through policy, should monitor the income side of the ledger and identify additional funds to be obtained through federal, state, or private sources. The board should have the ultimate authority for the approval of acquiring additional income.

Additional sources of income may be through investments. Safeguards for these investments should also be established in policy that states that investments will be in compliance with all appropriate laws and regulations. The board may wish to delegate the authority of making these investments to the superintendent or his or her designee, with the provision that a monthly or other regularly scheduled progress report of investments be given to the board of education.

Purchasing. The board may also wish to include in policy a guideline that would reasonably guarantee a purchasing system to provide safe, reliable products, materials, and services that benefit the educational program, and might further declare its intention to purchase competitively without prejudice, and to seek maximum educational value for every dollar spent.

Bids. Competitive bids or quotations should be solicited in connection with all purchases whenever possible. The policy might say that purchase-order contracts should be awarded to the lowest responsible bidder complying with specifications and with other stipulated bidding conditions. Procedures should also be developed to document reasons for a rejection of low bids that do not meet specifications.

Inventory. A statement on inventory should be included, to provide for responsible control over equipment acquired from public or private sources. Administrative control should be maintained throughout the development of a central property records system that will include centrally maintained records in sufficient detail to describe adequately the items of equipment and their location and value.

Money. School systems deal with large amounts of money, and this can cause great difficulties if proper precautions are not taken. A statement on handling of public funds should specify that any funds received from a student, parent, or other person must be acknowledged with a receipt. A proper record should be kept of all transactions, and all funds, without exception, must be deposited in an approved banking facility on a specified basis, such as daily. Receipts of deposits should be maintained and submitted to the treasurer of the board or other appropriately designated person.

Equipment. Identification of equipment and the use of such equipment should be clearly detailed. In many cases school equipment may be used to provide service to the private sector by an individual, resulting in a personal gain outside of the district organization. A statement should be made that the use of property, equipment, and services involved in instruction will not be deemed appropriate where a competitive disadvantage could result to outside vendors of similar services. The policy, and in turn regulation, is not intended to reduce or eliminate instructional activities required in program execution, but is intended to eliminate abuse that may occur intentionally or accidentally.

Safety. In addition, the district is responsible for the safety of personnel and students under its direction. Statements should be included concerning toxic substance abuse, safety committees, energy use, vandalism, and any other safety matters identified as district responsibility. A statement of policy to guide the retention and disposition of school records should also be provided by the board.

— PERSONNEL —

A specific policy for personnel should be identified to outline responsibilities related to recruitment and selection practices; appointments; physical examinations; responsibility and duties of personnel; probation; tenure; permanent appointments of staff; activities that deal with professional growth such as inservice education and conference attendance; absence; health insurance; fringe benefits; and civil rights compliance. In the classified category affecting civil service personnel, similar policy areas should be identified as those included for unclassified or certified personnel.

Teacher tenure areas. One area that may be of particular importance in policy is identification of teacher tenure areas. State laws or regulations usually identify tenure areas established in the state. Verification of these areas based on specific needs of a district may be included to state that all employees will be notified of their tenure area in writing and that employees will hold those areas based on tenure granted or seniority within the area. This may be important in relation to cutbacks that may be necessary in a district. If a person's tenure area was established at a specific time, then seniority can be identified in terms of the data included in personnel records. Management/specialist tenure areas must also be included, since states may be more specific or general in terms of identification of these areas. In states that leave it to the discretion of the board to include specific tenure areas under general categories of administrative certification, boards may have many single tenure areas, and reduction of personnel may be less difficult. If many titles are included in a single tenure area, confusion may occur in terms of who has the right to a position. It may be that the person with the least desirable background has the greatest amount of seniority for a position, thus reducing the effectiveness of the whole program. It is also important to include a statement outlining terms of evaluation and the process used for the evaluation of employees.

– STUDENTS –

Since schools are established for students, it is of paramount concern that boards identify policies for dealing with both elementary and secondary students. The statements should relate to attendance, activities such as corporal punishment, what to do in a crisis, special situations, and student behavior. Organizations such as student clubs should be defined and the process for establishing clubs identified. The management of student funds should be addressed, as well as policy on grading and transportation. A statement on continuing education is important, since most school districts provide this service either directly or on a cooperative basis. Civil rights compliance, safety and health of students, student records, and contagious disease policies such as those relating to AIDS, should be discussed in the policy document.

Issues relating to contagious diseases may vary considerably. Currently, it would be advantageous if policies relating to AIDS specifically were developed on a regional basis so that there is agreement within the region or county about actions to be taken when AIDS is identified in students or staff members.

– INSTRUCTION –

The area of instruction involves the programs or activities that are implemented by the school with relation to the activities conducted by the faculty and the students of the district. Items to be included are those related to instructional services, such as equipment, books and materials, and instructional resources for teachers, such as educational media. It includes such things as film previews and purchases. There should also be re-emphasis on the use of materials with copyright regulations. In some programs, work experience may be important in terms of students being required to have vocational or technical backgrounds. This will provide the board with an opportunity to document what practical experiences would be acceptable. A section should also deal with continuing education, since most schools provide programs in that area. A textbook policy may state that districts shall furnish students with all textbooks required other than supplementary review books, reference books, and work kits.

Further, the policy may state that it is the students' responsibility to maintain possession of textbooks and that a fine will be assessed to students for lost or damaged books. It may also note that course credit may not be granted to any student who has not completed his or her obligation with respect to payment for lost or damaged textbooks or workbooks; each student should be fully advised of this responsibility upon entering the district's program.

The policy might also state that a textbook or workbook approved for use and purchased with school funds should be adopted for a specific number of years. If a rapid change in curriculum or programs should make it necessary to adopt a new textbook before the prescribed number of years, special approval must be received from the superintendent. This would clarify to the staff the kind of limitations and processes used to deal with textbooks and workbooks. The change clause that allows discretion of the superintendent provides an opportunity for the staff to identify changes that occur in textbooks or technology within the period established by the board of education.

Another section that deals with instruction relates to film preview and purchase. This could be extended to all educational media. Examples of statements might include the following:

No film will be purchased for the district library without having been previewed by a user committee and recommended for purchase in writing. Purchase of recommended films by the district film library is solely for the purpose of making films available to program activities and in no way should be construed to mandate or dictate use of specific film titles by an individual school program.

Since school personnel frequently utilize materials from other locations and supplement their instructional activities with information outside of workbooks and textbooks, a copyright proviso is important, so the district can clearly state limitations in the use of copyrighted materials. Staff members should observe the United States Copyright Law guidelines and regulations regarding use and reproduction of instructional materials and program-related materials.

In the case of students who will acquire practical experience as part of their course work, the board of education should endorse the principle that actual work in various occupations provides effective and meaningful education.

– BOARD OF EDUCATION –

In the final section of the policy handbook, by-laws of the board should be included. Such things as organization, power and duties of the board officers, and methods of operation would be included. The election process for board members should be described, and also identifiction of advisory committees and councils that could relate to standing or ad hoc committees.

In relation to powers and duties of the board and its officers, specifics should be identified in terms of the duties of the president, duties of the vice president, duties of the clerk, and duties of the treasurer. In general, board power is corporate power. Authority to exercise it rests with the board as a whole and not with any individual member or group of members of the board. No member of the board has the right to exercise the authority of the whole board. A board member has authority only when meeting with the full board, unless he or she is specifically delegated the authority to act on behalf of the board.

Statements regarding the duties of the president would note that this individual presides at all meetings, calls special meetings as considered necessary or on request, appoints special advisory committees with advice of fellow board members, acts as an ex officio member of all committees, executes legal documents on behalf of the board, and performs other unusual and ordinary duties in the office.

The vice president will perform the duties of the president in the president's absence or if the president is unable to fulfill the duties of his or her office.

Although this varies by state, being a clerk of the board does not necessarily mean an individual holds an official seat on the board in terms of official action. Some states allow board members to act as clerks also. The clerk is usually elected by the board at the organizational meeting. The term of office of the clerk usually coincides with a one-year calendar designated by the state, such as July 1 through June 30.

In general, the board operates at the policy-making level, leaving the administration of that policy to its executive officer, administrators, and supervisors.

Board policies are statements that set forth the purposes and describe in general terms the organization and programs of the district. They create a framework within which the executive officer and his or her designee can discharge their assigned duties with positive direction. Essentially, they indicate what is wanted, and they may also indicate why and how much.

However, specific directions, giving precise details of how, by whom, where, and when things are to be done, come under the category of rules and regulations. This distinction between policy and rules and regulations does not imply that policy should deal wholly with abstract expressions of philosophy. On the contrary, statements of policy should spell out quite clearly what the board intends. The core of the statement of policy is the direction to be taken by the administration.

Since the board provides the administration with the guidelines for the operation of the district, it is therefore the responsibility of the board to develop specific procedures, regulations, and rules about policy that affect each aspect of the overall school program. The intention of this concept is to allow the administrative staff to work cooperatively with its employees in determining specific details for the implementation of board policy. The board may provide a general policy for the recruiting and hiring of personnel. A procedure or regulation relating to this policy might be as follows:

Supervisor

1. Determines if there is a need for the position, and if so, obtains a job description and completes a request-for-position form.

Assistant superintendent/personnel administrator

2. If position is approved, advertises and posts the position. Sends orientation packet to supervisor if needed.

Applicant

3. Completes employment application and, if for an instructional position, includes transcripts showing the number of credit hours for salary computations.

Supervisor

4. Checks references and interviews applicants.
5. Selects an individual and completes a payroll data sheet.
6. Forwards the payroll data sheet and employment application to the assistant superintendent/personnel administrator for approval.

Assistant superintendent/personnel administrator

7. Sends the "employment application" and "payroll data sheet" to the superintendent for approval.
8. Approves and distributes forms to various offices. The business office copy is sent to the assistant superintendent/business official.

Superintendent

9. Recommends hiring of the employee to the board. Files the original data in the master file. If there is any change, the superintendent will notify the supervisor and the various offices involved.

Board

10. Approves applicant.

Assistant superintendent/personnel administrator

11. Distributes a memo to all supervisors, notifying them of the new person, his or her location, phone number, and job responsibilities.
12. Reviews with the new employee the materials in the orientation packet and completes the personnel orientation procedure form.

Employee

13. Completes the required forms on the first day of employment. Data must be submitted prior to receiving the first paycheck.

Supervisor

14. Sends completed forms to personnel office.

Assistant superintendent/personnel administrator

15. Checks that all forms are completed and distributes them to appropriate offices. Collects transcripts.

Payroll

16. Makes adjustments to employee's pay.

Assistant superintendent/personnel administrator

17. Sends request for verification of employment and tenure status to previous employers.

Health department

18. Forwards a list of health physicals to the supervisor and assistant superintendent/personnel administrator.

The relationship between the policy of recruitment and selection established by the board, and the procedures and regulations established by the administration is similar, but also has a different definition in terms of role responsibility. As stated earlier, the policy statement is that of the board. The policy is general, and the regulations/procedure established by the administration are more specific and provide details for activities.

Another example is the case of providing a freedom of information policy. The policy generally identifies how to proceed within limitations of board of education authority as prescribed by law. A procedure may state that:

1. Any citizen may request examination of documents.
2. The district employee receiving the request refers the citizen to the person of authority.

3. The authorized person or designee:
   a. Releases information;
   b. Arranges for copy service;
   c. Collects appropriate fee;
   d. Forwards the fee to treasurer. Personnel files would not be released for inspection except with a written release from the individual whose records are requested. Student records will be released for inspection only with written authorization from the parent or guardian of the student whose records are being requested.

The regulation regarding this policy and procedure may provide more specific data:

1. The (appropriate) administrator is designated as the records access officer and the fiscal records officer. In the absence of this individual, the superintendent and the assistant superintendent are designated as alternates.

2. Persons seeking public records should make application to the records access officer on the application form supplied by that officer.

3. The records access officer is directed to make available to persons requesting records, those public records that, by law, are required to be made available for public inspection and copying.

4. No records will be removed from the lawful custody of any public office charged with the duty of maintaining those records.

5. In the event that any request cannot be met because records are being used for current working purposes, the applicant shall be advised of that fact and every effort should be made to arrange a specific time when the records will be available.

6. In the event that a question arises as to the nature of the records, if the public viewing of records may result in an unwarranted invasion of a citizen's personal privacy or may result in a disclosure of material that must be confidential to promote effective law enforcement, or for any other reasons that, in the opinion of the records access officer, are valid to promote the public interest while consistent with the law, the records access officer shall confer with the attorney of the district before determining if such records shall be made available for inspection.

7. In the event that any person is denied access to any public records in violation of the law, that person should advise the board of education

of the denial in writing and set forth the records requested, the reason for denial, and the fact that the fees for copying the records were tendered.

8. Location of records—all district records and documents will be available for inspection at (specific location). Student records will be available at the schools to which individual students are assigned. The inspection of individual student records will be accorded to the parent or guardian of the student whose records are requested. Students over the age of 18 may inspect their own records.

9. Time of inspection—records will be available for inspection during the normal business hours from 9 A.M. until _____ P.M. Monday through Friday. Persons requesting information must contact the records access officer at least forty-eight hours in advance, so that requested materials can be located and, if so requested, reproduced. Persons who request payroll information must allow a lead time of ten days.

10. Fees—documents will be reproduced upon payment of _____ cents for every page of information that is duplicated. Payroll data produced on the computer will be provided upon payment of _____ dollars. Other material reproduced on the computer will be provided at the rate of _____ per minute of computer printer time.

As one can see, procedure and regulations, as related to policy, can differ greatly. The key point is still that the process of developing the procedure, regulations, and activities is the responsibility of the administrative staff under the leadership of the superintendent.

The matter of having an approval system for disseminating new or revised administrative procedures may be relevant. The following list identifies the responsibility and the action necessary for the activity.

Administrative personnel

1. Identify the need for the development of a new procedure or for the revision of an existing procedure.
2. Notify personnel authorized to handle procedure.

Authorized personnel dealing with procedure

3. Review requests for procedure development.
4. Assign priority to each request.
5. Review priority assignment at each administrative staff meeting.

6. Assign procedure development to appropriate personnel dealing with the topic for change/revision.

Personnel assigned to new or revised procedure

7. Develop (or revise) procedure.
8. View completed procedure with key personnel.

Personnel in charge of procedure

9. Present new or revised procedure at administrative staff meeting.

Selected administrators

10. Critique procedures, suggest specific revisions.

Personnel in charge of procedure

11. Revise procedures as approriate.
12. Review procedures with superintendent.

Superintendent

13. Approve procedure as district operating procedure.
14. Authorize personnel in charge of procedure to disseminate procedure.

Personnel in charge of procedure

15. Order sufficient copies of new or revised procedure.
16. Plan orientation concerning new or revised procedure, as required.
17. Inform all necessary personnel of new or revised operating procedure.

Although this system may seem cumbersome and bureaucratic, it will provide the guidelines necessary for all personnel to deal appropriately with policy, procedures, and regulations that are related to district goals and objectives. Having an organized approach to deal with these items will make it easier for board, administration, and faculty to deal effectively with this process in terms of identifying the direction that should be taken for all activities guided and directed by the school.

— SUMMARY —

Members of school boards and administrators generally agree that the major difference in their roles is that the responsibility of boards is to establish policies, while that of administrators to put them into practice. Most also agree that it is difficult to separate where one role ends and the other begins.

Technically, policies provide guidelines for administrators to follow in the day-to-day operation of a school district. These guidelines are typically broken down into broad categories. Community relations policies often involve communicating to residents information relating to programs and activities taking place in the district.

Administration policies deal with guidelines for personnel involved in the administration of the schools, as well as management practices. Policies related to noninstructional operations involve questions of business and finance and the designation of individuals or groups responsible for them.

Personnel policies usually cover practices for recruitment, selection, appointment, job description, the maintenance of probation and tenure lists, planning, staff development, and benefit programs.

Policies affecting students include such matters as attendance, punishment, management of student funds, civil rights, health and safety issues, and recordkeeping.

Policies relating to instruction often involve programs, instructional services and resources, textbook adoption, and continuing education (if a district operates such a program).

Board of education policies include matters involving election procedures, the organization of the district, the responsibilities and authority of board officers and other members, and the role of the board as a group in relation to other individuals and offices in the school district.

— 15 —

Career Paths

The information presented thus far has covered various aspects of personnel procedures and conditions in education. This chapter considers the kinds of options and directions that people might take in terms of job movement in their own professional careers. Some individuals know very early in their careers what direction they want to take in the profession and within the organizations in which they work. Information has been presented that some school systems, because of their size, have limited promotional opportunities for their employees. As a result, some individuals may find that they have to relocate throughout their careers. Although size of school district does not always determine the movement of people in education, it is often an important factor in considering mobility.

— TEACHING OPPORTUNITIES —

Teachers may stay in one location for their whole career, or they may consider options that call for moving. Often these options are related to certification areas that vary by state, so the number of positions that teachers can choose from may be considerable, depending on their location. Other variables are related to personal factors such as change in marital status, need to care for an elderly parent, or desire to live in or near a particular geographical area. In such cases, district size may or may not be important; a factor such as the reputation or prestige of a district may have more to do with a decision to consider relocating there than other factors.

However, district size does have some effect on the number and variety of options that could influence an individual's decision to move. A teacher may take a position to gain entry into a school system. The job that this person is assigned may not be totally desirable to him or her, but may give the potential of moving within the district. A teacher may wish to teach in the intermediate grades, but finds that a primary-level position is the only immediate hope of gaining entry to a particular district. As a result, the teacher is willing to take the primary position, hoping that eventually an intermediate job will be available.

Grade-level mobility and the subject matter taught at a grade level, particularly in the early and later secondary grades, may also influence a person's movement. An individual may take a job teaching a certain grade or subject matter that is not his or her ultimate goal, but may provide potential for movement later. A teacher specializing in the early secondary grades may take a seventh grade assignment and wait to apply for a position in grades eight or nine, or perhaps in the upper secondary grades, based on subject matter preference.

The same holds true for the types of students to be taught. Unfortunately, many districts have allowed the most veteran, skilled staff members to teach the college-bound students, while new staff members are relegated to the low-track students. Survival with low-track students is tantamount to coming out on the brighter side of the "sink or swim" adage, but the experience may destroy the motivation of good teachers who become discouraged and never get beyond the first year in the profession. Even those who survive the first year may decide that the lack of potential for teaching less difficult students motivates them to stay only a short time in a position, until they can find an assignment elsewhere, either in or out of the profession, that better challenges their interests.

One area that is receiving a great deal of attention is computer education. By either state requirement or societal demand, the schools are being called upon to educate students to become computer literate. This may simply involve having individuals acquire keyboarding skills or may extend to the potential use of computers in the classroom for all subject matter areas. Students may be involved with simple programming or may be required to be able to access the computer for instructional use. Itinerant teachers may be employed to carry out this instruction in more than one school district, through cooperative arrangements with regional educational agencies.

Multiple certification. Due to the preponderance of graying staff in many school districts, personnel administrators have become more sensitive to the need to identify job candidates with multiple talents. This includes multiple teaching certifications (authorization to teach in more than one subject area), as well as the ability and certification to coach and to advise student clubs. Those doing the hiring are often aware that many older staff members have decided that the rewards of coaching and advising are not as great as they once were. Consequently, when all else is equal in terms of teaching ability, candidates who can provide help in other areas are often the ones most likely to receive job offers.

Salary. Monetary rewards are usually important to individuals as they look at job opportunities. A person with some particular certification or other special expertise may be sought by neighboring school systems to fill their needs. Such an individual may be offered compensation well above the level currently being provided by his or her present system. As a result, the person may be enticed by a higher salary to teach the same thing in another district. Movement is also a challenge, so salary and a new situation may be the overriding factors in deciding to change job location.

Chapter 8 (Compensation) noted that a teacher may be willing to accept less money if factors such as the rewards of a school system are great enough. However, the increased compensation offered to individuals generally should be significant enough to persuade them to give up the security they have in their present location.

Tenure and seniority. Although tenure may not be a paramount factor in movement, it is still coupled with security, and an individual may have to wait two or more years to acquire tenure in a new location. Tenure is generally not transferrable from one district to another within a state. Additionally, regardless of how highly regarded a teacher or administrator may be, certain factors such as lower enrollments and school closings may compel staff layoffs. Consequently, personnel administrators should be honest with staff members about their status in the district. To offer a job to someone who may be giving up a secure position elsewhere, knowing that the person may be laid off due to declining enrollments, would be highly unethical.

— CAREER OPPORTUNITIES FOR SUPPORT STAFF —

The factors cited are not limited to teachers. School system personnel include those administering and teaching and also support personnel such as those in clerical, maintenance, custodial, food service, and transportation positions. In many cases, support staff are covered by the civil service. Although systems may have career ladder opportunities, individuals may or may not be able to move, depending on the availability of positions from county or state civil service, or due to the requirement to pass an examination for a position.

A secretary may start out at one level and be elevated to higher levels in the same position, based on years of service or appointment to a certain job area within the school system. In some districts a secretary can move from one level to another, based on being assigned to a person having greater responsibilities or confidential levels in the school system. Therefore, people may move from employment in one area to employment in another area, based on the fact that they can advance in the new area but not in the old one. In some cases advancement is done by seniority and in other cases it is determined by need or interest. The collective bargaining contract may specify the terms of what a person can or cannot do, and also may limit the employer in terms of how far an individual can be advanced in the district.

A custodian may prefer an assignment as one of a number of custodians servicing a large school, or he or she may prefer to be the single custodian in charge of a smaller school. In addition, these persons may be able to advance themselves through civil service testing to titles such as head custodian, senior custodian, or lead custodian. Changes in title often bring more money, prestige, and responsibility.

Dealing with maintenance work requires a variety of skills from electrical to plumbing to construction, and other areas necessary to operate school plants within the district. A person having this background would be an asset to the school system, and it could eventually pay the district to offer a higher salary, balanced against cost savings that might be effected by that individual's good work.

Part-time personnel. Some positions, such as bus driver, do have limitations, and may be handled with part-time personnel. If the school district does not have supplementary assignments for an individual, the job of bus driver would be limited to time periods identified by the district. To fill positions such as these, individuals may be employed who have other jobs with flexible schedules or individuals assigned to shifts other than the times they would be needed by the district. Many districts have found it desirable to offer insurance coverage to persons in such positions.

— ADMINISTRATIVE OPPORTUNITIES —

Many teachers who wish to seek new opportunities outside the classroom look at options in administration. To make this move, certification requirements must be met. A teacher of a certain subject matter may wish to become a department head in the same subject area. In this case, skill, interest, leadership potential, and political affiliation and contacts within the district where he or she works may play a role in advancement. In cases where no other people are interested in being the department head, such movement is not difficult. In other cases a number of people may be interested in the position, and competition will be keener.

Types of positions. People hoping to move into administrative positions should consider their long-term goals, in addition to looking at immediate opportunities that may exist.

Some traditional assumptions are made regarding suitability for high-level central office positions such as superintendent and assistant superintendent. For instance, many school boards involved in hiring a new superintendent prefer candidates who have had prior experience as principals. Since successful school operation is considered critical to the overall success of a district, it is logical that the person in the superintendent's chair should have a good understanding of school organization. The same holds true for those who hope to become assistant superintendents. Having been a school administrator brings credibility to the assistant superintendent who has direct responsibility for the supervision of school principals.

Most people entering the field of administration are aware of the steps usually taken by those hoping to work their way up the ladder of school administration:

Entry level → School Principal →
Assistant Superintendent → Superintendent

Entry-Level Administrators

Coordinator, supervisor, and department chair jobs are generally considered entry-level or first administrative positions. In many districts these positions are part-time, and the individuals filling them teach part of the day and carry out their administrative duties during the other part of the day. Whether or not they are considered administrative varies according to the nature of the duties, the amount of time needed to complete the responsibilities, the supervisory nature of the duties (whether they have responsibilities such as hiring, evaluation, and termination), and the bargaining unit to which they belong.

Such positions may be considered entry-level, but many staff members aspiring to them do so with the idea of staying in such a position for the remainder of their careers. This is usually because of a commitment to their subject matter and the fact that the position allows them to combine the challenge of a leadership position with the opportunity to continue working with students on a daily basis.

The variety of non-instructional positions has grown in recent years.

Positions coordinating such efforts as computer education, gifted and talented programs, and drug education programs have required individuals to take responsibility for overseeing these initiatives. In some school districts the individuals responsible for these programs are required to be certified in administration; in others, teachers are placed on special assignment status away from or in addition to their regular duties. As a result, a burgeoning group of quasi-administrators has developed.

Remuneration for people in this group varies. If individuals are not considered full-time administrators, determination of compensation differs. In some districts, usually smaller ones, part-time coordinators continue to teach their regular instructional load and are provided a stipend for their coordinator duties. These duties may involve running periodic department meetings and collecting budget materials annually. The next increment of compensation may involve a stipend plus some release time from regular duties. For instance, the coordinator or department chair may receive a stipend and also be relesed from teaching one or two classes and/or given no supervisory (study hall or cafeteria) duty. Rationally, it would seem that increased compensation should be tied to increased responsibilities, but in many instances the duties and compensation are not necessarily logical, but are based on negotiated settlements and the past allotting of job duties.

Another compensation factor considered for part-time staff work is calendar. Some part-time staff work the teacher calendar; some work the teacher calendar plus one additional month, usually in the summer. Most work twelve months except for holidays and usually four weeks of vacation.

Another consideration involves an individual's role in evaluation. As members of the teachers' bargaining unit who are called upon to evaluate, part-time administrators can be placed in a contradictory position, since they may be asked to testify against members of their own union. As a result, some districts have eliminated the evaluation responsibility of part-time supervisory staff. The elimination of this duty has caused some districts to downgrade the supervisory role and lessen compensation for supervisory duties. Instead of having department chairs who evaluate, some districts have moved to department coordinators who do not.

In larger districts, coordinators or supervisors may be full-time staff members working out of the district office. In these instances, such staff members are usually considered administrative and often belong to their district's administrative bargaining unit. In some instances, this group may even organize their own unit. The role of such staff is often awkward, since they are usually directly responsible to either school principals or the district's assistant superintendent. Principals are not always pleased to have people in their schools conducting instructional business without their clearance and with the ability to direct them. On the other hand, when such staff have reported directly to principals, they have sometimes been in the middle of power struggles between school administrators who want more of their time to be spent in their respective schools than the shared administrators can possibly give. If the supervisors are dependent on the principals for job security, they may find themselves caught in situations in which they cannot please everyone.

Small-school principals and vice principals. Probably the most popular entry-level positions for people who eventually want to move up the career ladder in educational administration are small-school principalships and vice principalships.

Many smaller districts operate only one or two schools, such as an elementary school and a high school or junior-senior high school, or in some cases a single K–12 facility that houses only one full-time building administrator. Such positions provide a number of advantages to the person starting out; in the job market, the title of principal has a definite advantage over that of assistant principal. After three or four years in such a position, the individual who has been successful usually can look for a higher-level job as an assistant superintendent or even superintendent in a small district. The opportunity to move into a larger school as an administrator would also be possible. In sum, the title and responsibilities would provide flexibility in making later career moves.

The disadvantages are evident. The individual moving directly into such a position from the classroom or an administrative internship might not have an immediate role model; the superintendent or the other principal may be the only other administrators in the district, and they would be physically distant. The demands on any administrator, especially during the first year on the job, are tremendous. Learning district and school routines, becoming acquainted with personnel, assessing needs, and becoming familiar with students and community are just a few of the responsibilities that first-year administrators must handle. Doing so without a previous frame of reference or fellow administrator to look to for assistance greatly increases the challenge.

Vice principalships are often considered to be the "pay-your-dues" jobs that administrators take to get started. The role is synonymous with student discipline, but some principals are sensitive to the needs of their assistants and make an effort to see that they have the opportunity to gain different experiences. These principals realize that assistants are likely to move on after a few years, and want to be sure that they will be able to do so as competent, able administrators. As a result, the best vice principalships are those that allow these assistants gradual exposure and eventual hands-on experience with the full breadth of duties of a school principal.

Concerned principals also realize that vice principals can become very jaded in their view of students if all of their contacts are negative ones. As a result, some vice principals will be assigned duties such as advising a club or working with the district's honor students. Although this perhaps does not make a total balance, it may at least provide a refreshing change from regular disciplinary duties.

As noted previously, school administration is often a requirement for gaining entrance to higher-level administrative positions. The route through the vice principalship or small school principalship tends to be the traditional method for moving through the career ladder.

Alternative paths to administration. Other alternatives for gaining entrance to administration are also available. Areas such as social work, psychological services, and guidance counseling may provide the needed background for someone interested in pupil personnel services work. In most cases, teachers do not move into specialty areas such as these, as they require specific training, course work, and certification.

Athletic directors and directors of health and physical education programs are also considered administrative positions in some school districts. Certification requirements for these positions vary; some states require certification and others do not. In some instances a position may not require state certification, but a local district may require that the person in the position be certified.

Titles. Because of local needs, odd combinations of duties often become established in school districts. Small districts may not be able to justify a full-time vice principal in their high school and will therefore combine the vice principal's position with that of athletic director. This allows one individual to take responsibility for two jobs, and provides the board of education and superintendent with an answer to any queries that might come from the community regarding an overabundance of administrative positions.

Other combinations often exist as well: elementary principal/director of special education, vice principal/curriculum coordinator, elementary principal/director of elementary curriculum, etc. In some small districts the district superintendent is also in charge of the business office, or combines his or her superintendent responsibilities with overseeing a small elementary school as its principal.

When such combinations occur, most boards are sympathetic to the great demands placed on individuals who are asked to fill two roles and expected to do them both well. Although boards may be sympathetic, such concern may not necessarily translate into a large financial reward. However, boards may be willing to provide other payoffs. A change in title that does not cost the board more in terms of dollars may be acceptable. Those hoping to move up the career ladder are advised to take a title change that will enhance their resume. In other words, a title such as Assistant Superintendent or Director of Instruction will probably serve a person better in the job market than K–12 Principal. This is particularly true if the resume indicates that the person was a K–12 principal for a period of time, and then his or her title was upgraded. The implication would be that the person did a good job and was rewarded by the board of education.

Degrees. Many people wanting to make a career of administration face the question of whether a doctoral degree is a necessity. A large number of superintendents do not have terminal degrees and have nonetheless been able to pursue successful careers. By the same token, a doctorate is considered by many to be a necessary "ticket" to particular jobs. Many districts, particularly wealthier suburban ones, will require or prefer a doctorate. If an individual plans eventually to seek work in such a setting, the doctorate is advisable.

Many persons in administration are also interested in teaching at a college or university, sometimes as an adjunct to their regular jobs, or possibly with an eye toward doing such work on a full-time basis later in their careers. The doctorate is often a requirement to gain consideration for such positions.

Other decisions also come into play. Accessibility is a major factor. The ability to attend a university that offers the doctorate is a problem for some individuals. Cost is another factor that can only be answered on a personal basis. The belief that people with doctorates are better administrators than those without them has yet to be proven, so having a doctorate is no guarantee that a person will be better prepared to do the job as an administrator.

Many doctoral programs have residency requirements stating that candidates must spend a year on campus. For people working in districts that provide paid sabbatical leaves, this may be an attractive option for furthering their education and potential for advancement. For those who have to quit their present jobs or take an unpaid leave of absence, there is no guarantee that the doctorate will automatically translate into an immediate position. In fact, many districts include language in their contracts stating that anyone taking a sabbatical or leave must return to the district for a period of time, usually one or two years, before they can leave for another position. Such language often provides a penalty clause that says if the person does take another job before the time period has been completed, a payback to the district will be required.

Good doctorates/bad doctorates. Some individuals, in viewing their options, decide to earn a doctorate through an institution that is held in low regard by some members of the education field, specifically superintendents and board members. Reasons for pursuing a degree through such schools are often understandable; the institution granting the degree has no residency requirement or only a limited residency that can be met in summer or on some weekends, and offers course work that can be done on an independent basis. Whether it is worth the time and cost to choose such an avenue must be carefully studied. Administrators who earn such degrees may sometimes be barred from consideration for positions. As a result, having no doctorate may be wiser than having a doctorate that might be questioned.

Salaries. The topic of salaries for school administrators has been an interesting one in recent years. The disparity between teaching and administrative salaries has shrunk to the point where many veteran teachers can see little monetary benefit in moving into administration. There may the desire to make a move, but no financial reward for doing so. In many cases, individuals do not want to take a cut in pay for a new assignment that would have a longer work day and work year and carry added responsibility and stress.

The move into administration often means giving up the security of a teaching position; moving into a new home; and providing educational expenses necessary to obtain certification. A teacher who has taught for a number of years may be willing to make the necessary sacrifices to change career paths. Unfortunately, the longer the person waits to make a move, the more difficulty that arises in terms of financial rewards and expenses.

For those truly interested in administration but concerned with financial security, a longer view must be taken. It may be true that a veteran teacher will not earn more money initially when moving into administration, but the potential for growth must be weighed. The move to an entry-level job may mean no improvement financially, but three to four years later a move into a principalship or central office position may yield greater benefits.

Other benefits. In addition to salary, other benefits must also be considered. Moving expenses are certainly one consideration for the person who will have to move for a new job. Many districts are willing to cover moving expenses in part or whole for administrators planning to move their families. Doing so is a one-time cost for the district, without the cost of additional fringe benefits. By the same token, paid moving expenses can be a major financial help to a new administrator.

Other forms of compensation are also sometimes available. Many boards of education, especially those located in financially depressed areas, are concerned about the amount of salary they can pay their administrators. As a result, some are willing to provide other benefits, such as tax shelters and insurance programs, that will eventually provide cash to administrators.

Administrators often take a weak stance toward salary bargaining, since they lack the numbers of a teachers' union or support staff unit. Also, administrators consider themselves part of the district's management team and feel uncomfortable about bargaining with board members. As a result, many administrators have left themselves unprotected or have been willing to receive less than they should. A healthy, candid discussion with boards about the need for administrators to protect themselves and their families, and the education of boards about the stresses and responsibilities placed on administrators, should be a regular part of the process that takes place when administrative salaries are considered. As one veteran superintendent noted, "Isn't it amazing that we're charged with the meticulous care of a multimillion dollar budget and facilities, yet so many of us are sloppy about taking care of ourselves."

– THE ADMINISTRATOR SELECTION PROCESS –

The process for the selection of teaching and support staff was discussed at some length in previous chapters; the steps involved in choosing administrative staff differ. For that matter, the process for identifying new administrators may vary by position even within the same system. For instance, in choosing a school administrator a board of education may decide to have active involvement by teaching staff, support staff, and possibly even students and parents. On the other hand, a board may choose not to involve such groups, or at least to limit the amount of involvement, in choosing an assistant superintendent or superintendent.

No precise method of selection for various administrative posts exists, but the following section outlines some of the major roles played in the selection process. The actual steps and who is involved at what stage of the process will vary, depending on district procedures.

Hiring Entry-Level Administrators

An individual applying for an entry-level position such as a coordinator or department chair may find himself or herself meeting with groups from the respective department. Usually the recommendations of members of the department that has the opening are given a great deal of consideration. Staff from the department will be best able to decide, based on interviews and paper qualifications, whether candidates have a good knowledge of their subject matter and whether candidates' experiences are suited to the needs of the school district. Also, since department members will spend the most time with the individual chosen, their impressions of their ability to work with the individual are important.

Vice principals. In most districts the principal has a major say in who will be selected as his or her assistant. Since people in these roles are together more hours per day than most married couples, it is important that they be compatible. In some instances a district may ask staff members, students and parents to meet applicants for positions, and then allow the principal to play a major part in the final recommendation. This is sometimes reversed, and the principal and other administrators in the district will narrow the field down to two or three candidates they feel comfortable recommending, then ask the other groups to interview candidates and give their impressions.

Principals. Because of the important role played by principals in the instructional program, their potential to affect the lives of students and staff in their schools, and the possibility that they may remain in the district for a number of years, boards of education and superintendents generally play a major role in the selection of school principals. Although students and staff may have the opportunity to take part at some point in the interviewing of final candidates, boards and superintendents will usually retain their authority to make the final recommendation.

As the concept of teacher empowerment grows, some districts have relinquished to teachers everything but their legislated rights, and as a result the instructional staff in those districts make a recommendation for hiring that will subsequently be accepted by the board of education. Proponents of teacher empowerment support this process by noting that if a principal's role is to lead, those being led should have the primary say in determining who that leader will be. In addition, as the ones working in the school, they are the most sensitive to the needs of their school and consequently are best able to determine who will best meet those needs.

Critics would argue that allowing the decision to be made by staff members would result in the principal having loyalty to the staff rather than to the students or the district. They would be further concerned that the principal would be hesitant about taking a stand against a faculty member, even when justified, because it might affect the administrator's relationship with the rest of the staff.

Obviously, the arguments of both sides have merit, and no guaranteed right way of choosing will work in every case. The means and extent of involvement of various school community contingents will vary, but it is important to make sure that their involvement is meaningful and considered. The worst mistake that boards of education can make is to ask people to be involved and then appear to ignore their recommendations.

Superintendents. The selection of a superintendent is a process that almost always receives a great deal of attention in a school district. As with other positions, the process will vary, but boards of education will usually reserve the right to final selection. In some cases, boards conduct their own searches. Depending on the state, boards may use a regional superintendent or agency, or may use a search consultant. Each method has its advantages and disadvantages.

A board of education that conducts its own search is likely to become extremely committed to their new superintendent, regardless of the impressions of the rest of the community and staff. The immense number of hours required to do a search results in such a great deal of vested interest that board members find it difficult to admit they made a poor decision. Board of education members also have more difficulty getting accurate information on potential candidates than a professional educator would have. Although the hiring board is likely to find that members of other boards might be willing to share information with them, teachers and administrators in the field are likely to be more cautious. Board members are also likely to ask questions that are illegal and could result in other problems; in one case, a board member asked a female candidate, "How do we know you won't get pregnant and leave us in a year or two?" Finally, most board members have full-time positions that prevent them from putting in the necessary time to learn how to conduct the search process in a proper manner.

Many districts use a regional administrator or agency in the selection process. Such people are usually familiar with the district's makeup and needs and have experience in providing such assistance. In addition, since they are local themselves, they have an interest in seeing that a capable individual is hired. Some boards will shy away from this approach, due to a fear that the new superintendent will establish loyalties to the regional administrator rather than the local district.

Consultants have long been used by boards, but they also have their advantages and disadvantages. On the one hand, consultants who are active in the search business will have a network of people with whom they exchange information. This allows them to gather a great deal of information in an efficient manner. They also have networks for advertising and soliciting candidates. Finally, in working with boards they are able to provide assistance by instructing them on procedural steps they might take, and providing them with screening and interviewing information. One of the things boards like best about outside consultants is their ability to remain neutral. Once a candidate is hired, the consultant usually leaves the employ of the district. On the other hand, some board members see consultants as hired guns who have little personal concern for the district, and fear that such consultants may only be interested in adding another successful hiring to their list of jobs completed.

In reality, many boards tend to vacillate; if the departing superintendent was successful and well-regarded, and he or she was hired through a consultant, the board may want to use the same consultant in hiring the next superintendent. If the superintendent who is leaving was not successful, a different consultant may be used, or the board may decide to use a regional administrator or conduct the search themselves.

Interviewing Administrator Candidates

Staff members from both the central office and the school may be involved in the process of hiring building-level administrators. Questioning by school staff would probably be related to the activities that would be accomplished within the school as opposed to those involved in the execution of overall district activities. Specific questions by staff members might be based on incidents that occurred in the school under the principal being replaced, and may relate to topics ranging from student discipline to curriculum implementation.

District-level staff may ask questions dealing with the same topics, but from different perspectives. A teacher might ask whether a candidate believes in teaching cursive writing to primary grade youngsters, but an assistant superintendent for curriculum might ask what steps a candidate would take to determine where a program initiative fits in with the district's overall curriculum plan. Scheduling of staff members and students, course offerings, the number of sections needed to meet the needs of students adequately, treatment of the faculty and staff, and money questions may be dominant concerns in selecting a person to be involved in school administration.

The interviewing of central office administrators may be conducted by the superintendent or by the superintendent in concert with other individuals including staff, community members, students, and school board members. The questions asked in hiring central office administrators differ from those used when choosing school administrators, because of specific skills required for the job. If an individual is interviewing for what is strictly an instructional position, questions will probably relate to the activities included in the duty statements for that position: leadership in identifying programs, evaluation, supervision, etc. If a district seeks a business administrator, then questions will center on factors such as the process for maintenance of a budget, construction of a budget, supervision of those involved in the budget process, ability to complete state aid forms, procedures for budget refinement, and steps for presenting a budget to the school community.

Responsibilities

In larger districts a person may be specifically assigned as the personnel administrator. The role of this individual in hiring may only include involvement after a recommendation has been made to the superintendent by other administrators or may require the personnel administrator to be involved in the hiring of all people in the district, based on recommendations from other administrators in different parts of the district. As can be seen by the differing scope of responsibilities, questioning of candidates would be extremely different.

When a personnel director screens initial applications, a question to be considered is whether a candidate's background, knowledge, and personality fit district needs. This allows for a first cut and usually narrows the candidate field significantly. In some cases, people lack the certification required by law and can easily be eliminated. Others may lack prerequisite experiences that were advertised, and these are usually easy to discern and eliminate.

In the superintendent search process, the steps may differ in that the board of education may choose to receive input, either formally or informally, from other individuals or groups during the selection process. This can be done by giving various committees specific directions and responsibilities. Committees may be made up of separate groups such as faculty, community members, and administrators, or be integrated groups with representatives from each of the interest areas involved. A committee may be more directional than advisory, based on the preference of the school board.

Board members and district-level administrators seldom confer with the public on final recommendations about job candidates. Board of education members frequently feel that since they are elected officials, the ultimate responsibility for hiring a chief school officer is theirs. As a result, for better or worse, the final determination for this important decision does not involve input from other groups.

When a board of education does interview candidates for the superintendency, they are concerned not only with existing mission, goals, and objectives, but with potential changes in the district's mission, goals, and objectives that might be recommended by a candidate. The final candidates have the responsibility of learning as much about the district as possible and should be able to respond to questions relating to the district's current status and potential for the future.

The individual possessing the necessary skills and knowledge for the position must also be able to relate to other people. Therefore, board members also give a great deal of consideration to the candidate's ability to interact with various school and community groups. If a person can relate well to faculty but not to parents, the likelihood for success is greatly reduced.

– GETTING THE FIRST ADMINISTRATIVE JOB –

Preparation for obtaining an administrative position is often lacking for today's new administrators. For many, the only advice they receive is from a local administrator they know. In other cases, colleges and universities with educational administration programs may spend some time with students to help them prepare.

Getting a first administrative position is often more difficult than getting a first teaching job. Many people will refer to their ability to get offers for teaching positions, noting that they were offered almost every teaching job for which they applied. However, administrative positions are often more competitive and consequently more difficult to obtain. As a result, individuals may be required to take positions that are not their primary choices, in order to enter administration. In some cases, the position may even be one that a person finds less than satisfactory but that offers career potential. Individuals may wish to work in the instructional activities of a school system under the title of Assistant Superintendent for Instruction. However, they may find that because of their background and training, their business skills are notable, and therefore they may be offered a position as assistant superintendent for business or business administrator. As with teachers, prospective administrators often must take one job in order to position themselves in a district where they can eventually take a job they want.

In deciding to make the move into administration, candidates must be honest with themselves about what they will require in order to accept a position. One bad strategy that many candidates follow is "shotgunning" applications—that is, applying for every administrative position for which they might receive consideration. Persons involved in hiring administrators become wary when they learn that an individual is willing to take almost any position. It shows a lack of discrimination on the part of the applicant, and also indicates that the person may have no idea of his or her own strengths and potential to do a job successfully.

Before applying for an administrative position, candidates must ask themselves if they will actually take a position if it is offered. If a job offer is made and refused, an applicant may have difficulty in being considered for future jobs, especially if this happens on more than one occasion.

Preparing

Many individuals who are just beginning to look for administrative positions find tht they suddenly hear about a job, but are not prepared to apply for it. This lack of preparation often involves not having a resume prepared or failure to have asked appropriate people to write letters of reference.

Resumes. These omissions are easily remedied by planning. Prospective candidates should have resumes prepared that can be easily accessed. Many people have more than one resume, depending on the positions for which they may apply. For instance, a person who had an administrative internship as a vice principal, with a great deal of curriculum experience prior to and during the internship, might decide to apply for positions such as curriculum coordinator, director of special programs, or vice principal. In this case, the candidate might have a resume that highlights accomplishments in the curriculum area and another that highlights school administrator experiences.

Many administrator candidates find it advantageous to have their resumes on a computer program rather than sending them out to printers. In addition to the flexibility to handle situations like the one described, a computer allows the potential to add new experience as it occurs.

There is no single correct format for a resume. Common sense dictates that resumes should be easily readable and laid out in a logical manner. University placement offices are happy to work with candidates in the construction of a resume. In addition to content, presentation of a resume is also important. Resumes should be printed on good-quality bond paper and printed by laser or letter-quality printers. Resumes made on dot matrix printers using flimsy computer paper raise a question for those reading the resumes: if a candidate is not willing to represent himself or herself in as professional a manner as possible when applying for a job, how meticulous is he or she likely to be once hired?

Letters of interest. A letter of interest is always sent with a resume. The content of a resume is generally simple to provide, since it is based on actual experiences, but a letter of interest can be more challenging to construct. A letter should briefly introduce a candidate, highlight major experiences, and explain why a candidate's preparation and experience fit him or her for the job.

Reviewing opportunities.   Once an administrative job opening has been identified, potential applicants must determine their interest in and suitability for the position. Standard questions a person should ask him or herself include:

Is this a job I really want? If the answer to this is negative, it is best not to apply.

Can I do this job successfully if I am hired? Taking on a job that may result in being dismissed can critically damage a candidate's career; being successful is a must.

Are the salary and conditions satisfactory? A number of concerns may exist for candidates and should be answered before an application is sent. For instance, a minimum salary may have to be met. If the position is being advertised for a salary substantially below what a candidate must be able to make, it is probably not worth applying.

Districts should not post one salary and then hire candidates for another, since this could have a discriminatory effect. However, such practices sometimes do occur. If the advertised salary is below what is considered acceptable, but the job is highly attractive, it may be worth submitting an initial application. Those contacted for an interview may wish to investigate salary further at that time.

Common advice on salary questions is to refrain from talking about money before becoming a finalist. However, this may not always be the best advice, particularly if a position is a significant distance from a candidate's home. It may be appropriate, when contacted by an administrator from the district doing the hiring, for candidates to note their present salary or ask if they could be given a salary range. If the person making the contact is an administrator, he or she will probably understand the concern.

There is no right answer to this dilemma, and candidates have to use their own judgment on whether or not to pursue sensitive questions dealing with matters such as salary or residence requirements.

In addition to salary, other conditions must be considered. As noted, residency may be one. Another may be whether the position will lead to where the candidate hopes to find himself or herself eventually. If a candidate is hoping to become an assistant superintendent for curriculum, it probably is not wise to take a job as athletic director.

Going to the interview.   In preparing for the interview, administrator candidates should learn as much as they can about the district ahead of time. Information regarding labor relations, test and reporting data, the district's organizational chart, community makeup, and the other related information outlined in Chapter 5 (Orientation) should be reviewed. It is usually a good idea to find out what happened to the person who was previously in the position.

When an applicant is first contacted, it is wise to ask the person who makes the call for the names and positions of those who will be doing the interviewing. Sometimes first interviews are with only one person, such as a superintendent. Other districts may have a panel with a cross-section of people. The content of responses should not change substantially, but it is useful to know who the audience will be.

Finding out where the interview will take place is of course essential. Prior to travelling, a candidate should take the day off from work, or at least a good portion of the day, in order to be rested and prepared. The candidate should drive to the interview location when he or she first gets to the area, to confirm its location. After doing this, it may be worthwhile to find a restaurant where it is possible to have a leisurely cup of coffee and read a paper. A big mistake that many candidates make is to rush from their present job to an interview without taking the time to prepare for the questions likely to be asked.

Presenting yourself.   There are right and wrong ways to dress for interviews, but exactly how to dress varies by area of the country. A college placement office would be the most appropriate source for tips. In addition, a number of good books can be found with suggestions for physical presentation. Although recommendations for specific types and colors of clothes will vary, a general rule of thumb in education is to be conservative.

Interviews are often enjoyable experiences. Candidates are usually treated well, as the guests of those in the district. Candidates should also appear relaxed and act friendly. However, there is a limit to friendliness, and candidates must also remember that they are there for a purpose. Joking in an interview is not wise. A subtle poke at oneself may be acceptable, but a district is not looking to hire a clown.

Usually a candidate will be offered a cup of coffee and possibly a donut or cookie. Acceptance of the former depends on the confidence of the interviewee. However, food should be avoided during an interview. It is difficult to take a candidate seriously who has powdered sugar scattered down the front of his or her clothing.

The first few minutes of an interview are often the most crucial, as during this time an initial impression is made. A firm handshake of greeting, coupled with eye contact and verbal acknowledgment of people by repeating their names, are good ways to create a positive first impression. Some candidates have found it useful to draw an outline of a table on a pad, and then write down the name of each person interviewing them, based on seating at the table. This allows the candidate to call people by name during the interview.

Responding. Sometimes there is a tendency to overanswer questions during an interview. Candidates must be sure to listen carefully and respond directly to a question. Periodically a question may be asked to which a candidate does not have an answer. The worst thing someone can do is try to bluff through a response. A few alternatives should be considered. One is simply to say, "I don't know the answer to that offhand, and there are times during the course of my job that I may not have an immediate response available, but I will find out and have an answer for you by tomorrow."

Another method is to respond by saying: "I don't know the answer to that but I'll tell you the process I would use to get an answer." This is followed by detailing what steps would be taken. In some cases candidates will draw from their experiences and talk about a similar problem they had to deal with and how they did it.

Exiting. A candidate will generally be given the opportunity to ask questions at the conclusion of an interview. People who are considering changing their employers and possibly moving a family should certainly have questions about the job and community that they would want to have answered. If offered the opportunity to ask questions, it is wise to have two or three prepared.

Candidates often ask whether it is appropriate to talk with the job contact person after an interview. A brief thank-you note is always appropriate. A phone contact is usually not recommended, since it may appear that the candidate is being overly aggressive. If a negative decision is made, a candidate may want to ask how he or she could have done better. In some cases useful feedback may be provided; in others, interviewers will avoid giving specific responses to such requests.

The best response to not getting a job is to be gracious. Education in any state is a relatively small enterprise, regardless of state size. Those involved in hiring administrators tend to talk to one another and share information on candidates. A brief thank-you at the conclusion will leave a positive impression. Future job opportunities always arise, and the way a rejection was handled will be remembered.

Second and final interviews. In follow-up interviews, final candidates are invited back to a district for more in-depth questioning. This is an important time for both district and candidates. At this point a candidate should have a list of all questions that he or she may want answered. This includes potentially sensitive areas such as:

Were any problems left behind by the last person in this job?
Are you hoping to have someone fired?
Are there major changes being considered that could affect the labor relations in the district?
How are matters related to finances (raises) and security (reappointment, tenure, etc.) determined?

In addition, personal concerns should be satisfied before leaving a second interview. It may be wise to meet with a realtor in order to get an idea of housing opportunities and costs.

There are no hard and fast rules in the employment process. A person may feel confident, based on comments made in an interview, that he or she is going to be offered a position. Unfortunately, more than one person has been surprised when a district did not make an offer. A person should not be disappointed or feel at fault if not offered a job. Just being chosen for an interview out of a large field is a compliment; making it to the finalist stage is an even greater one. Those who are good enough to make it to this point in the process deserve a great deal of credit, and in reality probably any one of them could do the job adequately. Assuming that skills and abilities are equal, intangible factors involving personality and who is most likely to fit in, are often the determinants when the process has narrowed to the point of final selection.

Impact on Family

When an individual moves to take a job, his or her family is also affected, particularly in the case of married candidates—especially married candidates who have children. If a spouse is working in a job with growth potential, added difficulty is placed on the family. Unless the spouse sees potential for acquiring a similar position at an acceptable salary in the new location, he or she may be resentful of having had to sacrifice for the educator's career.

Children may appear to be less affected, but it may be extremely difficult for children in junior and senior high school to leave their present home. This is especially true when they have been in one place for a long period of time, or have to move to a district in which program offerings are less able to meet their academic and social needs. As a result, a parent seeking a career change should take these factors into consideration.

Depending on his or her final decision, a person may be locked into a position for a period of time that may not have been a part of the original career plan. The effects of these situations may result in a reduced interest in a current assignment or reduce the individual's interest in a change later on, since the person may see himself or herself as too old to move by the time the opportunity arises.

— REMOVAL OF ADMINISTRATORS —

The majority of people who take the step into administration do so with the knowledge that they may have given up any possibility of real job security for the rest of their careers. States vary in the protection they provide their administrators. Some states have no protection whatsoever, and administrators serve strictly at the pleasure of their board of education. In others they may be provided statutory protection through law and have tenure rights similar to those given teachers. In other situations administrators may work within a contract, and in some they function under a combination of these — statutory tenure protection may be accompanied by a local contract.

In reality, even when tenure and contracts exist, it is often simple for a board of education to terminate an administrator they no longer wish to employ. Law may forbid manipulating a person out of a job, but it does happen. Thus, if a board decides it wants a high school principal removed, they may determine that it would be in the best interest of the district to eliminate the principal's position and instead have a director of secondary education with some overall supervisory responsible for the high school with the help of assistants, but who is primarily a district office staff person. If an assistant superintendent for instruction falls out of favor, a board may determine that the position is no longer necessary and that two coordinators or teacher leaders could fill the major duties for less money.

An administrator must display loyalty to his or her employer, but should also be aware that boards of education change and that the board members who hire an administrator may be replaced by a new group in a few years. Unfortunately, some administrators fall victim to the phenomenon of believing that the agendas that were in place when they were hired will continue to operate even if the makeup of the board has changed. These administrators may find themselves valuing and believing in the need to move in one direction, when the board's values and desires are to move in another. This results in frustration for the administrators, who feel that the rules of the game were changed in the middle innings without their having been notified.

Veteran administrators take the time to make sure that they talk often with their boards about goals, priorities, and desires. Ultimately, administrators work for the elected representatives of the community. Although some community members do not always agree, especially when a sensitive topic arises in the schools, these board members have been placed in their positions to represent community feeling. Administrators may not always agree with their boards, but it is still the right and authority of the boards to set direction. Formal goal-setting sessions and regular dialogue at the board table are critical processes in which a superintendent must participate and then relay the word to his or her staff if these bodies are going to work well together.

– SUMMARY –

Various career paths exist within the field of education. For support staff, jobs tend to be more highly regulated and opportunities are often limited, due to state regulations and local contracts.

For professional staff, a number of opportunities exist. Many teachers now have the opportunity to remain part of the teachers' negotiating unit while becoming involved in career ladder programs. For those choosing to move upward in the education hierarchy, opportunities often begin through staff positions such as coordinator, supervisor, or chairperson. In addition, line positions such as vice principal or small-school principal are often available.

In many cases, opportunities become more available when candidates have had broader experience and/or more prestigious job titles. As a result, it can benefit individuals to upgrade their positions and titles within their present jobs when such opportunities arise.

This chapter also discusses the advantages and disadvantages of academic degrees, gives advice on procuring positions, and describes some of the methods used in administrator selection by school districts. It also provides a number of suggestions for seeking administrative positions and concludes with comments on the removal of administrators from their positions.

Index

Dismissal, *see* Termination

Employee assistance programs, 243–244
Employee data, 12, 247–255
  access to, 253
  background data, 248
  collecting, 248–251
  and collective bargaining, 253
  evaluation data, 248, 252
  forms, 249–250
  freedom of information, 254–255, 308–310
  processing, 254
  training data, 252–253
  updating, 251
Enrollment projections, 31–34
  cohort survival formula, 31–32
  worksheet, 34
Equal Pay Act, 86–87
Evaluation of employees, 140–141, 148, 187, 189, 224–225, 226, 244, 248, 251, 289, 318

Firing, *see* Termination

Garfield, James A., 3

Hawthorne studies, 5–6, 8
Herzberg, Frederick, 247–277
Hiring, *see* Recruitment; Selection
History of the personnel function, 2–8
  behavioral science era, 7–8
  era of productivity management, 8
  era of scientific management, 4–5
  Hawthorne studies, 5–6
  human relations era, 5–7
  origins of civil service, 2–4
  private sector, 4–8
  reforming civil service, 3–4
  in schools, 8–10
  testing, 6–7

Interviews, 66, 82–97, 251, 285, 326–327, 331–332
  for administrator candidates, 326–327, 331–332
  appropriate questions, 100–102
  follow-up, 333
  how many, 83
  legal considerations, 98–99, 104–109
  pilot, 94–95

planning, 83–85
preparing, 89–96
probes, 94
question bank, 99–100
rating form, 95–96
starting, 95
types of questions, 93–94

Jefferson, Thomas, 2

King, Martin Luther, 19

Labor contract, 82, 84, 139, 140–141, 145, 146, 148, 161, 179–180, 184, 195–230, 316. *See also* Collective bargaining
  administration of, 208–209
  bargaining unit, 199, 220–221
  dispute resolution, 209–219
  duration, 180
  interpretation, 218–219
  negotiating, 195–230
  and pay standards, 179–180
  and raises, 185
  sequence of activities, 199–207
  for support staff, 257, 316
  terms of art, 218
  writing provisions, 219–229
Labor relations, 11, 12, 84–85, 174, 195–230, 269–270, 280–282, 289–294, 331. *See also* Collective bargaining
Legal considerations, 65, 66, 72, 74, 79, 83, 85–89, 98–99, 104–109, 164–165, 168–169, 195–197, 207–208, 232–242, 249, 251, 254–255, 283–284, 297
  Bill of Rights freedoms, 232–235
  in collective bargaining, 195–197, 207–208
  and conditions of employment, 232–242
  discrimination, 85–89
  freedom of information, 254–255, 299, 308–310
  in hiring, 72, 74, 79, 83, 85–89
  in interviewing, 98–99, 104–109
  job posting, 65, 72
  political activities, 239
  search and seizure, 239
  sexual harassment, 237–238
  sexual misconduct, 235–238
  and tenure, 141–142
  in termination, 164–165, 168–169, 249
Levinson, Daniel, 278

340   *Index*